T0164648

THE LAST HORSE PATROL

By

Homer A. Taylor

Order this book online at www.trafford.com
or email orders@trafford.com

Most Trafford titles are also available at major online book retailers.

Photo by Sue Robinson

Printed in the United States of America.

ISBN: 978-1-4269-4435-2 (sc)
ISBN: 978-1-4269-4436-9 (e)

*Our mission is to efficiently provide the world's finest, most comprehensive book publishing
service, enabling every author to experience success. To find out how to publish your book,
your way, and have it available worldwide, visit us online at www.trafford.com*

Trafford rev. 10/18/2010

www.trafford.com

North America & international
toll-free: 1 888 232 4444 (USA & Canada)
phone: 250 383 6864 ♦ fax: 812 355 4082

PREFACE

Working a job that one enjoys is a rare privilege. Officers in the horse patrol would have worked for free if we could've afforded it. We had other duties and the U. S. Customs Service never really recognized our horses officially. Those in charge simplyloved our drug seizure stats. In fact, the U. S. Customs Service just barely recognized its Customs Patrol, even though its patrol was the most cost effective and most successful drug seizing agency in U.S. history through today's date.

This work doesn't cover dramatic shootouts because we had none. Actually riding upon a stashed load of smuggled drugs isn't all that exciting, except to a new recruit or at a Customs Patrol station where the stats were low.

From the time of its beginning in 1971, the U.S. Customs Patrol began winning the so-called "Drug War" hands down. The special agents of the Customs Service knew their seizure stats would increase but not to the level that was reached. The special agents conceived the Customs Horse Patrol because they simply didn't have the time to seize drugs, themselves. There were hardly 400 of them to work all the ships that were importing merchandise, plus the entire Mexico border. The money this handful of agents poured into the national treasury from penalties, paid by importers who cheated on import papers, reached into the millions each year. The veterans from Viet Nam needed work, and since the patrol's journeymen earned GS-9 wages versus the special agents' journeyman wages of GS-11's, common sense prevailed among Customs leadership. The time for the horse patrol was ripe.

The Customs Patrol dried up drug smuggling on the Mexico border by 1978; only a handful of smugglers remained on the border at the close of 1978, and they were slowly stopped through arrests and having their loads of marijuana seized. The smugglers had all moved to the east coast.

Six-hundred of the eight-hundred Customs Patrol officers moved to Florida in 1978 and '79. There, they began catching shiploads of smuggled drugs. Today, they have returned to the border.

We read where the U. S. Coast Guard seized tons of marijuana and other drugs. The Coast Guard received the credit from the mainstream news media. Customs took the last line as assisting in the seizure, if it was mentioned at all. U. S. Customs fed our treasury billions each year, so Customs didn't need the headlines. Other non-revenue gathering agencies like the DEA, FBI and U. S. Border Patrol needed the headlines to impress Congress each year for higher budgets. Politics were already fast at work on all levels of the U. S. Customs Service, and surviving them, was a feat unworthy of recording.

The fact is the U. S. Coast Guard, under the Treasury Dept., had no authority to seize drugs or search ships during the years of high drug seizures at sea. Thus, Customs Patrol officers had to be aboard the Coast Guards boats and cutters to affect the drug seizures legally.

By 1987, after thousands of tons of smuggled drugs, plus seized ships and boats, and hundreds of arrests, the U. S. Coast Guard received its own search and seizure authority, for the highly successful Customs Patrol had to be put to rest. It was about to become a history, that perhaps, never happened. In all likelihood, the patrol won't even be mentioned in history, which is a reason for this book.

Supervisory Customs Patrol Officer C.O. Tilton was the founder of the Horse Patrol. He received help from SCPO Weldon, who has no first name for this book. Weldon and Tilton had pull with the District Director of Patrol in Nogales, Arizona, who had friends in Congress. I helped in small ways, such as caring for the seized horses. Four of us rode in the overnight trips on the border. We looked for signs of smuggling on the ground. We found the areas of smuggling through the fence and documented each area. Slowly, the smuggling began to cease. The horse patrol wasn't entirely responsible for this success, but certainly a great part of it.

The officers' names in the book have been changed for various reasons. Weldon told me that it wasn't necessary to change his name, but he later said that he changed his real name after reading the rough copy of this book. Officers riding in the patrol were from the Lukeville, Seirra Vista and Douglas, Arizona stations. They were Tilton, Weldon, Garcia, Will Williams, Kem Shulton, Block, Jacobs, Johnny, Cracker, and myself.

Tilton took up golfing after retiring and is rather good at it. Williams and Shulton began working as background investigators. Weldon and Garcia took up cattle ranching since they were cowboys from birth. I have lost contact with the remaining officers.

With the exception of two Chapters, all of these stories are true. These two chapters are mostly hypothetical and could have happened in another world at another time. The events are not chronological.

I enjoyed writing the fun areas of these stories, and if you enjoy reading them, my real goal will have been met

Homer Taylor
Lubbock, Texas

In loving memory of

Sandra Jean Shelden Taylor

Chapter One

No Fear of Flying

Among SCPO Tilton's many duties was to keep the horses busy on the Arizona-Mexico border. He filed the paperwork for a three-day trip on the remote stretch of border between Nogales and Sasabe, Arizona. Most of this border area was mountainous and unsuitable for vehicles. Information had this area hot for smuggling by backpackers.

No one in the Horse Patrol had seen this portion of the border. We needed to know if our water wagon could travel that part of the border, and, if not, find water holes for the horses. We could hobble the horses at night on the rich grassland for their food. There was plenty of rain in the mountains, so we expected the horses would have sufficient water each night where we would camp. The only way to know for sure there was sufficient water in the pot holes for the horses was to fly over that portion of the border.

SCPO Weldon called the Air Support Branch in Tucson and then me. I was recently transferred to the Sierra Vista, Arizona station, a few miles north of the border. "Be ready to fly that afternoon," he said. "You know that Tilton and me ain't boarding an airplane."

I was thrilled to go flying. Weldon would also be sending a Customs Patrol Officer (CPO) from his Douglas, Arizona station. He said that his CPO would help keep notes and assist me in any way possible. I assured him that it wasn't necessary, that I could handle it. Nevertheless, he sent CPO Cracker, who was something of a pilot, himself, having taken lessons to fly or something..Cracker and I would be meeting the airplane at the runway in the Ft. Huachuca Army base at 1400 hours.

In the already written orders were the objectives/goals of the particular mission. Before we could even think of beginning if a horse patrol mission, one item had to be met. That was the planning of campsites and coded locations in the event we needed backup by helicopter anywhere along the border. The smugglers back then were never hostile. They faced little or no jail time under that strange administration. If we jumped a hot trail, we could easily give directions. To helicopters that could land in most areas in the unlikely event we had arrests.

Twenty border miles per day, plus any side trip investigations of trails each day were the miles allotted for the horses. We had to ride the same horses everyday and horses cannot completely rest overnight. We didn't want them spending their energy in one day. Light rides kept them fit for the next day. Our horses could gain weight on these missions in the slow pace we rode.

The Tucson Air Support Branch of U. S. Customs was happy to oblige us in any way possible. They wanted to know of any green houses in the remote area, also.

The written plan in the orders said that CPO Taylor, that was me, would plan the route. Weldon had trophies at home from riding broncs and bulls in rodeos, but was scared of an airplane! That brought me a great deal of chuckles. He needed tranquilizer shots and strong restraints lest he'd risk escaping while aboard commercial airliners. At times I laughed at Weldon until my stomach hurt.

Tilton also had his private license to fly but never bothered to keep the medicals and written exams up to date. He admitted to me once that he never fully recovered from air sickness. This proved to be a bargaining chip each time he had me under the hammer. *Airsickness? What a wimp!* Two of the toughest men in the entire Customs Patrol got airsick! They would never hear the last of it.

Weldon was naturally scared of anything that flew in the air or swam underwater. A mockingbird could make him run for cover. Yet he had rendered several arrestees unconscious with one blow each when they felt they could fight their way out of it. He was fast, as strong as most NFL players, yet he stood less than six feet and was almost slender built.

On the day of my mission I thought the perfect time for a flight over the mountains that spring would be in the afternoon, while it was cool with spring thunderheads brewing. We would have all our paperwork finished and could mimic dogfights in the air for the remainder of the day.

The airplane that picked Crackere and me up that afternoon was a Queen Air, a breath-taking beauty! That sleek, aerodynamically-engineered aircraft was built to fly, never to sit idly on the earth. Beech Craft had manufactured many perfect airplanes, but this beauty with her twin turbo props, exceeded the exaggerated titles like Intruder, Flogger, Foxbat, Hornet, but no more than a fearsome, dramatic effect.

Those aircraft were warriors. The Queen Air was regal! Her name even depicts it! When this majestic goddess spread her imperial wings, the clouds moved aside, and the sky gods kneeled in humble admiration. Denying her worthy stateliness bordered blasphemy. No sovereign lady moved with finer grace or greater eminence. No queen is more delicately adorned. It is, by all standards, elite, a beauty of pardonable pride, and so ravishingly adored!

The Arabs have a saying: "A camel is only a camel, but a Mercedes is a *car!*"

We aviators also have a saying: "A flying machine is only a machine, but a Queen Air is an *airplane!*"

Its fast lines suggested a gliding weightlessness, built to skim through the atmosphere like the shadow of a perfectly symmetrical shark speeding past a colorful reef. I was overwhelmed. It stopped exactly where we waited!

The door to her lovely fuselage fell open. Air Officer Don Heimer welcomed us aboard while the pilot did what pilots do best, remain seated and thumped all the gauges confidently as if he knew what all those gadgets were for. He whistled while patiently waiting for us to climb aboard. I nodded a hello. He ignored me and pushed more buttons and flipped every switch while jerking and twisting the yoke and stomping on the pedals. I was impressed by the inside of the magnificent aircraft as well as the outside. The engine noises at that present time came from the pilot.

Heimer showed Cracker the shotgun seat and asked me to sit on the left side in the passenger section. I was humbly overwhelmed and thought silently, asked, "I have a whole seat by myself?"

Heimer took a seat on the opposite side of the hall and asked if I knew how to adjust the windows.

I politely commented. "I'll just keep them closed. Thanks."

He grinned and showed me how to turn the handle in a circle at the round windows. I couldn't believe it! The tinted window went from dark to light and back to dark again just with him just turning the knob! Now that was some high tech know-how! I was sitting on the inside of a perfectly symmetrical airplane with adjustable tints on the windshields! Cars don't even have windows that can do that! Cars are really boring in comparison with this gallant lady of the skies. I also knew how to operate seat buckles back then but Heimer saved us time by buckling mine. They clicked like a professional invention. Beech Craft's brilliantly-gifted engineers had outdone themselves again!

He checked the snugness of the belt and explained. "It may be a little bumpy over the mountains, Homer."

The afternoon's heat currents and gusty winds over the mountains did prove a little bumpy that hot afternoon. But I didn't know how he knew that in advance. Actually, it was a little more than bumpy. It was outrageously rough! The demons waiting in the sky's dark recesses began to grow serious.

I wished I hadn't thumbed my nose at gravity when we took off!

We ascended into the wilds of the purple thunderheads boiling over the western mountain range and crashed head on into an invisible brick wall! Fortunately, I was buckled in tightly, lest I would've slipped from that seat in the same manner as having departed many saddles. A heavy, leather briefcase packed with maps zipped past me, hit the wall in front of me and bounced off the ceiling. An ice chest went bonkers and scattered sandwiches everywhere, leaving long swipes of mayo and mustard across the windows, specked with bits of tomato seeds. The pilot made everything right with a few words of wisdom over the intercom.

"I trust you two guys are firmly buckled in back there. We may be in for some mild turbulence."

Some predictor! *Mild* was an incredible understatement! Other items not fastened down had became airborne and bounced off the ceiling and walls, spilling all its contents: combs, pocket change, wallets, I.D. folders from our pockets, guns, and what looked like Customs Pilot Dillon's horseshoeing outfit. My stomach suddenly felt the need to empty its contents.

CPO Heimer risked serious injury to himself by fetching me the only sick sack on the airplane, a large, black garbage bag, the thirty-gallon size, fortunately. With both feet off the floor, at times, and grasping desperately to the tops of the seats, he eventually buckled in alongside me, not a second too soon. It got rough after that.

I don't know who the pilot was that afternoon but I do remember his sarcasm over the headsets, "Hey--Heimer, make sure that he uses that sick sack! I don't want 'im nastying up my airplane!"

"Hey--no problem, Captain!" Heimer replied. "He's using that sack all right. I mean to tell you, is he *ever it!*"

"Aw right!" the pilot exclaimed after Heimer had finally delivered his long and semi-dramatic soliloquy. "I sure hope there's no hole in that old sack. It's been on board for years."

"Looks like it's holding thus far, sir. If it ain't, you got major problems."

"Heimer! Make sure there's no hole in that sack!"

"Up yours, sir! If you want to wallow this sack around looking for tiny holes, come back here and do it, yourself!"

If the pilot was Dillon, we would have had an expert aviator. This guy, well, he was hitting every chug hole in the air! He tended his own chores after Heimer's last reply. Then, as if he'd almost forgotten, he customarily and politely offered to turn around and set me down at Ft. Huachuca. I wouldn't have it, of course, one of my greater mistakes. I explained that it was only a mild motion sickness and that it would soon pass. Then, I'd be up there with Cracker, plotting our course for the horses. Besides, it wouldn't take much over a half-hour to complete this type of elementary mission.

It required three hours. Even though the turbulence was mild, I soon lost consciousness, but not before dry heaves had set in and after I had personally witnessed the most spectacular wonders known to the greatest of aviators. I actually don't remember passing out. I remember different conversations at different times. Cracker had sent me several messages over the intercom:

"There's a good waterhole, Homer! How about this for a camp spot?" He repeated that nonsense many times.

Even though my eyes were tightly closed, and my head was buried between my knees, I always replied but with severely burned vocal chords. "Yeah--looks good. This's a piece of cake. Make a note of it."

I did open my eyes two or three times, but only for an instant. The first time I chanced a glimpse outside, a wing tip dug deeply into a canyon's wall, leaving a cyclonic trail of dust behind it for a half-mile. Boulders the size of automobiles were torn loose and tumbled into the gorge below. Huge scores of metal were ripped from the wing and floated down in no particular pattern. We were flying through a narrow canyon! When the canyon's wall grew close together, we were slowed down and almost stopped while the wing tips cut their way through the rocky walls. When the walls suddenly widened, we broke loose like a paper wad shot from a rubber band.

This went on for hours. The pilot and Cracker would sound off gleefully each time the g forces changed from zero to a plus nine and suddenly back to a minus nine continuously.

Nevertheless, the Queen Air was an element of the wind. She flew as her regal title commanded. She could right herself with an elegant shrug of her royal shoulders after having been slammed against a mountainside like a kid bouncing a ball off the side of a barn.

Gale forces of wind tumbled us end over end frequently. One time her majestic tail dug deeply into the rocky soil like a farmer's plow while we were inverted. Her spinning props whipped through the rocky soil like an eggbeater through the softest of cream. She uprooted giant saguaros, causing them to cartwheel behind us like runaway gyros.

At times I felt myself weighing as much as 3,000 pounds, then minus all my weight plus another few hundred pounds. Heimer's face would balloon like a pumpkin with his skin stretched tightly across his skull. Then it shrunk suddenly like he had no flesh on his skull. I already know what he would look like after he's been dead a couple of years. No improvement.

Closing up the thirty-gallon bag tightly around my face, I continued to tear out my stomach and silently scream through some of my greatest misery. I think my screams were silent. I heard nothing over the noise of us tearing apart. Surely no one could hear me. The bag's sides would be like a sapling's trunk at times and in the next instant like a huge weather balloon. It cushioned me at times as I bounced off the bulkheads.

Incredibly, my luxurious seat had ripped its anchor bolts from the floor. Since I was firmly fastened to it, I was batted around the in the fuselage like a ping pong ball, the long sack flapping and trailing like a black wind sail from hell. Map packs, carpets, hoof trimmers, rasps, a huge anvil, and horseshoes filled the air. I'd be flung into the tail section so hard that my seat would be wedged there before the torque in the fuselage ribs and stress bars caused them to stretch and twist like rubber bands until I was free. Then I'd crash into the instrument panel. I heard later that the pilot almost lost his temper:

"Heimer, can't you get a rope on him or something?"

Heimer, unknowingly to the pilot, had been rendered unconscious moments earlier by the iron foot stand that was used to hold up a horse's front foot while it was being rasped. Dillon should keep his horseshoeing kit at home! Heimer was bleeding profusely at the right temple with part of his skull indented. He'd be alright. One moment I saw him like that and at another he was sitting back and laughing at the pilot's and Cracker's stupid jokes. I couldn't join their glee with any type of word, except a grunt. I loved flying, the concept of it, anyway. It's a dignified way to die.

At one point in time, I thought I felt Heimer patting my shoulder as if I might've been a mourner at some dismal funeral. Although I never realized it at the time, I guess I was in need of some contact with the human race as we plummeted through the tunnels of hell. I appreciated his kind gesture but never did tell him.

When the terrible ordeal first began, I remember our pilot asking Cracker through the headsets: "Does he get this sick on horses?"

Cracker didn't reply straight away. The question was simply too complex. I could've answered affirmatively, had I been able. The same sickness arose when I sat on the porch swinging one afternoon with my wife. Well, not really swinging. We sat very still. Then one of the grandchildren suddenly pushed us from behind, I screamed and bailed out. I was born with a motion sickness that surfaces when turning corners in an automobile, but there's no call to go around telling it.

Another one of the pilot's ridiculous stab at humor had reached me somewhere in a vast, uncharted realm of darkness, lit brilliantly, occasionally, by psychedelic explosions, colorful galaxies, novas, all screeching wild tones of alien music without rhythm. Humorous digs in Customs are actually hard to miss, even when one feels himself as the only spiced buffalo wing at a redneck party.

However, both Cracker and Heimer found a great deal of humor in the pilot's remarks. When the pilot realized that he had finally influenced someone by his original genius, he also laughed. I joined them days later once my facial muscles relaxed. I never heard his complete sentence. Something like a glass of water sitting on the panel without rippling.

Suddenly, Cracker was slapping the sides of my face like a nurse waking a patient out of surgery. We were back on an air field near our vehicles in Ft. Huachuca.

I glanced around. "Well--we're home, men!" but I couldn't state it clearly. The strange voice from my vocal chords was being played in the slow speed of a tape player. What happened next wasn't clipped from the fantasy files. It's true, word per word.

"We got it, Homer!" Cracker proudly announced. "The mission was a success. We'll go over the proposed routes tomorrow to see if you're still in total agreement."

Not everyone realizes that one can go into complete shock from motion sickness. That fact is far over Cracker's head. I was realizing the fact very well! I couldn't move my feet or hands. All my blood was still lodged around my stomach, flattening it, which had caused it to empty. I was sufficiently conscious for conversation at a congressional level, but my acid-burned voice box was uncontrollable. I was, in all seriousness, paralyzed, completely unable to talk or move!

The Queen Air had righted herself. That bride of Satan had powers beyond logic. There wasn't a single ding anywhere throughout her precious body. Her metal surfaces were clean and glistened like the oily surface of a salt lake. Today, I'm sure that if we peeked inside her wingtip covering, we'd find rocks and other debris. A U. S. Army truck was pumping her tanks full of life-supporting fuel as if she had been on nothing but another simple flying mission.

Cracker and Heimer slung my arms over their shoulders and dragged me to my pickup. My boots' front tips skimmed over the asphalt's tiny pebbles behind me. Someone called:

"Hey--Homer! We still have a couple hours of flying time if you want to go back up!"

Even in the bleakest of hours one can always find a comedian.

They drove me to our home in Sierra Vista. My wife was at first alarmed when she met the three of us at the door. Then she quickly understood:

"Oh--he's been flying--hasn't he? You should've seen him after we rode the elevator out of the Carlsbad Caverns. He sat with his head between his knees almost an hour before he'd move. A park ranger asked if we needed an ambulance. I explained that he often dreamed of becoming a pilot."

My wife has been well protected, first by her dad, then by me. I still had no voice and my legs were too rubbery to walk. She had never met Cracker or heard of his tact. He said, "Yeah--well, you must be very proud of him. Where do you want us to dump 'im?"

They tossed me face down across the covers of our tumultuous waterbed. I could've scratched a few words of thanks from my acidic throat but didn't try. I was still unable to talk or move. It was five in the afternoon. I lay there without moving so much as a finger a full four hours, until nine that night, sleeping mostly.

Two weeks later, after I had sufficiently recovered, we began the border ride from Nogales to Sasabe by horse. During this time, the officers at Sierra Vista placed a twelve-inch statue of a pilot standing by his locker. All his flight gear were donned, even the leather helmet and lit pipe, but he was without his pants. The caption read: "Why--yes! I fly." Tied around the neck was a tiny sick sack. Even with this remarkable display, Sierra Vista CPO's Williams, Shulton and Block still haven't been offered high-paying salaries as comedians.

Chapter Two

Hopelessly Lost

How does one get lost while riding the border fence? The following is an endeavor to explain.

It was SCPO Tilton's fault. Perhaps SCPO Weldon had a role in it, or CPO Johnny. I think that I'm innocent.

The Douglas, Sierra Vista and Lukeville Horse Patrol Officers met at Sasabe, Arizona late that afternoon. Weldon and CPO Cracker were of the Douglas, Arizona Station. Cracker's personal horse was in the trailer with *Chola*. They picked me up, along with my personal tack, at my home in Sierra Vista. The three of us headed west to Sasabe, about forty miles southwest of Tucson. Weldon's old seized truck pulled the two-horse trailer.

Tilton would be pulling two horses from Lukeville in another Customs trailer. One of the horses would be the big palomino, Clyde. I always rode Clyde while working out of the Lukeville Station. Tilton would be riding the little buckskin appropriately called Buck.

Behind Tilton in a large military truck would be Johnny, who pulled the water wagon. His truck would carry our food, bedrolls and cots. Johnny was a map nut, who later, with the assistance of the U.S. Geological Survey, mapped the entire Mexico border and its nexus, giving a name to all the roads, washes, etc. He never got lost in the desert, nor did anyone else, except us. We had mountains and the sun as reference points. In fact, no one, regardless of how green they were to the desert, got lost. Out there, it just isn't in the cards.

Nevertheless, Johnny would stand for an hour by his horse and study a map if he ventured out of eyesight of the house. Mountain points meant nothing to him. Miles, half-miles, or "Over there," or

"At that intersection," meant absolutely nothing to Johnny. Words associated with his jargon of "Clicks" and *kilometers* were his language. He not only pulled the water wagon the exact distance for the horses, twenty miles, he wasted no miles on wrong roads over new territory to him. He might sit with his nose stuck to a map for eight or ten hours without moving, but he knew exactly where he was at all times and how many "clicks" he was from the nearest click in the middle of the map. North was always two clicks to the right or left. I think.

CPO Johnny always found a perfect place to camp, gathered more than sufficient wood for a fire, and had the water trough filled for the horses before we arrived. He also had the feed troughs full of oats and alfalfa ready for the four horses. So long as he didn't touch any of the food on board, no one wanted to shoot him.

He never volunteered to cook. We wouldn't allow him to touch our food. In fact, he wasn't even allowed within a yard of it. He ate from cans, sardines, chicken, fish, or anything that stank and caused buzzards start circling overhead. His cans of food would bring coyotes calling at night, ravens, and wildcats. If he cooked anything over a fire, he burned it. Water, he scorched it. But he would eat what he prepared. We only required that he eat downwind of us. The horses would eat downwind from him, also. *Pas* flatulence was frequent.

Sasabe, Arizona is a small town built around the U. S. Customs Port of Entry. It's built near a deep canyon that's full of tall cottonwoods and elm that turned the southern desert breeze fresh and cool on their northern side. On the floor was plenty of shade and green grass for our horses. The Great Sonora Desert is not one of desolate sand and rocks. Small to large mountains fill its eastern side with deep canyons green with heavy vegetation. Hundreds of varieties of small and large cacti mark the rocky slopes, and all this extends north of the border a few miles before it fades rapidly.

We would be leaving the Douglas truck and horse trailer in the seizure compound at the Sasabe Port of Entry. Our trip to Lukeville, slightly more than 100 miles by the border fence, would require approximately five riding days, more than that if we encountered any fresh tracks or sign of narcotics smuggling. Otherwise, it was noted and later reported to Johnny, who would figure the exact distance of the crossing on his maps in clicks and could estimate the traveling time of the smugglers within five minutes for subsequent trips in the event officers of the patrol wished to ambush them.

None of us knew the border between Sasabe and Lukeville, Arizona. We would be crossing the border portion of the formerly called the Papago Nation. Today it is the Tohono O'odum Nation. I guessed the border distance across the nation at eighty miles. Johnny knew the exact distance in clicks. Miles, to him, made no sense.

The five of us camped a mile northwest of Sasabe that night and would be heading west across the Indian nation at first light. This was at the slope of a single mountain, oblong to round at its base and extending 1,000 feet to the peak. The east-west border fence crossed this mountain at its peak. We could see the white marker highlighted by the setting sun. on its peak. That was a border marker.

I knew somewhere in Arizona that the east-west border turned sharply to the northwest somewhere around Sasabe. I never studied maps. Johnny knew exactly where it was but he never volunteered pertinent information. From that exact mountain, where the border crossed its peak, is where I realized the border fence between Arizona and Mexico actually became southeast and northwest instead of east-west as it appears on the surface.

Our federal government gave up a lot of land to Mexico due to our first surveyors that found better things to do than to continue straight west with the border. They knew they would be in for some wide desert further west, where the Sonora lost its beauty and became desolate and forbodding.

If Weldon and Tilton knew that the fence turned abruptly northwest, they didn't say so. Anyhow, so much for geography. I've never had time for it. There was beer to drink and liaison with the inspectors at the port of entry.

We camped that night at the ranch headquarters at the base of the mountain on its eastern side. We made our presence known to the ranch housekeeper then kicked out a clean place for a camp near the corrals.

We broke camp at daybreak and packed our gear and horse feed onto Johnny's camp truck. Tilton asked him to meet us at the nearest waterhole about twenty miles west.

Johnny is unique. Contrary to our promptings, he always had a cab full of maps that were always spread out where he couldn't see out the windshield. He consistently studied them--on the border!-- burning precious moments when he could've been doing something else, swatting flies, anything! He always folded them slowly and neatly, which always made me feel like I was sitting in a bed of prickly pear. If I ever used a map, one time was all it was good for. Folding them required a special skill, and anyone worth their salt would never bother to learn it.

Johnny lowered the edge of the square yard of a noisy paper between him and the windshield after we had all mounted that morning and voiced another of his many corny jokes that we consistently ignored: "Don't get lost!"

He chuckled and petted all the maps gently flat while humming to himself. If one could get lost in a narrow hallway between two walls, then the same could get lost on the international border fence. Johnny's humor never cracked anyone up.

We rode to the north about a mile or so, skirting the mountain and carefully watching for any tracks from smugglers that entered the United States from over the mountain. Actually, I thought we were riding north. We were gradually going west, slowly. There was an overcast. Remember that.

We planned to hit the border fence on the other side after riding around it's northern base and back south again after about a mile, which would be our border fence. Does that make sense to you? The fence was supposed to be east and west. We were to ride north a mile and around the north base of the mountain, skirt it to the west, and then back south until we reached the fence. Simple.

We would have done exactly that if the sun had been out...

Actually, what I was calling straight north along the base of that mountain was really northwest. It seemed north. No one contradicted my directions. Believe me, in Customs, people will contradict you if they even slightly disagree. The overcast was rare. None of us had seen one on this particular portion of the border. No sooner had we ridden to what we thought was the north end and slowly bent back toward what we thought was an obvious west in order to continue skirting the mountain, we hit this dilapidated, barbed wire fence. To me, it was at the north base of the mountain. It even appeared to run north, not west. Everyone agreed.

By looking at that fence, no one would have guessed it was the border fence, especially that far north! Besides, this fence had a wide road running through it. Wide roads don't run through border fences without a port of entry! It just doesn't happen. In fact, it was a wider caliche road at that point than the asphalt road that ran through the port of entry at Sasabe! The stringy gate had only two wires that were crossed at the middle. Millions of fresh vehicle tracks were under it.

Tilton said: "What in the hell kind of fence is this and where did it come from?"

Weldon said: "Looks too dilapidated and too far north to be the border fence. Homer?"

My word was always the tie-breaker between Weldon and Tilton, if I ever bothered listening to them. If I am an authority on anything it is on fencing. I could almost identify the owner of a fence by just looking at it.

I laughed and then made a solid pitch to burn some time. "Nowhere--and I mean nowhere!--does our international border fence get this pitiful! I mean, even a government contractor wouldn't ask to be paid to build this mess! This fence belongs to the laziest rancher that I have ever seen or heard of. Cowmen no longer afforded fences like these. So this property has to belong to a movie star or some pro athlete with more money than brains. Only *they* would allow their fence to get this bad."

I brought all facts to bear. They pretended to believe me. They'd always pretend to believe me when I talked negatively, which was often. So I continued:

"Look at all those tracks and the way the owner has let his gate run down. A real cowman has pride! When it comes to having a fence built, even the U. S. Government's contractors have pride. Men, this land belongs to a rich Arab or, perhaps, an ex-governor of Louisiana or New Jersey, someone too rich and dumb to know the difference between a fence and a string of spaghetti."

So we unknowingly crossed the international border and rode south along the base of the mountain on its western side, complaining about how our economy had gone south under Carter's administration. We expected to run into the border fence at any time. We rode and rode! We began to grow more anxious as we rode. I looked back, finally. The mountain was north of us! The border fence had eluded us! We were in Mexico, armed to the teeth, and probably better equipped to fight Poncho Villa than General Pershing's troops had ever been.

Actually, we had crossed through gates of three fences, none of which even resembled a border fence, definitely not built by the United States Boundary Commission. What we crossed were rancher fences, not some coke-sniffing movie actor's property or some retired pro athlete that still hasn't figured whether he was in high school or college when he was first told that he was too old to play ball with the sixth graders. The fence posts were chopped from mesquite and ironwood trees by hard working people. The men who twisted wire around the corner and brace posts wore spurs. It was built right. They were cowboy fence builders, even better than the city contractors that built fences for the U.S. Government. "Stout!" as they say in west Texas.

Later, much later, after much grumbling from the small group of esteemed colleagues behind me, we arrived at a road, a caliche road recently bladed.

"This ain't no border road!" I said, growing more tense by the moment. My horse stopped on his own and began grazing. He was in Mexico, feeling at home again.

For once, all three men agreed with me. As I looked back, they were a sorry lot to behold. They didn't shave that morning. Lord only knows when they last bathed. Then there were the obvious guns, chaps, hats caked with dust, and neckerchiefs. They looked more like extras in a spaghetti western than U. S. Customs officers. Clint Eastwood and Lee Van Cleef would've eaten their hearts out.

The problem was that the scowl on their faces really wasn't acting. They weren't posing for some director lost in their world's dilemma. Those scowls were directed at me!

No time to think of something sharp to say but I was thinking fast. The atmosphere had suddenly turned terribly amiss. They were alienating me as if I still worked for the U. S. Border Patrol. Even the horses were curious. All their ears pointed directly at me. I guessed the horses were anxiously expecting me to point to the ground in order that Tilton would suddenly explode into a crazy frenzy, thinking that I had pointed at a snake.

I could only think, from the looks of those riders, that it was a good thing we weren't in Mexico--yet we were! *"Oh-Lordy!"*

Cracker finally said, "I don't remember any road like this when we flew the border in the airplane. Do you, Homer?"

I didn't bother answering. I never even looked out during that airplane ride! A dig's a dig. Besides, I heard a vehicle approaching from the west. It was a truck with a rooster tail of dust stretching behind it a mile long. I'll settle this, I thought calmly. In fact, I had best perform a miracle before they pulled heat and shot both me and my horse dead.

The truck was a two-ton stakebed without sideboards, old and rusty. I inched my horse into the road and lifted my hand high. That truck not only stopped, it actually skidded sideways with all wheels locked tightly and scattering wild caliche rocks in front of them. The driver was alone, his white knuckles were glued to the steering wheel, and his natural dark complexion had paled a great deal. His voice was barely above a whisper. I failed to understand him, but I swore it was something how the news of an Iranian invasion would sound in Spanish.

Weldon, who speaks Spanish fluently, rode forward and asked him where Sasabe, Arizona was located. The man pointed back north and east after regaining his voice. "Over there, sir, about eight kilometers, more or less."

We had ridden almost five miles south! This man was only five miles away from the nearest telephone! We had exactly that long to beat him to the border. No time was wasted in spurring our horses into a hard run back to the northwest. The race was on!

I tried to keep up, but we had reached a mesquite grove, which would provide cover, so there wasn't any use in killing our horses. They would need their strength when the big chase came from 10,000 armed *federales*. None of my friends appeared concerned whether I kept up or not.

"Hey!" I shouted. "You can't reach the border by riding westward!" They didn't answer. They just kept whipping and spurring forward.

Now that I think about it, I should've just let 'em go. They had not only alienated me, they had actually tried to lose me!

"Don't you ever tell me which direction to ride!" Tilton yelled back at me. Weldon dittoed that. I looked at Cracker, who just grinned. Cracker was they type to hold his voice until the winner became obvious. I wonder if he ever wondered.

If not for the remoteness, we stood an excellent chance of being caught south of the border with guns and official U. S. identification. We needed permission from both sides of the fence to be in Mexico. If there was ever a time to have political clout in the federal service, it was at that time. Repercussions would be extremely damaging. Mexico was already ticked off at the United States for making them look bad with all their smuggling, etc., not counting millions of illegal immigrants we kept dumping back across the border each year so they could return and give the BP more stats.

I tried to explain that they were riding too westwardly, that they were actually riding deeper into Mexico, but they weren't listening. If we rode straight west, and if the fence was running northwest, we would ride further and further from the fence and deeper into Mexico! They resumed their long gallops in the wrong direction. I spurred around them and tried to physically herd them back north, true north. Even by riding due north, we would hit the border miles further west than where we left it. But they continued to ride westwardly, scared into real panic, no longer trusting me. Weldon and Tilton, my good friends, yelled something about not ever riding behind me again, or something like get the hell away from us and shut the hell up!

About two miles further, they pulled up and began to listen to reason. Their panic had momentarily subsided. That's the problem with people who seldom screw up, even their hysteria scares them. Our horses were blowing hard and needed a breather. What a pitiful mess we would've been if we were suddenly forced to run from the Mexican army. I pointed that fact out to them, but appreciation wasn't in their present *forte*.

By riding westward, even slightly north, we were now much deeper into Mexico than when we had met the truck. If the Mexican officials notified U. S. authorities that armed gringos were horseback in Mexico, U. S. Customs aircraft filled with FBI agents dressed in fatigues and armed with assault rifles would be flying over us within the hour. The U. S. Attorney General in D.C. would know about it, which meant the FBI would be typing out the charges against us before their next coffee break. Once they learned we were Customs officers, our Internal Affairs would hit us first with a chance to resign our commissions in order to avoid prosecution. After all, our violation wasn't deliberate, just stupid! We wouldn't need lawyers to defend us. We would resign without further embarrassment.

I know--I know! Armed federal officers of the United States are permitted to wear weapons in Mexico—but it happens with prior permission. There would be celebrated feasts and picnics in other federal agencies over our blunder, which had suddenly become all my fault! Every federal agent, then and for years to come, would have a chuckle at our expense. The FBI would not only gloat, every agent, including their recruits in training, would be obligated to tell our story to every reporter that would listen. *We had just gotten lost while riding the border fence!* I placed my hand over my eyes and tried to force myself to cry!

The FBI, a professional group, would never buy the truth of the matter. They would credit us with more sense and attach a motivation for the so-called blunder, like purposely violating the Mansfield Act for hidden reasons, like smuggling drugs while we rode the border fence. No one, according to them, could possibly be stupid enough to get lost by riding the border fence! In other words, we would have to convince them that we had made a very stupid mistake. That would further their reasons to gloat triumphantly for the next ten years! Our other choice was to face serious charges. Yet--they would never allow us the dignity of a firing squad. Suicide began to sound good.

Worse yet, if the Mexico officials caught us, we would be arrested and forced to spend uncertain periods of time in their jail and in national disgrace on both sides of the border...which wasn't going to happen. We were armed. At this point, let's appreciate the fact that we had not hired out to be arrested in Mexico or in any other socialist country. We would never stand still for what accompanies an arrest in Mexoco. This is why guns were invented. Over all, things just didn't look too good. But if I had to fight the Mexican army, I had the right troops. The army wouldn't stand a chance.

"Back north," I kept repeating and explaining from behind. "Actually, the quickest way to the border is to ride back northeast." If we keep paralleling the border like this, we were going to stumble into ranches, people, cowboys, and who knows what. We would, in fact, keep riding west and eventually hit the northern coast of the Gulf of California!"

It was a good thing we had stopped in the midst of that mesquite thicket. I saw two straw hats moving at the top of the brush about a quarter-mile north. Since they were riding west, I didn't think they spotted us. My horse, Clyde, was the tallest, so I could see better. I moved slow to the north, which was unnerving. Every second we spent in Mexico increased the chances of us getting caught there.

I explained that we would come in sight of the cowboys if we broke through the mesquite grove too soon. They claimed that I hadn't seen anybody and plodded around me. About a quarter-mile further they spotted the tracks of the cowboys and spurred their horses back behind me again. From then on, I fairly well had my own way as a guide, but without the respect that goes with it. The cowboy's tracks, it appeared, had also turned back north! Of course they weren't looking for us. The trucker hadn't made it to Sasabe yet, but he would be close.

We crossed many fences during the crucial two hours that followed. Tilton carried wire pliers in his saddlebags. I used them with a great deal of desperation. We didn't cut their wires, exactly. We attached them to the bottom of the posts by removing the stave wires. All four fence wires were virtually tied against the ground. That way we led our horses across the barbed wires without a mishap. The wires always sprang back into their straight and tight positions, almost, after we loosened them at the ground level.

I spotted the cowboys again at the brush tops after we had crossed the first fence. They still paralleled us and had, no doubt, ridden through a gate. It was the last time I saw them. Perhaps they had spotted us. We rode slow and straight north, keeping well inside the bushy draws and taking full advantage of all the natural cover.

We rode as silent as possible. There was no loud talking or allowing our horses to slap the rocks at a trot with their iron-clad hooves. At times, I caught myself holding my breath. It was necessary to stop, occasionally, to listen for other horses, a vehicle on some distant road, and for airplanes. I dearly dreaded to have U. S. Customs airplanes to come searching for us.

Approximately eight miles later, we caught up to the border fence. The Papago Reservation was on the other side. It looked good. We didn't start talking again until the border fence was cut and our surreptitious entry accomplished. We didn't even bother to voice an official declaration to one another that we all were U. S. citizens and that none of us had made any foreign purchases during our trip to Mexico. We were in the United States legally, so long as no one in Customs ever found out about it.

Even with the new country we just rode through, probably where no gringo had ridden since Pershing's troops, I felt tired. My hands trembled. It was great scenery south of the reservation, nice to ride in and to hear and smell. We even saw a few caracaras, a type of long-legged carrion eater, which resembles Africa's secretary bird. These birds don't get any further north of border but a few miles. The high overcast that kept our directions confused that day began to break up. The sun's rays hit us hard. Outside those two cowboys, there was no trace of civilization in that new territory. However fond I am of remoteness, I don't ever want to see it again under those circumstances.

As for the laws we accidentally violated that day, they're all administrative and contain nothing of immoral turpitude, hardly qualifying us as bandits seeking glory and adventure found in robbing and pillaging. So if there's any hint of either during our brief episode as outlaws racing through the wilds of Mexico, it's gratifying to know that my ten minutes of glory are behind me. I no longer have to wonder how bandits feel.

Regarding the international boundary fence back where it was in such a terrible mess and where we erringly crossed it, well, that was actually one of the places we were supposed to check out. To uncover places like that is what we get paid to do. The intelligence had originated from a Border Patrol aircraft. So we reported it later as we found it, omitting certain particulars, like knowing what the south side of the border looks like. The U.S. Customs Patrol in Tucson later organized an ambush at that border crossing and seized 200 lbs. of marijuana and a vehicle. From that one arrest and seizure, that particular road through the border fence quickly dried and faded. The Sasabe Port of Entry, for some reason or other, began to have several legal entries at night again.

Contractors have rebuilt the fence. It stands today, healthy, in the form of something built for the U.S. Government. As for the movie star, pro athlete, or Arab that may or may not own the property, he was in no way linked to smuggling activities or even remotely suspected for a second. It can and does happen to many honest land owners on the border.

Chapter Three

A Horse is Not a Horse

Have you ever attempted to tell a rock to move? Attempting to make sense to some authorities in the federal government is far more difficult.

In mid-1978, at least two years after the Horse Patrol began in Lukeville, Arizona, no real horse patrol existed in the Sierra Vista, Arizona Station of U. S. Customs. The prognosis was worse. It appeared as if the U. S. Customs Service, in its entirety, was run by federal employees.

I was transferred there in August of that year in hopes of bringing the drug seizure stats up with horses. Horses were the tool that beat the backpacking smugglers on the Arizona border in the late seventies. After working there fourteen months before transferring back to the Lukeville Station, there was still no horse patrol at the Sierra Vista Station. Worse, drug seizure stats remained at a most embarrassing low. I had failed.

Supervisory Customs Patrol Officer O. C. Tilton told our district director, when referring to Sierra Vista's low stats, that it was due to a lack of horses. The director said to fix it. Drug smuggling was rampant in all areas on the Arizona border where there was a lack of horses.

Douglas, Arizona, under the fine leadership of Supervisory Customs Patrol Officer Don Weldon. He kept Douglas's seizure stats respectful. The nationally infamous tunnel at Douglas, Arizona was yet to be discovered. The Douglas Customs Patrol Station kept a lid on the above-ground drug smuggling.

A horse patrol was the exact shot in the arm that the Sierra Vista station needed. Tilton and I knew it. So did the director. Weldon's horse patrol in Douglas cannot be credited with all of Douglas's stats, but it helped. The Douglas station was approximately sixty miles east of the Sierra Vista station.

Please understand that Horses were abundantly available for the Sierra Vista, Arizona Station. The U. S. Army kept about 100 head of "Rentals" at their horse corrals on the Ft. Huachuca Army base at Sierra Vista. Therein lay the rub. The Sierra Vista Station was physically located on this fine army base.

Not one horse at those corrals was suitable for Customs patrol horses on the border. When I first explained this to my boss, he cut me off by stating:

"Nonsense! A horse is a horse."

The case was closed. A horse is a horse is like saying a human being is a human being; therefore, all human beings can play football in the NFL. We are all Bill Gates.

Now my federal employee boss would accept my explanation of rental horses if it came from a higher office, like above the district level, all the way to "Region". So I called a man in Regional Headquarters and asked him to simply explain to my boss why rental horses were no good for U. S. Customs work. He was a bright man, so I thought. He felt that I was simply attempting to cause U. S. Customs an extra expense. I explained that the rental horses available to us were unsafe and too much of a problem to ride in order for us to patrol the border.

He said: "Nonsense, Homer. A horse is a horse."

"Listen up!" I said rather firmly, "A horse is not a horse!"

He laughed and advised me to listen to myself. I hung up on him. When it comes to brilliance in U. S. Customs, it reaches all the way up to the U. S. Border Patrol levels! Incredible! No one was left in our entire U. S. Customs Service that I could explain this simple problem. President Carter was federal employee, the big boss. Yet he would probably have to ask the Kremlin in Moscow if I were right.

Later, President Reagan would have listened and suitable horses for the patrol would be made available within the hour. But he was still a few years away.

Rental horses for the Sierra Vista Station slung their heads, fought the bits, danced sideways, and were completely ruined by inept riders. No rental horse, once he has had an untrained horseperson aboard him for a couple of hours would ever be worth anything for anyone other than for rental to the public. These inexperienced people were taking their lives in their own hands when they mounted a rental horse. Of course, some of the horses still had the ability to think, but even the best ones in Ft. Huachuca were far from being suitable for our patrolling the border.

I asked to borrow horses from the Sells and Lukeville Stations. Tilton, who was in charge of both stations, laughed so loud that I had to hang up on him. My fellow officers at Sierra Vista, Customs Patrol Officers Williams, Shulton and Block were all smart men. They would ride and handle horses according to instructions, if the horses obeyed their commands. Block was enough of a horseman that he wouldn't mount a rental horse if his pay was doubled. He drove the truck and trailer for us and laughed each time we saddled up.

I offered to purchase horses from my own bank account and allow Customs to feed them and pay for their shots and shoes. No way! U. S. Customs wasn't about to feed my personal roping horses! Roping? Me? Roping requires a lot of time and practice, plus a little talent that I never had. My spare time, outside of 60 to 70 hours per week of work, was spent with my family. Besides, I couldn't throw a rope into a hand dug well. I was and still am the sorriest roper to ever draw wages on a working cattle ranch. I could ride most bucking horses on any big outfit but tossing a loop over a speeding bovine requires the ability to throw straight. I told my friend this at region.

He said, "Nonsense, all cowboys can rope.

There you have it! Why that man resigned from the U. S. Border Patrol is still a mystery.

Management loved non-thinkers in the field. They believed the patrol should rise to an investigative level, not to regress fifty years to the feeble mentality of Horse Patrol Officers—even if it meant no drug seizures. This was our tax dollars at work. It hasn't improved!

Drug smugglers on our Mexico border are not interdicted from investigations! One has to get in the field and ambush them. No Customs Officer went undercover in Mexico and joined the smugglers just to rat them out. Customs Patrol Officers interdicted the smugglers on the border. In order to do so, we had to be where the smuggling took place. It's a rather easy concept. Most four-year olds can grasp it.

Another thing I disliked about renting horses (for free) from Ft. Huachuca, were the Civil Service employees hired to care for these horses. They instructed the riders briefly on the rules and allowed them to ride in the forest without a guide. The people renting horses rode them for pleasure? *What pleasure? What happened to all our rocket scientists in this country?*

The army was willing to rent their horses and trailers to U. S. Customs for free. Free! Who would even think of paying the army to ride such pitiful bear baits in the first place? Except for my work as a little kid for my dad, I'd never ride a horse without being paid. The pay I received from U.S. Customs wasn't enough for me to ride a cursed rental horse! But I did.

The horses were hauled in the best trailers money could buy. However, most Customs Patrol vehicles were seized from smugglers that could barely burn a half-tank of gas before a tow truck was needed. The best we could get out of our seized vehicles was to start and run, far less of all the requirements. Stopping those seized vehicles with real brakes posed a problem. Equip them with trailer brakes? Disaster! About half of Customs vehicles stayed in the garages to be repaired by mechanics who loved to simply collect money from the U. S. Government, which was performed more easily than cheating old women who knew less about a car than they knew about playing football. The majority of mechanics working on Customs vehicles didn't even know how to attach trailer brakes on a vehicle. They could make out the paperwork that said they mounted the brakes if we paid them money. Federal employees never question the integrity of vehicle mechanics. Good liaison with the public was imperative. Enough said. We drove inferior vehicles at a cost.

The horses and saddles were also free at the rental stables at Ft. Huachuca. That was good enough for the Sierra Vista Station's Branch Chief's approval. The Branch Chief was in charge of our office and the one in Douglas, Arizona. It was just one slap in the face after another!

SCPO Weldon would never argue for me on the subject of rental horses. He claimed that his hands were full at his station of patrol officers who loved for the union to buck management at each and every opportunity. Besides, Weldon had never ridden a rental horse in his life, so what did he know? I hadn't, either, until I arrived at Sierra Vista.

Just to rub it in, Weldon, my good friend for years, told me personally that he would never ride a rental horse, nor will he allow his family to do so. He was completely in favor of putting some of his union leaders on rental horses. Weldon is a good man who worked hard for his wages at all times.

By all outward appearances, my boss had a point, even if he was wrong. A horse is a horse, an undeniable, indisputable, scientific fact but it was wrong! Rental horses were and are nothing but menaces to society.

First, no one but curious or inexperienced people will ride a rental horse. Fact: There is no such thing as riding for pleasure! It cannot happen! A child might ride behind a parent and enjoy it, but that's as far as the pleasure goes. I explained this to my boss. He scoffed. "A horse is a horse."

I set my foot down and told him in my best boy scout voice possible. "A horse is not a horse! There are horses and there are four-legged brutes that look like horses. The rental horses are handicapped with a lack of discipline, self worth, stamina, and can do nothing but sling their heads, ring their tails, dance, prance like a Mexico parade horse and then run like hell toward the barn."

He stated that his word was final.

Why are rental horses wrong? Once a horse that is trained to respond to reasonable horsemanship, children can ride most of them. However, when a mature person that knows no more than a child about riding, mounts a normal horse, the horse expects to be given the correct commands in a reasonable time with the right amount of pressure applied, what is reasonable and prudent for the horse. An inexperienced rider doesn't realize what he/she might be doing to the horse's brain and training without commands applied correctly. Everything is too extreme and wrong from the horse's point of view. The horse becomes confused and tends to panic.

A horse is a highly sensitive animal. It is simply at a loss at what to do or how to respond with inexperienced riders. The horse is suddenly given harsh commands, none of which he knows or recognizes. All horses expect to be given one command at a time, also. He'll usually figure out what's up from the circumstances without too many following commands. A horse never expects to be jerked up by the reins and be kicked harshly to go at the same time, unless, of course, he's a parade horse in Mexico. He does not expect to be kicked into a dead heat race out of the clear blue with no warning or warm ups. Most horses never see a race track. Normal horses are never jerked about or kicked roughly. Breaking these few simple rules confuses the most docile of horses, and it will overwhelm them. In the meantime, the horse hears harsh tones from its rider, such as: "Stupid hoss!" Horses tune in on tones as well as any dog or domesticated animal.

Horses will usually panic or simply take advantage of their riders and run for the barn. It's an escape mechanism. But if he gets away with it, he'll make it a habit, especially with a rider that doesn't know what he or she is doing. Thank goodness for the barn! If the horses didn't want to run for the barn and get this maniac off his back, they would run in any direction and keep running until exhaustion. They might even buck or start running sideways with their heads in the air, expecting to be manhandled by the bits. Even the so-called "Dead-mouthed" horses have sensitive feelings in their mouths. They simply hide the pain and start running to escape from their riders, mentally or otherwise. Running for the barn is the only thing that makes sense to them. People hanging on tell stories for decades on what a stupid hoss he once rode. The horse remembers only what he did the last time to escape his dilemma, running sideways or running to the barn. Oftentimes, they won't even leave the barn. Really, that's as simple and complex as rental horses get.

I attempted to explain this to those who were in charge. I received a simple fact in response: "These horses are gentle. CPO's Williams and Shulton can ride 'em. You can, too. You can also drop hints for Will and Kem in how to control their horses in the event they have problems."

"Beam me up, Scotty!" I could no more control a rental horse anymore than I could cause a flaming meteorite to change directions! I have limitations! A horse must always be willing to cooperate before anyone controls him! That's actually what the training is all about. Horses are never controlled. They simply agree to cooperate instead of bucking, rolling, or rearing up to fall backwards in less than a heartbeat. Rental horses that do this can suddenly be on his back before any experienced rider can think what is happening. A rider can be riding along and suddenly the ground slaps the back of his head and back with 1,000 pounds of horse on his chest.

Furthermore, rental horses are extremely dangerous in the back country, for these horses can, at anytime, suddenly decide to split, go 10-8 in Code 3 in any direction at any given time. We needed quiet horses that can stand still and move only when prompted. When we gallop, we don't act like Hollywood heroes bent over and whipping and spurring for the camera as if we're trying to save a lady in a run-away wagon.

However, Will and Kem needed no help or suggestions. They were oriented, which only added conflict to my problem.

"So what's your problem, Homer?"

I turned to Kem Shulton. "Can you see tracks on the ground from one of those rental horses?"

"Sure!" he answered.

I turned to Will Williams. "Can you track from one of these horses?"

Will stated firmly, "I don't track nothing! I don't like horses. Tracking is not what I'm paid to do. If I never straddle another horse, I'll try to survive the shock."

I looked at Block. He grinned and shook his head negatively. "I'm staying out of this."

I said, "Okay, Will. If you need a day or two to think about it, go ahead."

Will could care less if a horse was a horse or a camel. Someone once said a man never gives his task at hand his full 100% until he was handicapped in some way or another. I was handicapped. The Sierra Vista Customs Patrol Station was about to go another few months without an interdiction of smuggled drugs into the U. S. Simple logic.

One needs to understand that the necessities of interdicting smuggled drugs into the U. S. included the correct working hours, meaning twenty-fours per day, or when the situation called for it. Going to work on schedule five days a week and announcing it each time over the air did nothing but give the bad guys an advantage. Horses with riders and out of uniform shifted some of the advantage to our side. Being spotted patrolling the border fence in vehicles in wide open country gave the smugglers our habits and working hours. Like the illegal aliens, they entered behind us after we passed their crossing places.

We needed horses to parallel the border about a half-way between the highway and the border. We never needed to patrol the fence. We needed to patrol miles north of the border or simply short of the highway that paralleled the border. We needed to watch for their tracks and take whatever action necessary. We were to ride in different directions in paralleling the border and on different distances from the fence. Most of all, we needed sound and sensible horses. But above and beyond all else: We desperately needed to stop announcing going to and from work on the air! This is not so difficult for the average mentality.

Worsening matters, renting the horses was altogether a full time job. In order to rent them, we first had to wait until the civilian employees that worked for the army to open their office at Eight A.M. We lost two hours of valuable daylight right there.

Whoa! Did you just ask, "How about checking them out earlier?" No way! We were told that we would respect their working hours or go somewhere else for our free riding privileges. I desperately wanted to go somewhere else.

We had to rent a horse trailer to reach the border in a timely manner. The same man who inspected our truck dozens of times earlier, inspected it to make sure that we had trailer brakes, which were there in show only. We signed their stupid rental agreements. We checked out the tack with valuable time lost. They trusted us to not steal saddle pads and bridles, and saddles. Talk about irony! Nothing they had was worth stealing, not their saddles, bridles, bits, pads, or horses. I liked their big barn. No one but the federal services and their civilian contractors could afford such a monstrosity.

The civilians who work for the military and federal officers can co-exist when there's a common goal. There was no common goal between me and those highly overpaid stable hands. A more friendly and hospitable attitude could be found in a Saudi Prince after he caught an American trying to kiss his sister.

I respectfully requested to look through their corral for our horses to ride instead of them bringing our two horses to us. Of course I could. Now that was progress!

I found ten horses in the entire *remuda* of 100 that looked like they could carry a man a half-day under easy and slow riding. Unfortunately, these were the exact horses that were used by the "Company B Troop," the group of riders that rode in rodeo parades all over the southwest as they represented the famous Buffalo Soldiers of the old west. They wore the old blue cavalry uniforms of the original Buffalo Soldiers. Ft. Huachuca was still the home of the original Buffalo Soldiers in spirit only. In other words, these horses were not for rent.

If those exact horses of Company B weren't going to be used within the week, I could go ahead and choose them for the day. Otherwise, I'd have to use their remaining wastes of skin and bones. I got to use two of them once during fourteen months. They were decent horses to ride. But the Buffalo Soldiers were jealous of their mounts and didn't want Customs Patrol Officers riding them.

So we rode what they brought out to us. It ruined my day. The horses were gentle on the ground and loaded into the trailer without protest. That's the extent of the intelligence after having been driven quite mad by riders that knew absolutely nothing about riding and issuing commands to a horse. Horses should never be subjected to such abuse. If the animal rights activist had an ounce of intelligence, renting horses would cease to exist.

The border fence crossed mountains that belonged to the NPS and the Iron Mountain Ranch. An old friend from northern Arizona was foreman of that ranch, Paul Alasteuy. He offered to loan us good horses to ride. I refused his offer. Customs wanted us handicapped for reasons of their own, all of which boiled down to dumbuttedness. My arguments had only strengthened their resolve. Paul told me that I was the same as always, bull-headed. He was positive that he could talk sense to the branch chief and my boss. There was no use in frustrating him, too. We rode the stupid stable horses as ordered.

The civilian Civil Service employees had purchased, for the army, more than 100 head of rejects that local ranchers had been selling them one and two at a time for decades. If they bucked, the army didn't want them. If they died, they were buried where the army chose to bury them. Most were gentle, some ill bred, yet they were still hot blooded and spoiled rotten by the people who paid money to ride a horse. One could bring no worse mental agony to a horse than handing an inexperienced rider the reins for a couple hours without the strict control of a cranky horse wrangler. Renting horses in the open that way needed to be as unlawful as hitting the horses' knees with nine-pound hammers.

As for interdicting smuggled drugs, we could have walked with poodles on a leash and performed a better job. No one can track while riding one of these barn-crazed plugs that knew noting but to fight the bits and to run in circles. They danced sideways, slung their heads, twisted and spun in circles. If an officer was suddenly forced to shoot from the back of one those brainless crow baits, the bullet would have struck the shooter between the shoulder blades. They could spin and run at the same time, and that would be while they were striking our noses and chins with the tops of their heads. If I tried to stop and study the ground my face would receive a fast swat by a long tail. Rental horses, as the entire world knows, except the management of U. S. Customs, are kosher for dog chow only. Hunters up north use them as bear bait.

Any rancher that would sell a horse to a rental outfit is as ruthless and unjust to the horses as any horse abuser who would tie it to a post and whip it with chains. But ranchers loved dollars more than they loved their horses that weren't suitable for ranch work. This way no money was involved by having a vet to put a horse down or having to buy a bullet to shoot it. Sell it to the army for a dude horse was the American way among the ranchers in that area.

Each time I rented those horses, henceforth known as fleabags, I had to grovel in front of the civilian personnel in charge of the horses, which was sufficiently humiliating for anyone inside one day. For example, I wiped my feet before entering their clean barns. I not only had to sign for the horses, tack, and trailer, I had to sign a paper that stated that I was not renting the horses for pleasure! For pleasure! *Wasn't there someone this side of Heaven that would give me a break?*

It turned out to be no laughing matter to them. I learned this after the first rental agreement transpired. Two of them filed a complaint against me for being rude (laughing in their faces). I was only laughing at such a ludicrous suggestion. In fact, I almost lost my breath laughing so hard and slapping my knees. I didn't ask them if they were kidding but once.

They liked Kem Shulton. Kem had tact as did Will and Block. For once, accidental or not, I had done something right and cleared myself from having to deal with those good people. Kem could see no difference between them and any other civil service employee, but he liked people, a trait that I could have and should have practiced.

At the end of our four-hour day, which was all the time we were allowed if we were to complete their paperwork and go through the rituals. For example, we *actually* had to sweep out the horse trailer and hose it down with water each time we used it! That, too, exceeded the boundaries of good sense! Again! Anybody--everybody!--knows that you just don't do that!

When a stock trailer gets too dirty to use, you give it to your brother-in-law, sell it, or junk it, and buy a new one. That's been the tradition for decades, and here these guys were breaking another age-old custom. I've yet to meet a civilian working for the military that could eat a bowl of cereal without verbal instructions.

I owned a complete set of good tack and always have, but I would never strap it aboard a dude horse, rental horse, fleabag. In the 1920's some starved out rancher in California had discovered that he could rent his riding horses for money. He called the customers "Dudes."

Had it not been for the paychecks that Customs provided my poor family, I wouldn't have ever stepped aboard a dude horse. Did I think that I was too good for them or something? Oh—yes! Absolutely! Honor and professionalism sometime fall miles apart.

Contrary to Congressional tradition, federal officers patrolling our land border by horses saved taxpayers a bundle on gasoline and vehicle maintenance expenses.

Then it happened! Oh-how I detested that day!

Will Williams had wisely claimed annual leave the day when we were assigned to ride the border horseback. Block drove the trailer to where we unloaded the horses on the border and agreed to meet us ten or fifteen miles further in three or four hours. By that time, the remaining of the shift would be spent turning the horses and trailer back to the U. S. Army. More valuable time lost in using those rental horses! Atrocious.

There was no small wonder the drug smugglers were walking all over us!

33

Fortunately, Kem Shulton loved to have fun on the job as he did riding. Instead of calling into the Branch Office by radio and giving them our exact positions for the day, we lied.

Why? Because the drug smugglers monitored all of our radio transmissions. We stated that we would ride the border west of the mountain for a few miles and call it a day. Then we headed for the opposite direction, straight for the eastern flats.

Kem wasn't the least upset while his horse slung its head and swished its tail while dancing sideways. My horse was a blur that day. I didn't know where we were or what direction we traveled. I suffered from motion sickness and had much rather be aboard a stinking camel! I had to remain focused on dodging the top of his head and often grabbed his tail and tried to yank the hair out by its roots. I finally managed to tie the tail to the back D-ring of the saddle. That saved my face for awhile. It never occurred to me to tie the tail with a rope between his back legs that was anchored to the cinch underneath. One doesn't think on days like that.

That's the way it went that day. After two hours of misery for me and a total delight for Kem, he stumbled onto a visible trail of south-bound smugglers. Fresh! Illegal immigrants never walk south. They walk north. Drug smugglers walk south after they had delivered a load to the highway. We back-tracked them three miles north toward the east-west highway and found where a load of marijuana had been smuggled from the time we called in our lies on the radio.

To help convince management that a horse is a horse and it doesn't matter what type of horse it is, Kem had discovered the tracks! I hated that! If my strict code of ethics and principles were trampled any further, my chest would have caved. *Kem found those tracks by accident!*

Kem did all the tracking in a fast gallop, while I attempted to will myself into dying. A fast gallop suited our horses just fine. We were north-bound toward the corrals, even through the corrals were twenty-five miles distant! That's where our horses were headed.

I asked Kem to rein up prior to reaching a brushy area close to the highway and scouted the area all around prior to entering the brush. I scanned the ridges overlooking the brushy area carefully for a sniper. This was a common practice in the event of armed smugglers were guarding the load. The load was well hidden in the brush, all 600 pounds of it. I rode the perimeter and found the tracks of a guard, but he was long gone or had gone invisible. So long as he didn't shoot at us, he was free to go. Getting a conviction on a guard over a load in those times would be a miracle.

Block picked us up. A trooper from Douglas arrived to pick up the load and haul it to Nogales. It was a happy day for the Sierra Vista Station. For me it was losing the war.

Kem and I helped hose down the trailer and hung our tack where we found it in the huge barn. Kem turned in the paperwork. The employees greeted Bock and Kem but ignored me.

That topped the end of a perfectly miserable day, getting beat in the field and at the horse corrals. I had set about to wash the horse trailer to the point of where one could eat off the floor! It had to be inspected by one of them. The man nosed around, sniffed, grumbled to himself a couple of minutes and sighed as he motioned me to go unhitch it. So many times we had to hose it down again due to a small twig no bigger than half-toothpick was imbedded in the floor.

Our boss was grateful for the marijuana seizure, yet he was at a loss in why we didn't do this once a week. My youngest daughter could have drawn him a picture of why we didn't. I took the advantage of mentioning the type of horses we had to ride. That was as factual as I could get. He didn't want to hear it. I was a lost cause, because Kem had just proven me wrong.

We could, indeed, track men on rental horses. Kem deserved a pat on the back before he stood in front of the firing squad that I silently wanted him to face. If I were Japanese 100 years ago, I would've sunk a dagger deep into my gut and gone to Heaven in harmony instead of suffering the loss of the biggest challenge of my life.

Chapter Four

A Slow Learner

One group of backpacking smugglers (mules) used one trail into the desert once too often. The mere $200, the price of a mule to carry the marijuana across the border and deposit it at a predestinated place on the north-south highway, lacked excitement for one smuggler. His need to live the dramatics one finds on television. It almost cost him his life.

Lukeville, Arizona. They smuggled right under our noses two to three times per week. I believed we were actually passing each other on the trail. I counted five and six sets of the same tracks each time we tracked them. Each set of fresh tracks appeared to be two to five days old. They walked on their tracks north and southbound and to the side of the trail that would extend a quarter-mile in width at times. Since tracks appear fresh in the desert several days, to stay on the same set of tracks for the group of five or six was challenging. Of course, we also contended with the illegal immigrants that also used the trail.

The smugglers often walked single file in rocks or in a sandy wash for a mile, then on hard surface, then back to the wash for miles. Sometimes they would spread out and walk side by side over a span of several yards.

While we rode north on their trail, they were walking south close to their trail. They could hide in the brush or in a wash anywhere over a space of ten miles while they hiked backed to Mexico. I suspected this by watching my horse. He would alert on something for a second and then it was over. I have stopped and ridden in circles to search for a man or men lying under the brush dozens of times. Then, my horse might have simply spotted a critter taking refuge in the brush while we passed.

It's most important to ride a decent horse while tracking. He needs to keep his head still, except to expel a fly or some other pest. He needs to move exactly as he's urged, slowly, bit by bit, or else move at a normal pace, whatever the situation requires. Once the horse and rider understands one another, a tracking team is formed. I liked the discipline the Mexico cowboys taught our horses before they were turned into drug smugglers.

It was this group's arrests in early1978 that marked the decline of the first wave of narcotics smuggling through the Lukeville Station's jurisdiction. This group also gave us the most trouble.

Each of the five, perhaps six, was difficult to track. They walked backwards, on one foot, hopped, skipped, and hurdled rocks. They walked on rocks. Their shoes were almost alike and I never found more than five prints that I could memorize with confidence. Had there been seven, I wouldn't have been surprised. Never were all the tracks readable at the same time. They drug tiny marks over one or two of their plainer tracks, each way, to simulate a blowing twig or grass stem, just to make them look older. A track can appear fresh in the desert with no wind for a week. I often had to put my foot down alongside a week old track before I could notice the difference. It was slight. From a horse and at first glance, it was difficult to tell the difference.

Backpackers of this particular group smuggled approximately sixty pounds of packaged marijuana on their backs once and twice weekly into the United States for several weeks. They, and others, paralleled the last trail a few feet and crossed over old trails to confuse us. They'd spread out at times instead of single file. The illegal immigrants always left a trail of litter behind them, cigarette butts, plastic milk cartons, orange peelings, etc.

Backpackers, on the other hand, carried nothing extra. If they had water, it was stashed along the trail. The sixty pounds they carried over a distance of many miles was a sufficient load. I have put sixty pounds of rocks in my backpack and duplicated these guys the best I could in order to learn more about them. I needed water. Lots of it, and my load grieved me unmercifully in the rougher terrain.

In the sizeable boulders, the smugglers always stopped for a rest. I found their crushed filter-tipped cigarettes pushed down between the igneous boulders on each trip. I tossed all of them away in order to determine when they passed. We could determine the times they smuggled, or close to it, from this method. Mexico's laborers, especially the smugglers, always smoked. That's a given. They could well afford the vice. They also had stashed water in the boulders. We found it and drained it on more than one occasion. Was that endangering their lives? The well-traveled north-south highway was only a quarter-mile to a mile at any given time, so I didn't think so.

By dumping their water, we forced them to shorten their distance and move to the highway for help. If this meant abandoning their loads of marijuana, so be it. However, they still beat us at this. They began to carry their water on their packs. We were forcing them to be stronger from the extra weight.

SCPO Tilton and I tracked them from the border several times over many miles to their many stash sites without success, and we hardly missed them an hour. They and their loads were gone by the time we arrived. They delivered their loads over a two-mile stretch alongside the north-south highway. The U. S. Border Patrol, who seldom stepped outside their vehicles adhered to the highway in hopes of finding their stash areas.

We worked well as a team, Tilton and I. Blind luck provided him the opening he needed while he worked alone that day. Other officers believed that Tilton had a special gift in seizing loads while alone. Some claimed that he could go to sleep in the desert and the backpackers would drop a load next to his cot. He seemed that lucky. Tilton always made his own luck.

These mules were gluttons for punishment. After delivering the loads alongside a predestined spot on the north-south highway, they sometimes jogged the entire distance back to Mexico. This could be up to fourteen miles. Of course, this meant they delivered at night. If they delivered in the daytime, they walked back south over the same trail, careful to dodge us riders. I've seen their southbound tracks where they walked, stopped, jogged and run.

Mules (backpackers) didn't have to think really hard to beat us. The country was big and there were a lot of backpacking smugglers. They simply made the deliveries when no one else was about and when they thought they had the best chance of being successful. They found their best time, two to four in the mornings when most of the officers were asleep. They delivered behind us as we tracked them north from a previous time. They knew we had to saddle up and wait for sunup before we could track them.

But how did we know when they smuggled? A Customs Patrol Officer we called Big Sam, an ex-special services veteran. He worked the Midnight to Eight Shift and would check for their sign at four or five each morning, five days a week. If he found the tracks, he called Tilton, the supervisor, at home and woke him. Tilton would then call me. We would drive twenty miles south to where we kept the horses. After saddling and wishing we had breakfast or some coffee to start the day like normal people, we found their tracks at daylight and began tracking them north.

Backpackers and the drivers of cars that drove south from Phoenix or Tucson to pick up these loads delivered by our backpackers were also called mules. The mules are the poor-boy jobs that always melted the hearts of Arizona's judges. For that matter, federal judges loved them to a point where I'm sure they've set up college funds for them. The loads would be found at predestinated areas. Mules from Tucson or Phoenix received 200 dollars for the night's work. That, of course, went to feed their families and the parents and grandparents of the families. The fact that they looked like they were raised in prison and had the prison tattoos from Mexico and the U. S. didn't matter to the judges. It didn't matter if the arrestees had records miles long, judges pitied them. Judges shot darts of hatred with their eyes to the officers that arrested them.

Mexico is a socialist nation under a dictatorship that elects its dictators each six years. Each elected president designates his followers. Another is chosen to simply run against him with no chances of winning. In fact, the second one makes sure his campaign will not get him elected. Voters will vote for the chosen man that is to be elected president. The news media does that for us but we don't face governmental harassment if we don't abide by their judgment, not yet, anyhow. Mexico's government hasn't changed, except in name, since the middle ages. The poor were kept that way, under control, no guns, and starving. Each revolution earned the country a new dictator that knew only the socialist philosophy. It's a fact of life. It's unlimited power to those in office.

So why do we bother to arrest the poor souls? We would also starve if we didn't have a job. That's the nature of the beast in the land of the free bordering a socialist country.

Not to worry about our arrested drug smugglers. The judges turned them loose as fast as they were arrested. Anyone but an honest taxpayer can melt the heart of a judge. A mule can apologize to a magistrate within hours after an arrest and be released within seconds. Pedophiles have learned this art decades ago. I guess the mules learned it from the pedophiles.

Defense attorneys are still paid by the taxpayers to make sure that no civil rights of the smugglers have been violated. Under the Carter Administration, a mule would practically volunteer to be arrested just for a day off from work. He faced no jail time. Nevertheless, we never noticed such irony and we never knew when we might have to go to court. Going to court meant that Search and Seizure rules had to be strictly followed. I didn't mind that so much. Search and Seizure rules practically wrote themselves under our Constitution. The U. S. Constitution is much easier to read than U.S. Search and Seizure regulations written by lawyers that never learned to use the English language properly, so I simply obeyed the Constitution in all my activities. Unless the Search and Seizure laws were stretched, stepped on, ambiguous, and written with nouns interchangeable with verbs and unheard of adjectives, the defense attorneys wouldn't have a job in our system. Anything wrong found in court with our seizure, we'd know how to dodge it the next time. Or—we could talk our federal prosecutor into fighting it because they don't know the Search and Seizure laws any better than the imbeciles that wrote them. If we actually studied the laws as instructed, we'd have no time to work. To simplify this, I cannot read junk writing that's called laws unless they make sense and are not ambiguous in six different directions. Neither can lawyers. They bluff a lot. Only another attorney will challenge bluffs and affirmations, however. After all, the court is our final step in the justice system. It needs to be operated correctly. That's why lawyers own it.

The lack of prosecutions was really no problem for us, until the White House changed from liberal to conservative. Then, when the smugglers knew they faced real jail time, they became hard to arrest and would physically attempt to avoid handcuffs. These were rumors. We had no real problem with smugglers until one of our guys, years later, was murdered by a mule in 1986.

In the meantime, no smuggler has ever fought seriously with me or with other officers at my station. They only scuffled harmlessly to get away. If one of them ever seriously fought with me, and if I won or survived, which was doubtful, the Rodney King Civil Rights violation in Los Angeles would have appeared more like love pats. That fighter would definitely be hurting for a long time, providing he lived passed the lesson he would receive—providing I was able. I was fond of my children and no dirt bag was going to make them orphans. I could care less about the defense attorney's practice in assuring the arrestee's rights were not violated if an arrest ever became that physical.

Tilton, who shared this philosophy, was seriously tested the day he arrested this group of strong backpackers. It is for this reason that I would never be a city cop. Those people are grossly underpaid for the dangers they face daily.

We had two officers working the Midnight shift that would spot the tracks of these mules. Big Sam had a partner that night. They cut the sign at the border and notified Tilton.

These mules also possessed a great amount of physical strength. That fact is solid. However, one will have to admit at least one of these backpackers wasn't the smartest mouse in the maze. He inspired this story--not Tilton or any of his incredible and uncanny blind luck!

I'm not an expert tracker. I have seen better trackers in the U. S. Border Patrol and in our officers at the Sells, Arizona Station. SCPO Weldon was a better tracker than me. Unlike Hollywood, no expert could even begin to tell how heavy a person was when he left tracks on the surface. Anyone claiming this might as well claim that he can tell what the person was talking about at the time he made the tracks. It simply doesn't happen! When I'd point to a significant track, Tilton always asked me the man's name or what he was thinking about while he made the track. If Tilton wasn't arguing, he was practicing sarcasm.

It was that day of blind luck for Tilton that my wife and I had to take our six-year old daughter to Tucson to see an ophthalmologist. It happened two times each month. We had been doing this for a year, so my days off were scheduled on those appointment days. Otherwise, I had no days off. Everyone worked seven days a week.

It was that day, a Friday, after the 300-mile round trip to Tucson, we returned home to find pictures of familiar footprints tacked to my front door. Under the prints was the scribbled message: "Five arrests and 300 pounds of marijuana! Thanks for getting the hell out of my way so I could catch those guys! --Tilton."

That was Tilton, my friend. He loved to have me to suffer through all of his warped sense of humor.

My wife had a chuckle. As for getting the out of his way, he was absolutely correct. It was me, however, who always told him the exact same thing during each trip. I'd beg him to go back to the house in order that I could concentrate on tracking those people, that I didn't need his witty remarks. We suffered through each other's jokes and always kept the bitter side of reality within easy reach. He actually pretended to listen to me during the serious moments of tracking those people. He also claimed that he never learned much.

I was sick at heart, but our trip to the doctor was worth it. The entire station would soon learn of his victory, even though the emphases would be placed on *my failure* to catch them--not *his luck* in catching them! No doubt about it, I was in for a thorough ego bashing. He had caught them alone and he'd darn socks for the Merchant Marines on a stinking Greek freighter before he'd ever let me forget it.

He, alone, had nabbed our elusive group while I was vacationing in Tucson, as the story first broke among us. It's a simple story, so recalling it didn't require notes or a lot of special memorization on my part. After the big routine, congratulatory remarks, and handshakes at the Briefing Room, we all settled in to hear what happened from the hero, himself. A few officers were already in the office by the time I arrived. Tilton didn't want to tell his story but once. After that, I lost count of how many times he told it.

Big Sam wasn't in attendance. Big Sam, later an excellent narcotics officer in Florida, said that he already knew the story and skipped the debriefing.

"Big Sam and I saddled up at sunup," he began, "just like Homer and I did for weeks. Big Sam had already spotted their new sign during his midnight shift--as he always did for me and Homer. He has excellent eyes for tracks, as we all know. He said the freshest sign was further east, so he followed that set north. I disagreed, and, as it usually turns out, I was right. Those Big Sam was following were illegal immigrant tracks. Big Sam not only fell behind on his horse, he got about a mile too far to the east and stayed that way. I tracked them alone up to Milepost 70, where the big, west-bound wash intersects Highway 85.

"Now--as we all know--Homer is a slow tracker. He and I together have never tracked them that far and that fast before. At the big wash, Milepost 70, I thought I heard voices where my trail was going to intersect the highway.

"I reined old Buck back to a slow walk. As we neared the wash, I thought it would be just my luck to be on a cold trail. The voices, naturally, would be those of picnickers from Phoenix. But as I got closer, they were all speaking Spanish and I could smell their stinking Mexico cigarettes and smelly bodies. Buck snorted. Anyhow, they talked so loud that they didn't even hear me until I suddenly emerged from the brush practically right on top of 'em!

"I had already pulled heat and was pointing it directly at their lips. All five of 'em were laying on top of their packs of marijuana, smoking and relaxed. They were waiting on the load car from Tucson, which was already running seriously late. They didn't jump up or run or anything. They just gawked. I could tell by their faces that they wanted to know where the hell Homer was. It was almost like they never had anything to fear whenever he was along.

"None of them spoke English, and I know even less Spanish. That was okay. Once they saw the heat, the silent language was automatically universal. I motioned for them to stand up and walk over and sit down by the highway. They did exactly that. I doubt if they would have obeyed so quickly if Homer was there. Homer is fluent in Spanish, providing he's talking with a three-year old that doesn't have a vocabulary larger than forty words. I have never seen him make anybody from Mexico move as fast as I made those guys move.

"Anyhow, the tallest and nearest smuggler, sort of innocent-like, walked slower. I suspected he was the leader of the group, and I suspected that I might have to shoot 'im. He was working his way in my direction as I followed them the short distance to the highway. I watched his back and knew that he was about to jump me. Buck suspected the very same thing. He tensed up just in time. That backpacker suddenly spun and sprang toward me like the blur of a charging leopard. It happened just like Little Buck expected. I didn't even have to dodge! Old Buck did it for me. All I had to do was ride. The smuggler missed me a mile, but I didn't miss him! I just automatically reached out and tapped 'im on his head with the barrel of my .357 as he was going down empty-handed.

It had all happened before I realized it! That sucker had just received the biggest 'V' in his skull that any man has ever received from the barrel of a pistol. It had to be three inches long and about that deep right between his ears! I had bashed his skull in as far as his nose, crumpled his forehead, and spilled brains everywhere. That's what I was thinking and it scared the blazes outta me!"

I had to interrupt Tilton at this point. "For goodness sakes!" I said.

He paused to let his mistake soak in on us slow people.

"We'll be hearing about this!" I said. I was watching Tilton tell the story and laughed with the others laugh each time he gut-shot me. But we all groaned at this point of the story. I added: "Nobody--and I mean nobody!--NEVER!--EVER!--hits anybody on the head with the barrel of a gun! That's one of the biggest no--no's the ACLU and other bleeding hearts have ever dreamed up! No gun barrels! Shoot 'em first! Period! I doubt if Wyatt Earp ever did that. Really! A gun barrel across the skull in the heat of battle is instant death! How did you know that he wasn't just asking for a cigarette?"

"You didn't really hit him with your gun barrel!" someone gasped while we all clutched our chests.

"I did." Tilton was unshaken and perfectly confident. "Homer, actually, is probably the only one that would ever do anything that dumb, but he was safely sharing a wine bottle with his friends in the shade of the dumpster behind the Tucson Bus Terminal at that very moment! I had to go it alone. Now, let me tell you, that guy dropped like every muscle in his body had suddenly stopped functioning!

He spilled down on top of his feet like Beetle Bailey does when he's crowned by Sarge. I had bashed that sucker's head in like it was an egg!

"The other four backpackers stopped and looked at me. I could hear them thinking, 'He didn't do nothin'!' I motioned for them with the gun barrel to sit down next to the highway, which wasn't ten feet away. They did, like, within a fraction of a second. They actually bounced and slid on their bottoms next to the highway! I looked down at the dead man. He was in a fetal position, holding his head and groaning! Thank goodness! I had just won myself a reprieve from being tried for murder in a federal court by a Democrat judge! Right then and there I made myself a solemn vow to never, never, never hit a man on the head with a gun barrel again! That was out. I was lucky that he lived."

I interrupted Tilton again. "Well done, Tilton. Can we go home now?"

The other officers laughed and urged him to continue. They wanted to hear him rip me apart a few more times. Tilton's troops always had high morale at my expense.

I said: "I don't suppose it occurred to you to just hit 'im with a coiled rope."

That remark rattled Tilton sufficiently. He raised his voice a few octaves. "I wasn't out there in my spare time killing the National Park Service's rattlesnakes with a rope! I had pulled my heat to effect an arrest. If they ever get around to sending you to the academy, Homer, they'll teach you things like that. You use your sidearm in felony arrests instead of ropes."

I argued that Wyatt Earp never really hit anybody over the head with his eight-inch gun barrel--but I don't know that. I said, "Wyatt knew better. Gun barrels crush skull caps. Of course Wyatt Earp never had to worry about the ACLU or a liberal judge, either."

"Just let me tell my story!" Tilton snapped. "That guy squirmed around a bit on the ground and then he was on his feet as fast as lightening! Little Buck shied away again and saved my life the second time. Sure enough, before I could even think, I had chopped 'im on the head with the gun barrel the second time! 'Damn!' I said.

"He rolled into the fetal position again, holding his head with both hands, groaning and gasping for breath. This time I just knew that he was holding his skull cap together with his hands for sure! I had gotten 'im square between the ears in exactly the same place with my gun barrel the second time!

"Oh--yes!" Tilton scolded himself for our benefit. It was all the reprimand he would ever receive. "I didn't even hit 'im purposely the first time! It just happened the second time, too, before I even realized it!"

"So what happened then?" Johnny asked, imitating the attorneys that would be asking the same thing in the Deposition hearing weeks later.

"Well, I holstered my gun and yelled my head off tryin' to attract Big Sam's attention, that's what! He was still a mile away, still tracking the same group from another trip they had already made. I reached inside my saddle bag and called him by radio. About five minutes later he answered."

Johnny asked again, this time snickering. "Did the guy jump you the third time? Did you smite 'im with your gun barrel the third time just like Homer would've done?"

"Nothing like getting interrupted!" Tilton growled. "Anybody else care to say anything juvenile? Homer, do you care to make anymore dumb observations? I can remember the whole story without any of you guys' prompting. The man got up but he kept his head down and covered it with both arms. He groaned and sobbed. Lone lines of spit was trailing him. He drooled all over everything. He flopped down in the middle of the rest of them. One of them asked him something, and he answered negatively. Probably if it hurt or something like that.

"Big Sam came racing in on old Speck and pulled back on the bits like a roper training his horse to stop. He wanted to know what the hell I was doing over here when he had their sign over there! He was madder'n hell. I told 'im that he may have their sign over there but I had their bodies and marijuana over here! That really ticked Big Sam off. He got down and inspected the design of their shoes then swore it wasn't the same ones he was tracking. I just told 'im to go get his own smugglers, that he wasn't any better at tracking than Homer."

"Was it the same ones?" Johnny asked.

"Yes! Damn! I tell a good story and you don't even listen! It was the same group that Homer and I have been tracking two times a week for the past ten years! All I had to do was wait until I could get some decent help so's I could catch those guys."

Johnny snickered again, "Doesn't sound to me like you had any help at all!"

I braced for the next remark.

Tilton took his time and grinned broadly while I was trying to shush Johnny, who had opened the door for Tilton to gutshoot me again.

"Since you asked, I have to say that having Homer out of my way was something like hiring four good men!"

"Is that all there is to your story?" I asked without laughing with the rest of them.

"Yeah! You want to hear more or what?"

"Well," I said while getting up. "It sure wasn't very interesting. Even if you knew how to tell a story, it still stinks. The context was disarranged and your delivery lacked gusto. One would think that if you were going to call us all together, you'd at least organize your speech."

The smile left his lips. He always kept his waxed handlebar mustache looking like a pair of longhorns on a barroom wall. Proud! It suddenly fell straight down into a dippy-mean Ho Chi Min's. His lips were an upside down muleshoe. "Well--I'll tell you what! Things really didn't get this boring until you got back from Tucson!"

I glanced at Johnny. He was grinning at the fact that Tilton had gotten me twice within ten seconds. It would've been a chore for me to think up a good comeback inside a week. They all knew it, so Johnny rose to leave.

The five mules actually remained in jail overnight until the judge released them on their own recognizance at the preliminary hearing 24 hours later. The 300 pounds of marijuana went to the DEA to be burned. The smuggler didn't tell anyone that he got thumped on the head twice by the barrel of a .357 magnum. Crybabies and wimps among bandits in Mexico were never common. Had he been a U. S. citizen, he would've successfully sued Customs for millions.

About a month later, Johnny and I stopped by the intersection of the wash and the highway at Milepost 70. No doubt about it, old Buck had saved Tilton's life at that very spot. Twice! The only reason he had related the story to us, of course, was to recognize the fact that these guys, given the chance, can and will kill you if they think they can get away with it. I was sorry, in a way, that Tilton didn't hit the man harder. On the other hand, it was hard enough. He didn't cry about it in court. However, he might be wearing a steel plate in his head at that very time.

There would be no more smuggling here for months. I looked down and found a half-buried, fully loaded Mauser. It was a .380 automatic. It had been lost about the time Tilton had caught those guys and was in good shape.

Not many criminals will challenge a professional officer holding a .357 with a .380, not even one out of five in this particular group of mules. The little automatics are nice weapons for ladies who can latch their fingers around it while they're being strong-armed.

I said, "He could've killed Tilton with this thing."

"I dunno," Johnny said, slightly amused. Now if the mule could've shot a rattlesnake with it and then threw the snake at Tilton. That would've killed him faster than a bullet from this little pea shooter."

I was proud of Jiohnny for saying that. He usually kept such comments to himself. He was slowly but surely learning negative humor with a hint of sarcasm, a positive sign that Tilton and I were good for the man's character.

Chapter Five

The Blunder of the Decade

I don't know who it was that made up this crazy rule of never turning a horse loose in a strange pasture or corral without first checking the entire fence. Everyone knows to do it. It's plain common sense. It doesn't matter how large the pasture or the corral might be. Check it. Only God is capable of forgiving this failure. The first thing a horse or horses are going to do after wallowing and eating is to check that fence of the new corral or pasture. If there's a flaw, it will be found in short order.

One spends a lifetime trying to learn all of the rules, then dies short of success. The end result: One stupid mistake will undo a lifetime of abiding by the rules.

I refer to myself as a cowboy in these chapters, but the truth is that I've only worked in the profession a few years. I've wasted my money entering rodeos in the riding events, bareback, saddle broncs, and bulls. I was bucked off many times. While I made all the local rodeos, I worked on a large cattle ranch as a cowboy. The truth of the matter is that I've never been called a cowboy by a cowboy. I've heard real cowboys call men recently deceased "Cowboys" many times. In the cattle world, the term cowboy is a word of honor and prestige. Yet movies and television use it to describe a rebel, an unmanageable cop with gusto or a dummy. An American hero of the 20th and 21st century, Rush Limbaugh, uses the word regularly to describe an airhead that made it big in politics. These character types lack the substance of integrity, honesty, dedication, loyalty and hard work. So much for the trashy pieces of mankind, the word cowboy was born and it will die as a word of honor and great achievement.

Every redneck with a black t-shirt and big hat is not a cowboy, nor is the present President of the United States, who has been filmed in a decent hat and boots, both worn with dignity. He still fell short of the mark. So did John Wayne. As they say about some men in aviation, "He might fly an airplane but he sure the heck is not a pilot."

When cattle and horses are involved, there aren't enough colleges, years of experience, and men in the world to teach any one man all the rules, yet all violations of the rules are filed away in the files of *dumb-buttedness,* and, like the violator, he is never forgiven. No one wants that. No cowboy has ever escaped it.

My small mistake is remembered as "The Blunder of the Decade!"

By now, I suppose you think that I'm going to confess to a violation and that this story is about my breaking one of the basic rules. Okay.

Actually, it wasn't my fault. The NPS ranger shoulders the full responsibility. But since he has never claimed to belong to the cowboy profession, it's okay. Perhaps I should not have belonged to the profession, either. It was hot that day.

Ranger Dexter and I were riding near the *Quitobaquito* area on the Mexico border, a day trip. He had straddled a horse less times in his life than he had fingers, yet he learned fast, other than sitting sideways in the saddle once his bottom became scalded after an hour or so. He didn't wear denims like I suggested. His rough uniform was supposed to suffice. As I told him earlier, it won't and it didn't. He may have looked like a softie, but that PhD had a tolerance for pain.

We rode on to Williams Springs, three or four miles across country, northwest of *Quitobaquito* where I had parked the trailer. I was learning the names of plants and how they adapted to the tough climate in southern Arizona's hottest desert. He used the words *evolved* and *adapted* as if they aren't synonymous.

We rode across a wide but shallow wash near Williams Springs. The wild burro had pawed holes in the wash three feet deep in search of water. To see animals go to this extent of having a few sips of muddy water was not only heart breaking but baffling. There were water tanks every ten miles or so in this area of the desert. Most all are well hidden and known only by the wildlife and the desert's caretakers, such as Ranger Dexter.

"Why did they dig these holes?" I asked. "Williams Springs isn't but about a half-mile away."

He was reluctant to answer at first, for he had been saving me from learning a few more facts about our unfair world, or better stated, our socialist national park system. "You haven't heard? Well, it's no big secret, but then, we want as few people possible to know about it."

I was really confused by his low key monologue. No one was within fifteen miles of us!

What he was avoiding telling me was that Williams Springs, a water hole for wildlife for centuries, had been fenced off from the wild burro! The wild burros were being trapped by cowboys at the easier accessed water holes. I demanded to know the whole story. It wasn't a pretty picture, and he was no longer my friend. I allowed him to continue to sit astride a Customs horse when I should have left him afoot in the desert and let him suffer like the wild burros. They were trapping them in the interior of the national monument while I unknowingly worked in the same area!

What he explained was that the wild burros were being removed from the Organ Pipe National Monument. Two professionals were contracted by the National Park Service to trap every last one of the wild burros without the public knowing about it. The burros, he claimed, had been here since the era of Spanish explorers, yet they weren't native to federal lands. How's that for twisting facts? Where dollars are concerned, facts can completely disappear!

First, I'm not convinced about our equines being brought here from Spain and Europe. I know, most all the books state that they were. It's taught in college. I am convinced, however, that we have always had equines in the western hemisphere, just as we have had species of elephants, rhinos and camels, all native, right here on United States soil! Yet all of our species of asses in the United States are imported from Spain? I don't think so!

All the wild burros' water holes were fenced off! The man-made waterholes were fenced with one-way gates into a large corral. The burro that didn't allow itself to be trapped inside a corral would die of thirst. It could either die of thirst or die fast at the hands of the killers at a pet food factory. The holes we saw dug were of burro already dying of thirst. I was hopping mad. No one had the moral right to commit that atrocity and I'm not even an animal rights activist! The only tree I ever hugged was when I climbed it.

Ranger Dexter openly agreed with the NPS, that the wild burros should be removed from all federal lands. It was probably his idea, he and the dog food companies. I can only imagine that a part of Congress cashed in on this, also.

The lingering wild steers from the last rancher on the monument were also being trapped. Some of those steers were as large as horses, perhaps larger, and maybe ten or fifteen years old. Their split hoof tracks were larger than the size two shoes for my big palomino.

"You're working for a mighty poor outfit." I informed him of that with prejudice. "Did you not know that there are equine fossils, along with many elephants and camels found in North America?"

"No." He didn't argue but he definitely thought that I should be slightly more open on the subject.

He said, "Those fossils are of extinct species in North America and perhaps a million years old. The burros were introduced to this country a hundred years ago by prospectors."

Whoa! "These wild burros are the same ones the Mexicans raise. Any prospector from the east would have a larger breed of burro. No prospector wanted the small Mexico donkey to pack all his gear. They do that in the movies."

I was correct. All the wild burros I saw were of the Mexico breed. They were here before the white man came. They were here thousands of years before this cattle ranch was made, unfortunately, into a national monument.

He wanted to calmly discuss the subject and continued to do so. "Of course, white men purchased the burros from the Mexicans after they decided they would prospect the desert. The Mexican burros derived from the Spanish explorers. Everyone knows that."

"Not everyone," I told him.

We rode without my voice raising one octave. "These burros are living fossils of what you claim are over a million years old. The Mormons claim there were horses, elephants, and all the species belonging in the camels' genus over here as mid-eastern people populated both the North and South American continents, which was about seven centuries prior to Christ's crucifixion.

He became self-righteous at the word *Mormon*. He said, "I'm a Lutheran, myself. I take no stock in what any religious organization might claim in regards to science. I didn't know you were Mormon, so I apologize if I've offended your beliefs."

He was riding little Buck and I silently willed the horse to run him into a *cholla*. "I'm not Mormon! I was born and raised a Baptist, which is why I know everything there is to know about all the religious sects claiming Christianity, including the Mormons, Jehova's Witnesses, the Lutherans, and the Catholics! I've read the Mormon's book, and they mentioned horses right here in North and South America slightly over 2,500 years ago!"

"I can't help that. I choose to follow what science has proven."

"Science have proved absolutely zilch about the equines! It's all theory. Besides, the Mormons have just as many scientists as the Lutherans."

He was becoming exasperated. He wasn't dressed for the sun, anyhow. I suggested we drop the subject and ride to Williams Springs to assess the damage. I wanted to find just one dead carcass. Then those cowboy trappers and me, whoever they were, would be having an understanding.

"By the way!" I said in hopes of blowing away the dark cloud hanging him. "Tilton, Weldon and I are going to be camping at Williams Springs soon. Then we'll ride by horse further west to Papago Well. If we don't find anything of Customs interest, we'll be returning on the third day."

He thought carefully before responding, considering the practicalities of us using horses instead of vehicles and what we would do if found anything. "Ah--yes, I suppose that will be an interesting trip."

I rode the new fence that surrounded Williams Springs. There were several natural springs in the area. All of them were fenced. The one where we would camp would be close to the large ironwood trees where the house of the Williams family used to stand decades earlier. It was difficult to see every inch of the fence on the south side due to the contractors having stretched the wire through a grove of tall mesquite. *I had ridden the fence and found it flawless.* I could not, however, ride through the mesquite—not without a great deal of difficulty.

Tilton, Weldon and I rode the approximate twenty miles from our corrals to Williams Springs. We arrived there late in the afternoon and built a fast gate inside the newly constructed fence.

Weldon said, "I'll ride the fence."

"Go ahead," I said, "but it's okay. I just rode it about a week ago."

It's impolite to ride over an area that's already been ridden, so he quickly turned his horse loose. "Damn, I ain't never did this before, but if you say you rode the fence, then it's been ridden."

"You can take it to the bank," I added with confidence.

"I'd ride the fence if I were you, Weldon," Tilton said. "Homer's been talking like a federal employee for about a year now."

If Tilton could find no one to argue with, he'd start one between two other people. We both ignored him.

We built a fire, heated C-rations over it and immediately became nauseated from the stench. They taste better hot but they stink beyond belief. I had extra drinking water and horse feed stashed in a garbage can well hidden in a mesquite thicket nearby. We had no water wagon on that trip.

Later, in the twilight, I found a broad clearing, one completely clear of big rocks and vegetation. I dropped my saddle and bedroll on the bare ground. That's not a good idea in the desert, for scorpions, T-rexes, and other man eating beasts can ruin a night's sleep. They're everywhere in the desert. No one should sleep on the ground. The water wagon always carried our cots and pillows. I used my saddle for a pillow, which is quite comfortable for the first two hours. After that, it's anything but comfortable. One has to be dead tired to use a saddle for a pillow all night long.

Two hours is about all the sleep anyone was going to get that night, anyway. A dark cloud suddenly blocked out the moon and stars, which is perfectly normal. It was about to rain a few drops, enough to make dew on the limbs for all the tiny creatures to partake, something science hasn't learned about yet, by the way. It rains a few drops almost every night throughout all the seasons in the desert. *All* animals need water to survive. They have fresh water daily to drink in the desert form these tiny rains. No animal depends upon insects and smaller animals for moisture. If anyone would stop and think about it, animals, birds and reptiles, need moisture for digestion, blood, eggs, and organs. The cloud grew heavier and heavier. Someone's barometer was definitely showing the little Dutch boy with an umbrella. I could visualize us being swept into a wash by a flash flood in another half-hour.

I shouted over Tilton's and Weldon's deafening snores, who slept about twenty yards apart, which is why I slept at least fifty yards distant. "It's going to rain!"

"Homer, shut the hell up!" Tilton yelled.

That's all the time he had to respond. A bolt of lightning struck a rocky mound nearby with a tremendous bang of thunder at the same time. I could've sworn the saddle jumped with me.

Weldon joined Tilton's sarcasm. "Well, if it ain't goin' to rain, it sure the hell's goin' to be a thunderstorm! Now both of you shut the hell up!"

That's all the time he had, too. Lightning kept our entire area well lit as if we were at a disco club where the noise is even greater. The deafening roars and strobe-like flashes were continuous. The rain that followed was more like Niagara Falls dumped on us all at once. The ground was flooded within seconds. It didn't let up. Of all the times I've slept on a cot in the desert, I had never been rained on like this. The first time I slept on the ground, it rained all night long!

Tilton kept a large fire going throughout the night. I hung my wet mummy bag on a limb nearby, along with the saddle blankets. Weldon was under a tarp, which was folded over him. Water flowed under his tarp. He would soon be floating away, drowning in inches of water. Weldon had a bad back. Once asleep, he could undergo surgery without waking up.

Little, greenish centipedes always come out after the water recedes in the desert. They're everywhere, every few feet. Thousands of them swarm and crawl over everything. They're about the size of a kitchen match. One stung me once, and I scratched the place for about a week after it quit hurting. Weldon didn't have long to sleep before he would be swarmed by centipedes.

Yet he snored off and on all night. The next morning he claimed he was drowning and didn't sleep at all.

The hours passed with Tilton feeding the fire that night, soaking wet, shivering and cussing. The centipedes would be out by the millions the moment the water moved away. I didn't like sitting on the wooden limb of the ironwood with my feet on the ground, but Tilton didn't seem to mind. I kept quiet about it.

It got lighter. The rain stopped like it started, all at once. The stars disappeared with the dawn. I said, "I ain't hearing Walker snore. Maybe he drowned."

Tilton said, "I ain't heard the horses all night long!" He kept saying that. What bothered me was him asking repeatedly if I were sure that I had ridden the fence in its entirety, which I had.

What worried me more was that I wasn't hearing the horses, either. Weldon finally said, "Homer, I ain't hearing the horses!"

I said, "If you only know how much you sound like Tilton, you'd shut the hell up. I know how to ride a fence. Both of you shut up!"

Both of them took turns at saying, "Yeah, we'll shut up after we find that hole in the fence."

It got light enough to see. No horses! I got sick to my stomach. No one makes a mistake like the one I had just made! I had apparently missed a hole in the newly constructed fence!

We had breakfast with Weldon mumbling something about me walking the twenty miles back to his vehicle, whereupon I'd drive it back here to Williams Springs where he would be waiting by the fire, then he and Tilton would ride back in the truck while I would be tracking the horses by foot. The little centipedes came swarming by the millions and disappeared a half-hour later.

In the brushy area, the horses' tracks clearly were one way all the way to the hole in the fence, the big bush. Inside the bush there was an obvious cut by someone that didn't like the fence anymore than I did. Perhaps it was Ranger Dexter, who remembered us using the corral that night where the water was located. The hole was hidden right in the middle of the bush where it must've been a bugger to see by the horses. The problem was, if Ranger Dexter had not cut it, the wild burro failed to find it. It was too well hidden. Our horses found

58

it right where the wires were cut. Ranger Dexter was definitely no longer my friend.

Both Tilton and Weldon agreed that they would've missed the hole if they had ridden the fence, maybe. The rule was that when one rides a fence, one sees every inch of it, including what was through the bushes.

We hid our saddles and equipment in the brush by the stash of drinking water and horse feed, then began our twenty-mile journey across the damp surface of the desert, on all four of the horses' tracks.

Tilton carried a handheld radio, which he used on top of a mountain about a mile into our hike. They were both tired. The dispatcher in Los Angeles read the transmission through a network of mountaintops between us that contained antennas for Customs and Border Patrol. The dispatcher telephoned Tilton's home, as requested, and notified Mrs. Tilton of our dilemma. An hour later she met us on the road to Quitobaquito in Tilton's truck. Her two little ones were inquisitive. Both Tilton and Weldon pointed toward me.

The four horses, three saddle horses and the pack horse, crossed the road to the border fence about two miles west of Lukeville, Arizona. They were on their way home in Mexico to starve all over again. Horses are forgiving creatures and never forget their roots.

Buck, *Chola* and Clyde were gentle but still had to be roped, even in a corral. The pack horse, the devil in disguise, old Speck, was wise beyond his years. I had no faith in catching the horses.

We tied a lariat to a post and stretched it ninety degrees from a fence post at waist high and moved the horses into that corner. Old Speck had none of that. He ran around us, but the other three huddled at the corner while I precariously roped all three one by one.

After retrieving our saddles, we rode them to the corrals late in the afternoon. This was barely in time to miss the second rain within twenty-four hours. Highly irregular for the desert!

Weldon has never forgotten about me failing to ride the fence, as it was a basic rule. I tried to tell him that Ranger Dexter had cut the fence after I had ridden it. He didn't buy that.

It went on to rain twenty-seven inches in the desert that winter and spring of 1977 and '78. Our brand new port of entry was flooded from the many weak areas of the roof. *Good enough for government work,* so the contractors claimed and quickly declared bankruptcy as tradition requires following all multi-million dollar projects.

Also, from that time forward, we used the water wagon and tied our horses to the shady *palo verdes* for the long rides that would last up to a week.

Chapter Six

Mistaken Identity

Customs Patrol Officer Johnny is one of the nicest human beings the traveling public or anyone local can meet. He's the most non-threatening human being in law enforcement. He's six feet and probably tops the scales at 150 with rocks in his pockets. His appearance and personality, however, are deceiving. Nothing frightens Johnny. He's far too intelligent to argue or allow any punk smuggler suspect push him into any type of physical or verbal argument. He was twenty-seven when the Customs Patrol picked him up from the Special Forces after he flew home from Viet Nam.

SCPO Tilton asked me to show him the desert. In doing so, I had the most boring chore of waiting while he studied maps at every intersection. He would stand for a half-hour sometimes, sorting out each hill and its relation to each mountain on his set of many maps. In a week he knew our desert as if he had grown up there.

He had a problem with the desert, however. The sun attacked his ruddy complexion each time he stepped outdoors. The sun penetrates the tiny holes in straw hats and will burn one's scalp in a day's time. Straw hats have to be the Guanajuato straws or a felt hat made in America. Johnny chose the felt made by one of the finest hat makers in America. It had the typical cowboy's four-inch brim, but it was brown. He actually needed to wear the silver belly (gray) like me. Then--of all things!--he turned the brim down like some phony farmer's picture in a magazine selling organic fertilizer! He reminded me of a bad guy in the movies--only worse!

I cautioned him against wearing that hat if he ever had to stop a tourist in the desert, or, for that matter, a suspect while wearing it. He was offended and quietly asked why. I spent the next half-hour explaining the concept of brown and black hats worn by bad guys in the movies since the 1930's. The good guys wore white hats like Gene Autry. The public carries a subtle image of these colors and automatically identify the bearer of a dark hat as a bad guy. He didn't argue. I thought I had reached him. I suggested he wear a silver belly since felt white hats are extremely rare. When we returned to the station, he respectfully told me that he'd be talking with SCPO Tilton, the head honcho at our station. I was second in command. I had, somehow, violated his civil rights.

Tilton backed me. Johnny thought we had conspired against him. He continued wearing his brown hat with the brim turned down on the horses on patrol, which posed no problem. The public seldom saw us—if ever. I asked him again not to wear it when driving a Customs vehicle. He said that I'd have to order him, and once I did, he'd have me in front of a reviewing committee, so I ordered him to not wear it. I urged him to find the same style of silver belly. He didn't. I didn't write him up. He didn't file a complaint. Then one day it happened.

A tourist walked into our office wanting to see a supervisor. He was a bird watcher that had stopped his van on the border at night and had spent a goodly amount of time there attempting to record the call of a poor-a-will, or something that flies at night and eats flying insects. Johnny pulled him over for a border search since he was leaving the border nexus. The tourist was scared out of his wits and rightfully so. He said, and I can quote:

"This cowboy or farmer-looking man pulled me over that was wearing a scary brown hat and driving this beat up old wreck of a Cherokee Chief that needed painting. He showed me his identification and badge. Man, I almost had a heart attack! He said that he was one of you guys. You guys...don't...usually dress like that, do you? I mean, actually, do you drive beat up contraptions like that?"

I assured him that it was one of the best U. S. Customs vehicles in our compound and it was seized from a well-known smuggler.

I called Johnny in and told him what happened. I told him that he'd better not be seen in that damned hat ever again! During a campout hardly a week later, his hat blew into the fire and was ruined before he could retrieve it. We shouldn't have laughed so loud. A week later he had another just exactly like it and wore into the field with the brim turned down and stopped another car before Tilton or I learned about it.

This time it was a couple who lived north in the state and was visiting his wife's parents on the reservation. Johnny and some overzealous kid from inspections did the stopping. The kid, being a former inspector at our port of entry, was never *deprogrammed* from Inspections. He took no guff off any tourist. He had the right to do this and that, so he searched their car whether they liked it or not. Johnny, in the meantime, talked to the man and his wife in his usual soothing tone. This was done from underneath his turned down brim, and, well, that was that! To simplify the matter: we were toast.

The man was still writing letters months later to every senator and congressman in Arizona, state and federal, and to every office Customs office that had ever dreamed of opening.

Tilton and I were called on the carpet in the District Headquarters. Tilton walked into the director's office shouting at him, wanting to know why the hell he was taking up our time, that it was a long drive from our office to his, and much more. The director listened and let Tilton have it, straight and to the point. "Get rid of that damned hat or get rid of the man wearing it!"

Tilton turned to me. I shrugged and said that I didn't know what he was talking about. No one wore a sloppy hat where we worked that I knew about. Furthermore, we'd be keeping whoever it was he was talking about, unless it was the kid from inspections. I'd turn him back into Inspections in a heartbeat.

Johnny was too valuable to undergo the firing process. Besides, Congress and the Supreme Court were too busy to mess with judging the firing of a federal employ under a liberal administration like Carter's. So I mentioned sending the kid back to inspections.

Tilton didn't want to get rid of Johnny, either. So he asked our district's director how he knew that twenty-four year-old kid from inspections wore a lousy hat. We were perplexed.

The director first made it plain that we'd be keeping the ex-inspector, that the Inspections Division didn't want him back, since the man had wanted to leave and that he also knew someone important in the state or federal government.

This time I really laid it on Johnny. The hat was gone or he was gone! The choice was his. But deep down, he knew he had at least a couple more complaints in the future before we got around to writing him up. I was willing to give him two to five more times, but he was going to have to change hat colors and style. It was that clear.

Then we had the El Salvadorian Incident months later in 1980. Reporters and freelancers filled every motel in Ajo and Lukeville, Arizona. This brought tons of reporters from all over that seemed to think stories were abundant out in the desert. They lasted for weeks.

During this time, Johnny approached a car in the desert that was well off the road and parked immediately next to the border fence. This was at 0200 hours. Johnny had watched the vehicle since Midnight and approached it much like a phantom. Johnny could sneak up on Indians, antelopes and deer in broad daylight.

The driver was sitting behind the wheel in the darkness, an ideal suspect for drug smuggling. He was silently listening to music on his tapes. He thought no one was around for miles out there in the stillness, and the music fairly well destroyed the desert's tranquility. That, alone, told Johnny that smugglers had better sense, but Johnny overlooked nothing. The windows were up but cracked.

Johnny tapped on his window. The man bumped his head on the roof and spilled all of his cameras. He turned his face to Johnny's light, which was held with one hand while his other held his revolver inoffensively.

Once the man settled down, and after Johnny was satisfied he was a freelancer from a city far north in Arizona, he advised the man to move on, that he could get hurt in this drug smuggling territory. Johnny stated it friendly enough. The man agreed, but he had gotten a good look at Johnny's credentials and that stupid brown hat he wore at 2:00 AM!

There was no complaint, just an article in some liberal rag of a newspaper somewhere in Arizona. Johnny's name wasn't mentioned but his description was right on.

It's no secret during these crazy times that there are journalists with intelligence. However, few intelligent ones seemed to report for a liberal rag. The "drive-by" (Rush Limbaugh's term) paper was definitely starving for subject matter.

This writer, naturally, knew nothing about his subject. He was wrong about everything he wrote about, from the stars to the desert's sagebrush. Johnny, however, stood out in the article like a tumble weed in a rose garden. I wrote the paper and blasted its lack of facts and sound journalism. I don't know whether the truth scared the editor or not. I never received an answer.

I said, "Johnny, you and that hat are going to get us both killed."

He said nothing, but I knew that he didn't believe me. Not long afterward, my prediction almost proved true.

Johnny and I worked the highway in a vehicle, his wreck of a Cherokee Chief that had been taken from a smuggler years ago and was the best vehicle in our Customs fleet of seized cars. Johnny kept it in good running order because he was a fair shade tree mechanic. The fastest way to lose the use of a seized vehicle belonging to U. S. Customs was to let a professional mechanic touch it. My seized wreck was in the shop, as usual, costing taxpayers thousands and still not working, and it never would. Customs wouldn't be satisfied until we had spent (lost) at least $30,000.00 to a professional garage that would spend the profits on nothing but tattoos for mechanics and grease to spill on the floor. We set up on the highway leading north of the port of entry after the border gate was closed at Midnight. He was wearing his brown hat while I was giving him fits about it.

About an hour after the port closed, here came a northbound pickup from Mexico. It had come from the direction of the border! We turned on the red lights and fell in behind it. I noticed the license was local. The Sector radio operator in Houston told us who the pickup belonged to before we pulled it over. There were five men riding in the cab!

Since I was the passenger, I stood alongside the passenger door with a shotgun. I didn't think about reminding Johnny to leave the hat in the car. He stepped out and did the talking. He brought the driver back to where he could use his headlights. The driver was feeling brave or *muy macho* on the border after a few beers. He stood with his chest puffed and his feet spread. I didn't like his stance, belligerent voice, or anything about him. Then the other four circled around Johnny, all *macho* and standing offensively, popping their knuckles and acting like they were getting ready to unwind. *Oh-boy!*

Johnny, as usual, wasn't the least bit concerned. He continued with his interrogation. The driver and his crew had been asleep in the parking lot at the Visitor Center because they were all too drunk to drive. They were going home when we stopped them for no reason at all. They didn't like that. I could hear most of the conversation. They were far too loud and still not totally sober. Johnny rummaged through the pickup and was satisfied they were telling the truth. He returned to the pack and told them they could go. They weren't ready to go.

They circled and began crowding Johnny. They nudged him with their chests, like the manager nudges an umpire at a baseball game. Johnny simply stepped back and caused the man behind him to move. Johnny was a cool operator. I wasn't.

I shouted, "Hey!"

Since no one paid any attention, I shouted again. By the third time, I was ticked. They all turned to me, although I was behind the headlights. I said, "There are two us--not one!"

"So?" About twenty voices sounded at the same time, although there were only five men. A couple of tough guys walked toward me. That was better. I had seen a Burt Reynolds movie once where Terry Bradshaw was playing the villain. Terry had a bunch of tough guys against Burt's two or one. Burt said, "So, do you want to go get some more guys?" Now that was funny! I laughed and couldn't wait to try it out. There was my chance and I had used it!

One of the tough guys approaching me said, "What about it?"

I said, "So do you want to go get some more guys or what?"

No one laughed except me. That's still the funniest wise crack I had ever heard in a movie. They didn't think it was funny at all. I couldn't calm down soon enough. They all came to me, leaving Johnny writing alone on his pad, copying names, etc.

Then I thought, *what now, Burt?* No answer. What Burt did was knock one of Bradshaw's teeth loose. That's what happened in the movie. Now which one of those dudes was I going to hit first? Actually, what I did, fast, was to open the door of the vehicle and toss the shotgun inside and locked it from my side. These guys didn't deserve shooting. They just needed a lesson in manners, and I sure wasn't about to let one limp away and get his hands on the shotgun! They surrounded me and asked what I meant, and I told them. I also told them to stand back and not crowd me like they had crowded Johnny. The best defense when outnumbered is a good offense.

Then--thank goodness!--they began to complain to me. They weren't doing anything wrong and wanted to know why they were stopped. I didn't answer, for Johnny had already told them that. One said, "You just doin' you job, right?"

I looked at the man firmly and then another. "Don't ask me that. I pulled you off that man who was outnumbered."

So far, so good. The offense in words was working well. They weren't being wise or loud. Perhaps I had read them wrong from the beginning.

One of them asked, "Who are you guys?"

"We're the Customs Patrol. We..."

"You the Border Patrol, man, or what?"

"No! Now you're trying to get smart with me. I told you that we were Customs! Don't call us Border Patrol. I don't like it, and I'm sure they wouldn't like it, either, although Customs is two steps up from the Border Patrol."

"Well, if you ain't Border Patrol, who are you?"

I said, "Johnny, did you tell these guys who we were?"

"Yeah, I told 'em that we were the Customs Patrol. I also told 'em why we stopped them. What's the problem?"

I turned to them. "There you have it, guys. The party's over. You can go now." I motioned with my hands. It was do or die, then. They left slowly. They kept turning around and telling us that we were going to be reported to the Better Business Bureau for stopping them without a reason. I waited for the stragglers to move on then almost fell backwards. I asked Johnny to unlock my door from his side, that I was having a panic attack.

It was time to go home, anyhow. We had worked since three the previous afternoon. Now it was early morning. As we drove home, Johnny chewed me out. He said that he had everything under control and that he was doing fine. I wasn't needed until he was assaulted physically. Well, I saw it differently and told him so. I would have done the same thing again. One doesn't wait until things get physical. One has to act, sometimes, to save things getting physical, which is what I did.

Johnny said, "Where did you hear this, 'Go get some more guys' crap?"

"Burt Reynolds," I said.

He grinned and shook his head sadly.

I agreed. That was pretty dumb, but it got their attention.

We went home and had a nice sleep, waking up about ten the next morning, refreshed. Tilton, however, was awakened by a U.S. Border Patrol investigator, who lived near the copper mine and knew the bunch of workers that we had pulled over hours ago. The five drove straight to this investigator's house and banged on his door at 0300 hours! They raved at him for two hours. He got no sleep! That was Tilton's message at 0500 hours.

Titon was awakened at five by this investigator, who raved at poor Tilton for an hour, according to Tilton. It reached the point where he grew tired and told the investigator to bug off, that he'd take care of his officers that were pretending to be Border Patrol agents.

He waited until we showed up for work before he raved at us. Actually, we confirmed what he already knew. No one knows who or what the Customs Patrol is or was. We were seldom in the papers or TV when we made a drug bust. The reason being, we were under the Treasury Department and didn't need to impress Congress for a budget. All Tilton wanted to hear was that we had identified ourselves properly, and why I had asked them if they wanted to go get some more guys. I'll stand my ground here, since Tilton needed to be educated in this tough guy stuff.

"If Burt said it, it's got to be right. That's all there is to that. If they don't want to use it at the academy, it's okay by me."

Tilton asked Johnny if the brown hat was worn. He answered affirmatively, but I could tell he was finally getting the picture. Johnny didn't come across as an officer of the law. He never wore the hat again at night after Tilton talked with him alone in the office after I left. I guess we finally *larned* 'im!

Chapter Seven

Fidel Castro's Bluff

This is one of the few unpleasant times of the horse patrol era, but an extremely sad time for our country.

In the mid 1970's the arrogant Fidel Castro puffed his long cigar and rounded up thousands upon thousands of his hungry citizens and dumped them upon U. S. soil. There were boatloads. Castro, in a typical and cowardly communist tradition, did blatantly violate our national security when he effected this embarrassment upon our even more embarrassing Carter Administration. The U.S. Immigration and Naturalization Service, regardless of the laws it has attempted to enforce for decades, had no voice in the matter. The mighty voice of the press robbed the I&NS of its duty and dumped the matter into the hands of inept politicians. We were suddenly faced with approximately 100,000 plus illegal immigrants from Cuba, and the man who drew an enormous salary to be President of the United States, didn't have the guts to stand up to the most arrogant but harmless communist dictator alive.

Our president, extremely fearful of the press and the Kremlin, didn't want to enforce the laws in his own country. Our sovereignty had just been breached by a communist thug. President Carter had no intentions to do anything but cater to the voice of the national news media and tell his country that the people of this great land had spoken.

President Carter's loyalty was firmly imbedded into our news media. He had zero respect for our U. S. Constitution and Congressional laws, through his actions and inactions that I witnessed. Apparently, he felt that he was too small and insignificant to make the decision to send the illegal immigrants back to Cuba, but the Kremlin and their arrogant puppet in Cuba was big enough to break our laws and violate our nation's laws. Socialist reasoning!

Being the Christian he proclaimed to be, Mr. Carter ignored his Biblical teachings and opened our door for the poor immigrants instead of providing them money, food and clothing before sending them home. Thousands upon thousands followed that first shipload. Our president failed to fix the wrong in Cuba, which is the Christian way. We are our brothers' keeper.

No U. S. politician wanting to keep his job bucked communism. Outside strong conservatives and libertarians, they still don't. Communism, according to the Monroe Doctrine, is not even allowed in our western hemisphere! President John F. Kennedy was the one who first ignored the Monroe Doctrine. Unfortunately, it's been a forgotten item since that time.

Instead of bombing that cigar-smoking communist windbag into oblivion and feeding and clothing all the poor in Cuba, President Carter welcomed the second phase of illegal immigrants from Cuba. He couldn't go wrong by adhering to the voice of the mainstream news media of the United States. The Fox Channel was yet to be made public.

Our President Carter wanted peace with the communists, which can only come, according to his view, by appeasing them. He received much assurance on this philosophy from his teen-aged daughter, who, no doubt, was more suitable to be president. It appeared as if the news media was perfectly willing to ignore our own laws to abide by the dictates of Marxism.

The news media tossed the pros and cons around about ten days, disregarding our nation's laws that fully covered the non-dilemma. Phony or dreamed up compassion was the news media's plea for mercy. Moscow praised our president's decision to accept them. Our president felt much better. The illegal Cubans would remain in the United States.

However, I'm pleased to write that contrary to the national news media's and Washington's socialists' hopes, these very immigrants turned out to be far better U. S. citizens than the run-of-the mill liberals. They were notcertain votes for the Democrat Party. They already had a bellyful of socialism under Castro.

Of course, new immigration laws had to be written to appease the communist dictator, which automatically allowed illegal immigrants from Cuba to permanently remain in the United States if they landed on U. S. soil. U. S. Border Patrol in boats have been physically pushing Cuban boats away from our shores since that time.

No one really knows the total of the illegal immigrants from Cuba, but our news media told us approximately 150,000. They were free to become legal immigrants and later citizens that can vote for the party that brought them to the United States where freedom reined. Not all of them did that. Ex-President Clinton was not the first man to fail to bribe liberal votes from illegal immigrants that were to be made into U.S. Citizens. This brilliant idea was born by ex-President Jimmy Carter.

"Poncho" Fidel proved himself correct in his assumption of our country's cowardly refusal to protect its sovereignty. Many other shiploads of hopefuls from other poor nations under inept governments, Haiti and Jamaica, were turned back, simply because they lacked Moscow's support.

There's a saying within our socialist system when facing a dilemma: "Take action and you'll face problems. Do nothing and you're home free."

What a cowardly concept allowed within the great walls of the best structured government in the world! Our federal officers are paid to protect our sovereignty and to uphold our Constitution. U. S. Presidents and Congress are no exceptions!

The news media wasn't interested in federal officers in the field enforcing any of our laws unless a sensational story might surface. It had no use for us, unless they could catch us sneaking around with girl friends on the job or taking bribes.

Following President Carter's decision to do nothing about the illegal Cubans in the United States, the news media has yet to make Ex-President Carter into a national hero or a legend of his own time. He received the Nobel Peace Prize for other reasons that simply being a communist bozo. The Nobel Peace Prize has lost its meaning and prominence.

I have to admit to agreeing with the communist dictator in part. Both Fidel and I had and have zero respect for President Carter. In fact, I wasn't alone in this attitude. I was sitting well within a majority of co-workers, peers, and other U. S. citizens.

Soon after this nationwide blooper, I was called into SCPO Tilton's office. He had an out of town supervisor sitting opposite his desk. A private training seminar in handling troops was in order, no doubt. Tilton had trained lots of first line supervisors. I had a day off, but receiving a call at home meant something was up, and I was always eager for work.

Like most everyone, Tilton was thoroughly disgusted with our so-called president's decision over Cuba's illegal immigrants. After helping myself to a cup of coffee from his thermos, I sat down. Had I known about the hammer he was about to drop on me, I would've never answered his call. Tilton wasn't the type to drop unexpected hammers on anyone, and I trusted him. This time, however, it was different.

"Homer," he said straight forward and without remorse, "pack your bags. You're going to Florida for a few weeks or months to help process those illegal immigrants that Castro just dumped on us."

I stood dumbfounded for a moment. I looked at the visiting supervisor, who sat like a stone. The office was as serious as death. Tilton wasn't grinning. He still wasn't grinning after a long wait. I was in no hurry. I wasn't laughing at his sick humor.

It was left up to me to make any sense out of this situation. We were not immigration officers. We were Customs! This wasn't even under Customs jurisdiction! The Immigration and Naturalization Service's U.S. Border Patrol had mad it clear to U. S. Customs that we were to stay the hell out of their jurisdiction years ago. *That was just another stupid statement originating within that agency.* We ignored it, of course. However, the time to respect it had arrived!

I finally started to speak but Tilton interrupted. "This is a Presidential Order!"

Actually, I planned on saying something intelligent like, "Let's talk about this a moment." However, it came out like this: "Presidential Order, my horse's rear end. I ain't going."

He continued as if I had said nothing. "Be ready to board the airplane Monday morning in Tucson. They will have your ticket ready. Someone from here will drive you to the airport."

I sat down in total shock, completely numbed. My stomach churned and tightened into knots. I desperately needed to run home and kick our old tomcat into the next county. Instead, I stood up, poured my moderately warm coffee into his trash, and said more clearly, "Read my lips. I-ain't-going!"

No one had ever disobeyed Tilton nose to nose before. He was embarrassed by that fact, then regretful about what I had just forced upon him, which was to place me on indefinite suspension.

His face was red as he looked up at me. His great handlebar mustache that proudly curled at the ends into a complete circle suddenly dropped straight down into a "Ho Chi Min." I've heard him chew on officers before, and he could care less about anybody's dignity when they screwed up, but it never went any further.

"*Whaat did you say?*"

These words are exact. They are as clear today as they were when it happened. "You heard me. I'm not going."

It was a tense moment. I know what I would have done in Tilton's place. He didn't dream up that order. It fell on him. His only choice was to take my badge and gun. I attempted to pump slack into the tension.

"Tell your cowardly President to process the Cubans, himself. He and his dippy cabinet of cowardly lapdogs that let the Cubans break our laws. Let them deal with the Cubans." (I did not use the word *dippy*.)

Wrong as it was, legally, I was morally correct. That meant a great deal to me. All of that morality my parents had instilled into me from an early age, plus twenty-five cents, would buy me a quarter's worth of chewing tobacco in our federal service. Morality was dead in my part of our federal system.

The Ho Chi Min curled back into its original status. "Oh--for a moment there, I thought you were going to disobey a Presidential Order by refusing to go to Florida."

His humor didn't change a thing. He was still going to have to place me on indefinite suspension as soon as he reported my reluctance. The suspension would be with pay for a few days, depending upon how long it took to search the manual at District, then it would be without pay. Refusing a Presidential Order pays rather poorly, even if it was a blanket order for hundreds more of patrol officers of U. S. Customs.

Arizona is politically split in north and south districts. I was sure that I could win my case in northern Arizona, where the state's premium newspaper in Phoenix would sway the court of public opinion in my favor. Tucson's newspapers, on the other hand, would want to publicly execute me. A few rich conservatives in Phoenix would pay for my lawyers, I'm sure. I'd have to apply for a change of venue, of course. Any federal judge in the city of Tucson would demand a prison sentence and a stiff fine for any federal officer refusing that president's order. In my case, the socialist judges who loved making laws in our land would likely reinstate hanging by the neck until dead.

Tilton explained it the way it was explained to him. "The Immigration Service (U. S. Border Patrol) can't handle the work load and still perform their daily tasks. Therefore, they need help. That would be us."

I kept quiet, strongly suspecting the Immigration Service had told the president exactly what I was going to tell him through Tilton, which would be telling him to go find a lake. I had the guts to obey the laws of the land but I would have no part of unconstitutional practices. I don't care who gave the order.

Tilton understood my reluctance, but he had his duty, so he continued. "What's happened has happened. No one can change that, so God help us. There's going to be hundreds of officers that speak Spanish from all the federal agencies to fill in for the immigration officers. The other Customs officers that can speak Spanish are going, so just what the hell makes you so special?"

I wasn't special, just morally and principally minded. Instead of choosing a federal service for wages, I could have hired out as a janitor at the local churches. The pay would have been better, anyhow.

At the level of our field office, I felt more of a traitor. I kept still, not wanting to say anything more to worsen matters. I wasn't going, and that was already carved into stone. The way I saw it, President Carter was the one that belonged on indefinite suspension without pay. He was the one who ignored our nation's laws. I didn't belong to his type of people and I never will! *Ultimate boss?* Carter was the boss of his cabinet and no one else. I doubt if his wife even took him serious. What he had done, in my opinion, called for immediate impeachment. Our country wasn't founded on his cowardly mentality, and it certainly won't survive on it!

What President Carter and I have in common is that we both worked for the federal government, or, at least, I did. Following that, I don't even think we even belong to the same species.

"Don't do this to yourself!" Tilton cautioned. The other supervisor from out of town was silent but his eyes pleaded with me to snap out of my moralistic stance. After all, it was the seventies and this was a federal service!

Tilton bore down on me. I think that I sat back down because my knees couldn't hold me up. I had just tossed nine years of federal service out the window. My instincts were: "Feed your family! You can't prove anything by making an example of yourself!"

I forgot the exact phrasing after that. The words came too fast and numerous. He went into all sorts of indignant language and cut absolutely no one on this side of the Canadian border one inch of slack. The other supervisor sank down in his chair and lowered his chin with a ton of guilt on his shoulders.

My response about two minutes later is also minus exact phrasing, only the bottom line: "You can tell President Carter, through all the channels, to take a leap. I'm not going. I will not suffer the indignity of helping Carter seal his cowardly and unconstitutional mistake!"

Tilton didn't buy into that, either. He accused me of not wanting to spend more than one night in Miami. Not a bad assumption. That city, its county and counties surrounding it, had somehow found their way into the dark recesses of my mind, where they remain today. He snatched up the telephone and dialed his supervisor with our rotary telephone, the most modern technology in Lukeville, Arizona at the time. I didn't like what he said, which weren't my words at all.

"Take Homer off the Spanish speaking list. The horse's butt can't say anything more in Spanish than 'Good morning' and 'go to hell!' He'll only screw things up in Florida...Yeah, I thought he cold speak it, too. I know...I know. He always claimed that he could. Yeah, he was probably fired from the Border Patrol because he couldn't speak Spanish well enough to pass the Five and Ten_Month Exams. He just hasn't ever admitted it."

The director in Nogales didn't buy it, but he agreed with Tilton. Then Tilton's face turned red as he listened. The great handlebar mustache drooped straight down again. After a moment of hearing how incapable he was at controlling his own troops, he repeated every word of my message to both him and President Carter, which just happened to the District Director's sentiments, also. The director literally detested to be chewed out by his inferior officer, Tilton, which happened a lot.

Tilton had just saved my career, with the help of the District Director. I wasn't placed on suspension, but my message to the president never got any further than the second office from the bottom. Frankly, I was relieved. I was the only federal officer, to my knowledge, outside the U. S. Border Patrol, that refused to go to Florida. However, Customs and other federal agencies sent officers to Florida to process the illegal into legal immigrants. Most of these officers could not speak a word of Spanish. The U. S. Border Patrol, did, indeed, have a few officers there, along with Immigration inspectors.

I know you're wondering if I were reprimanded for refusing the Presidential Order. Thank you for that. All levels of supervisors in my district felt much better after they had a shot at me. Was it placed in my folder? I can't say. I didn't go anywhere near our district office for about two years. I have never reviewed my personnel folder since that time. It was almost four years before I received a significant promotion.

My legal refusal was based on supporting our Constitution and because I detest socialist politicos like Carter. I detest socialists in the state levels of government, also, plus those in the counties and cities. But what can one expect of right wing radical like myself?

I personally know that many young couples from Mexico, penniless and holding infants in their arms, have been moved out of dirty apartments in Delano, Tulare, and Porterville, California then deported to Mexico. Through the sixties and early seventies, I'm sure there were hundreds of thousands of them.

In Florida, during that processing of making them legal immigrants, many young men from Cuba, separated from their women by recently structured fences, stood behind their stockade and committed lewd acts while U. S. citizens passed on the street. They were arrogant and shouted obscenities to everyone passing opposite their wire stockade, according to officers that related this to me. I asked each one why they even went there in the first place. Their answers were the same. It was what they were told to do. Told to do so?

What has happened to our country's pride and morality? What if they were ordered to shoot their grandmothers? Would they stop and consider their orders?

Unfortunately, I've seen a few Customs officers that I highly suspect of following any order whether it was morally and/or Constitutionally correct or not.

There is no pride in socialism. You will hear criticism and complaints from them, never solutions. Do Al Gore and Al Franken have pride? Where is it? Nothing that emanates from their mouths is related to pride or intelligence. You'll hear a lot of whimpering, screaming, and excuses in why things aren't going their way. No more.

Here is what the inept administration under Carter failed to do in this situation: He could have easily fed, clothed, and put a little money in the jeans of all those people, then sent them home with a message to Fidel Castro to treat his people with respect or else face the consequences of a few Cruise missiles.

Like it or not, such is the way in dealing with communists. You must slap them down or be slapped down. They have no friends. I'm a right winger, sure. As far as being a radical, radicalism comes in the name of cowardice and bowing to socialist dictators and communist nations. We had just experienced a "Sellout" to communism. That's radicalism.

In dealing with the deportees from Mexico, there have been hundreds of U. S. Border Patrol agents that have dug into their personal wallets and provided a few dollars to many penniless women with infants in their arms. I personally know this happened. None of them allowed an infant to pass them without providing them personal aid from their own pockets. Many of them gave up their entire allowance more than once. It wasn't a fun job, but some of them did their moral duty in a Christ-like manner. They remained loyal to our nation's laws and to the taxpayers of the United States. This was and is morality at work.

I personally doubt if President Carter has ever known morality.

All the immigration officers going through all of the academies were forewarned that deporting some deportees would bring them to tears and heartaches. That's an understatement! Very little satisfaction is found in the U. S. Border Patrol's job of deporting people.

President Carter and company were never warned that their jobs would bring them heartaches and tears. In fact, they couldn't even handle the job of deportation!

My eyes flooded one afternoon in the interior of southern California. Corcoran. This was prior to my transfer into the U. S. Customs Service. My partner and I had accommodated a man who wished to pick up a few things before we hauled him to Bakersfield for deportation. We found his wife and infant daughter, who was two months old. My youngest daughter was two months old at that time. The wife began crying. They had no money hidden away that we found. They did have a few diapers.

I couldn't bring myself to load them into the van. She might as well have been my wife holding my own child! I could not have stood still in that man's shoes. What I felt almost caused me to collapse, literally. I called my partner aside and suggested that we overlook this couple. I already knew that once we overlooked this couple, the news would grow fast. Even without bribes or money involved, overlooking anyone could and would end our careers. The very people you overlooked would tell others. Had we spared this couple deportation, they would have become our worst enemies! My partner showed me how he cleared his conscious by pulling out his wallet and offering the man a few dollars. It would buy them food while in Mexico. They may return, and they may not. If those tears were real from the wife that day, that couple would never return to the United States. She was devastated.

Our government could have given that family a bit of money instead of fattening the bankrolls of socialist politicians in Mexico City that put that woman in that situation in the first place! What a stupid way to run two neighboring countries!

It may be easy to sit back from a distance and say that it wouldn't bother you to deport some people, but I'm here to say that it will bother anyone that isn't psychotic. Hearing a woman cry in a tough situation, especially with a baby in her arms, is a situation that I want to avoid for the rest of my life!

I still desire to be the first volunteer to shoot Castro, legally, and if that hair-lips U.S. Senators like Rangel, Boxer, Kennedy and company, then they should know that today's plastic surgeons are fairly capable but probably wouldn't work for a federal voucher. After shooting that fat-bellied dictator in a delicate area, I would have been happy to toss all of his ivory dominos into the pool. I would have stood at his 'fridge and eaten all the food his cooks provided that day before I burned his mansion to the ground. Then I would've given all his chickens to neighbors.

On the other hand, I have more respect for Fidel than ex-President Carter.

Did you just think, "Who cares?"

I care! I'm not proud of feeling that way about any President of the United States.

How many times have our State Department dug into our national treasury and presented billions to foreign socialist dictators? Hundreds of billions of dollars have been given to men in office of socialist governments. How many bites of food did one citizen in all those countries receive? Were the poor ever fed? I think not. How long can this tough country of ours last with this type of immature mentality?

Could I have run Carter's administration any better? Oh—yes! Much better! So could you. My midget horse could have run it better, so could the two donkeys in the pasture and the wild tomcat that hangs around the barn.

Chapter Eight

A Canadian Affair

An old cowboy philosopher raised his head from the bar and announced, "Gentlemen, lawyers that cannot succeed go into politics." Since he heard no confirmation or argument, he resumed his nap.

The antagonist in this story claimed to be a Canadian attorney. Keep in mind, also, that some Canadians visiting the United States are natural lawyers.

The dialogue presented here isn't exact, but given the simplicity of the circumstances and what is clearly remembered, it's fairly accurate.

I rode my personal horse almost seven hours that day, mostly by the highway running straight north of Lukeville, Arizona. I was patrolling for new stash signs between areas where the smugglers had once used. I had not found evidence of a smuggled load of drugs in over a year. The loads used to be stashed next to the highway and left to be picked up by a vehicle from Tucson or Phoenix that same night or day.

It was early in 1986, a sad time for me. The Horse Patrol's short era was drawing to a painful end on the Mexico border. It irked me to see a winning force against drug smuggling be terminated by bureaucratic politicians in my own service. The reason for terminating the Horse Patrol was that we lived in the Twentieth Century. *That's it!*

I would soon abandon my horse, which cost the taxpayers one dollar and fifty cents per day. That included, food, medicine and a professional to shoe the horse each six or eight weeks. I would soon be transferred to some Air Branch in Florida or Houston to work the radar in a jet that used 1,200 gallons of fuel just to leave the runway! In cost effectiveness, my arrogant leaders' math was tantamount to their knowledge of stepping inside from the rain. From what I heard thus far, the U. S. Customs Air Branches no longer interdicted smuggled drugs as much as they did in the past. This was prior to President Reagan's stamping out the bureaucracies in the federal government, which amounted to mere shuffling of desks and titles with a raise in pay. Our federal government grew under President Reagan and has slowed very little since that time.

We had interdicted many loads of marijuana with the horses. When the U. S. Customs Air Stations first operated inside the patrol, it paid its way in seized aircraft. But when U. S. Customs decided to drop the patrol in order to meet the President's demands to end bureaucracies and start growing behind the scenes, these same airplanes and pilots fell under another division, one that did not patrol. Consequently, Customs aircraft almost completely stopped interdicting drugs.

It didn't matter. The pay was better. I told myself that I was just biased and bitter. Besides, all was well within my jurisdiction of the border.

One local drug smuggler recently stopped me in the local grocery store. We had failed to catch him with anything other than illegal immigrants. He only claimed to have been smuggling drugs for local citizens. I doubted it. He was no more than a mule, anyhow, strong in the arms and legs with a minimum amount of body fat. He told me that I could relax, that he was no longer in the drug smuggling business. I asked him if he were rich and retiring. He denied having any money and actually hit me up for a loan of ten dollars for gas. Not a problem.

I reported to him that he had stopped smuggling at the wrong time. I didn't tell him that I was working my 80 miles of border alone, but I did tell him that I was being transferred inland. That would leave the Mexico border wide open in my area. The U. S. Border Patrol doesn't work to interdict smuggled narcotics other than those times when they accidentally interdicted at their highway inspection stations.

He said that everyone he knew had stopped smuggling or else moved their operation to Florida. The Horse Patrol team could not have received a better compliment. *If only they were there to appreciate it!*

He not only failed to understand what I was telling him, he didn't believe a word I told him. In his mind, the U. S. Customs Service could not be that stupid. But he failed to understand President Reagan's cabinet addressing the "Stamping out of federal bureaucracies." He thought my news was only a ploy to get him to smuggling again so he would eventually be caught. I left him with the fact that he would only have to worry about the U. S. Border Patrol if he wished to resume his drug smuggling trade. He looked at me if he thought I had completely lost my mind.

A hand-held radio was carried in my saddlebag that day. It worked well in the desert's remoteness, but I saved the battery for emergencies. The boss in Tucson tried to raise me several times a day while I rode my horse, but I claimed to be unable to read him in the wilderness.

The latest Customs Directive to land on my desk via the U. S. Postal Service was written by a U. S. Customs lawyer. It was signed off by a deputy commissioner. This was only a few days ago. I received word of it inadvertently from a special agent who had just resigned from the patrol for a raise in pay, just like a few hundred of us before him. His heads up message was that I'd soon be calling a Tucson judge for a search warrant before I could look in the trunk of an automobile here on the border. *Nonsense!*

I explained that lawyers had been trying to kill the U. S. Customs Search and Seizure authority for decades, and such an ill move would endanger national security. It would never--ever!--happen unless some thoughtless inspector inadvertently searched a D.C. politician.

"Well," he insisted, "it would be wise to always call a judge before you look into the trunk of an automobile out there, Homer. That's what it suggests in the Directive. I'd hate to see you fired this late in your career."

So typical of special agents! The man hadn't been a special agent but a month and he was already running scared because they were brainwashed into believing all Directives and Memo's from Region and Washington. They didn't realize that a majority of them were written by some high authority's brother in law that had been put on the payroll for personal reasons, none of which included a plan to further the service. I had better things to do than bend to the whims of every attorney who wrote a Memo just to handicap the field officers. I advised him to take a couple aspirin and relax. People that read Directives and Memos from Headquarters lived a very nervous and insecure life. If a change was to be made, which is rare, my boss would be on the horn making sure that I had the word.

I haven't seriously read a Directive or a Memo in years. They existed to keep the paper manufacturers in business. If something ever did accidentally come up and I missed it, I would simply fall back on my standing excuse: "Nobody ever tells me anything around here!"

I was contemplating searching vehicles late in the afternoon while knowing that it was time to call it a day. My horse usually let me know when he was tired or too bored to work. I think he was about to do that when we both heard a vehicle moving at a high rate of speed. It was coming from the dirt road paralleling the border fence to the west of us. My horse pointed his ears and lifted his nose in that direction. I urged him into a brief lope to be at the intersection where the road met the highway before the car reached it. My horse knew I was responding to that sound and he was ready to stretch his muscles!

No one in their right mind speeded on that road in the desert unless it was a smuggler scared out his wits. A plume of dust rose rapidly from where the road practically touched the border fence. I patted his neck and told him to save his strength, for we might have a high speed chase on our hands if the vehicle reached the highway. No response. The only time that horse ever had a sense of humor was when I was at the brunt of the joke.

I wore no uniform, but a badge and I.D. were made ready, clearly visible in the hand that held the reins. My revolver filled the other hand and was held behind my back. I'm not a fast-draw artist. The horse stood at full attention in the middle of the narrow road seconds before the car reached our intersection. It was late in the afternoon and the sun was in our eyes, but the badge would be shinning directly at the driver. If he ignored it and attempted to ram us, he may or may not see the bullet speeding toward his head.

In no time, the speeding van rounded the corner and applied his brakes upon spotting my horse. He had to be doing fifty or sixty mph! The brakes locked and the vehicle skidded precariously on the rocky road to what we called a "Hollywood" stop. My horse moved out of the way, even though it wasn't necessary.

The van stopped completely. My badge was held in plain view and the revolver remained out of sight. A lady occupied the passenger's seat. The driver bounced out.

"What da hell's going on? Who da hell ah youse? Get da hell off da road!"

This rude behavior only derives from the citizen who is confident that the official is a genuine law enforcement officer. His words and action convinced me that he had seen my badge and knew that I was an official. Officers are always fair game to the air-headed portion of the general public.

"I'm U. S. Customs Patrol, Sir, and I am presenting my credentials to you to save any imminent mistakes in that regard."

"Really? Haven't youse evah heard of official vehicles out heah in this dis pile of waste?" (Not his exact wording.)

I don't remember his other words because I wasn't listening. He wasn't armed and I couldn't see the lady's arms well enough. The rest of the van was dark to my view. The potential danger of a common vehicle stop was still present.

"We'll cover the details later," I said. "Right now, walk back to your driver's door and stand there between me and your lady friend."

"Wife!" he corrected and began to approach me still pointing his finger and raising his voice.

I watched the van over his head and almost yelled, "Walk back to the driver's door and do make haste, for it is your number one priority. In other words, you'd better do it now!" I don't know what I would have done if he failed to respond. It had never happened to me before. He was about to enter a shoving contest with my horse, who can back up a Dallas Cowboys linebacker. Well--perhaps not.

He said, "Who aw youse and why'd youse stop us?"

"I stopped you because you were driving at a high rate of speed on this dirt road, and..."

"What? What'ah youse talking about? I wasn't speeding'! What aw youse, some kind of prehistoric traffic cop nut or somethin'?"

I began to relax. He wasn't a smuggler, unless he was terribly good at his trade. Drug smugglers were scared out of their minds at this point. New Yorkers and Bostonians were often of this attitude if they felt they were stopped for no good reason. No one has ever expected them to like it. And, frankly, I didn't have to enjoy their irritating manner, either. It just made my job easier and more pleasant.

Being loud and disrespectful was far from a smuggler's profile on the border. Unless, of course, his armed protection were in the van and out of sight. "Tell me how many people are in your van, sir."

"Deah's one. You'ah looking right at her. Wha's da mattah, youse can't count dat high?"

I stepped off the horse while I thinking I heard him snigger behind me in horse language, not that I speak it. I kept the driver between me and the female passenger easy enough. The revolver was still behind me. "May I please see some I.D. from you and your wife?"

This, of course, was fuel for more idiotic remarks. It was the quiet, polite and scared ones that frightened me. In these early times in a vehicle stop, if the bad guy thinks he can win, he's apt to do exactly that.

"Aw youse gonna write us a ticket fo speedin' o what? What did youse say youse were, U. S. Bodah Patraw?"

"U. S. Customs. Walk to the back of the van and open the door and stand there in the doorway until I say differently. Any fast movement of any kind is going to cause me to think someone is going to be waiting with an automatic weapon and ready to start spraying bullets. This is an official order and not a request and I do hope you speak English sufficiently to understand."

"Oh--what a bright boy we have heah! I thought youse said youse wanted to see our drivah's licenses. Whatta-yuouse-tink I am, anyway?"

"Don't stop until you're in the middle of that open doorway. Believe me, you'll be the first one hurt in the event all hell breaks loose."

I peered over his shoulder and saw scattered clothing and two pieces of luggage on the floor. Good enough. I took his I.D. and walked to the lady. I holstered the weapon and said, "You can relax but stand where I can watch you."

He did with a great deal of threats and lectures about not appreciating my tact and threatening to hurt him when there was no reason. I fished the hand-held radio out of the saddle bags.

"Was youse gonna shoot me?" He saw me holster the .357."

"Did I have to shoot you?"

I never once, during my career, feared that I had to shoot anyone. If the occasion ever arose, they were already shot or else I had missed and the second bullet would also already be dispatched, providing I wasn't already dead.

He remained quiet while I asked Sector at Houston, Texas to run the names and license plate on the rental van. Houston reported shortly that my two suspects were Canadian citizens and presently resided in Quebec. This mixed up and phony accent of his from New York and Boston sounded far too ridiculous to be Canadian. Apparently, he had studied law in one of the two cities and loved the way they talked. This I learned later. Another moment expired before both names came back negative all the way around. My call had priority over all radio traffic on the Mexico border due to my remoteness; otherwise, we would have had to wait several more minutes.

"Hop in the back, partner, and open those two suitcases where I can see inside them."

"What? I'll do no such ting!"

"Do it now!"

"Oh--I love dis! A genuine tough guy wit all youse boots, spurs and cowboy hat! Youse don't have a wawrant and no probable cause to stop us but youse wanna search us? Whose laws aw youse workin' undah, George Wassington's?"

"I take it that you consider yourself an authority on our history and laws, seeing as how you're a Canadian citizen, you have to be an attorney. Correct?"

"I am! But since we're practically twin countries, our larws in illegal searches ah close to da same."

I was watching his eyes as he talked. He was serious as far as I could tell. I didn't want to argue but I did want to let him know that I wasn't intimidated by his 1960's mentality. "If you were a lawyer, sir, then you'd probably know better than to challenge an officer of the law on the border. Most good lawyers keep quiet when they're playing in another man's ball park. *Know-wotta-I-mean?*" I can speak a little Boston, myself.

"Youse's an arrogant bastahd!" he said. "Funny in yous's own small way. I can have you up on chahges if you even think about searching us."

I physically turned him around the same time I ordered him to and spread his legs. He didn't spread them fast enough, so I kicked his ankles until he responded favorably. My horse backed to take the slack out of the reins to be as far away from me as possible in the event of a sudden wrestling match. Nothing like loyalty in one's animals. He'd also love to get away during the melee and leave me to walk back to the corrals. I patted the man down while he protested. The first part of the search was completed. Now he was genuinely irate without a phony front. He was red-faced and tight-lipped.

"Now you can get in the van and open that luggage before I call for a warrant. It won't get here before noon tomorrow. We will be waiting for it right here."

"I'm telling youse, man. Dis's a mistake."

Both pieces were half empty and contained no bags or anything suspicious. I had no longer began to search these suitcases by the time my horse had pushed me aside in order to look for an apple, candy, or any type of a free hand out. I edged him back gently after he had a thorough smell for food. That horse would eat anything!

The man said, "What da hell is dis, a sniffin' hoss?"

"Yes, sir. One of the best on the border. Horses have a better sense of smell than dogs and are far more accurate and faster. I'd say your van is completely void of anything that I'm paid to interdict. After we check your glove compartment and have my horse has a sniff your wife's purse without her opening it, you both will be free to go, sir."

"Helen, look! Dis heah's a sniffin' hoss jus like a dog, only he's a hoss! I've nevah seen one. So dis's why youse's ridin' a hoss instead of drivin' a cah! Right?"

"Excellent deduction, sir."

She said, "Wonderful!" as she held her purse toward my horse's nose. He had several short sniffs in search of an apple or candy. It was a good thing that he didn't smell candy in there. I've seen him go crazy for chewing gum, also. The glove compartment and under both seats were clear. The horse did sniff the glove compartment and under her seat. Actually, he did try to get to a wrapper on the floor from some old goodie.

I returned their driver's license and climbed aboard my new sniffing horse, who was somewhat out of sorts for not being fed a bite of anything. He'd eat a boiled egg or a bologna sandwich in a heartbeat." I had to give him worm medicine often.

I thanked them for their time and asked them to please drive more carefully. I heard the husband rattle off more threats of a complaint and possible lawsuit against the U.S. Bodah Patraw.

I had to grin and dug out my I.D. and badge again. "You've got to be a lawyer, all right. This reads, 'U. S. Customs Patrol.' Are we clear on this?"

"I will be adding' dat remahk in my complaint. I knows lots of Bodah Patraws on the Canadian bodah. All o' dems nice people. Youse really should do sumpin' about dat rotten attitude. *Ya know wotta I mean?*"

I chuckled at that. My wife had told me the same thing for years without my ever understanding why. My conscious didn't hurt me for searching this innocent individual one bit. It's easy to understand a short temper from the innocents while they're simply touring the border. But that's the cost of living in modern times in the 1980's.

No one wanted to be searched but I wasn't so sure that they were innocent before the search. I began to hear more and more complaining about my rudeness, illegal stop, and ordering them around from that yahoo as I rode away. He was no more a lawyer than my horse. He informed me again that I had no right to be doing what I was doing, especially searching their van *wit* a sniffin' hoss. Like today's airport security, it seemed as if I was paid big bucks to harrass innocent people and let the bad guys alone.

"I stopped you because you were speeding from the border nexus

I searched you because you denied speeding on this hazardous road.

That covers both the stop and search. Do you have any questions before I leave?"

"Yeah! Who's youse boss? Whas's 'is telaphone numbah? What's 'is address?"

I said nothing and turned my horse, who was readily willing to leave the harsh tones of the man. Horses are sensitive and literally despise harsh voices of people. I had already heard this phony tell me what a poor host and representative of my country that I had been. He was wanting an argument to use as fuel for a real complaint.

He raised his voice as I was leaving. "If we were in Canader, I'd have youse brought up on chahges!"

"In Quebec?" I said without looking back. "I'd believe you. You'd probably win a nice civil suit, too."

"How's dat? Whatch youse sayin'? Youse insultin' my country?"

"No sir." I had to look back for this to watch his face. "You're doing okay by yourself. I almost forgot to say that I sincerely apologize for any inconvenience that I might have caused you!"

"Das spost to make it okay? We'ah filin' a complaint!"

I rode straight for Lukeville a mile south where the horse trailer was waiting. I tied the horse to the trailer and stepped inside the east side of the huge port of entry to wash my face and hands. I also had a long drink of cool water.

What happened next is accurate almost to the word. The west side of the port of entry was open to the public. The man and his wife did not see my horse and trailer on the east side of the huge building.

This was definitely one of those times where truth is stranger than fiction. I dusted my clothes and was leaving my office when a knock sounded at the western door to my office. It was an inspector. Behind him stood the two Canadians. Knowing that particular inspector, he probably riled the Canadians even further.

I made no move to turn on the lights because the guests weren't worth the expense of the electricity it required to light the room. Besides, I could see fine. Surprisingly, the inspector was apologetic.

"This man and his wife are from Quebec, Canada, Homer. They have a complaint against one of your officers. It seems they were stopped for nothing and accused of smuggling, speeding and all sorts of harsh words spoken by the officer."

The inspector also knew that I was the only officer working out of my station. He was digging me as if he believed every word they said. Inspectors were professionals at irritating tourists as well as anyone else within ear shot. It was their way of self-preservation against a daily horde of ill-mannered people they had to appease daily while searching their luggage.

I asked the gentleman to be seated opposite my desk and placed a chair nearby for the lady. Then I said, "Now, then, tell me about your experience with one of my officers. Start at the beginning, please."

I was joking, of course. They had to know me! It wasn't that dark. My hat and sunglasses were off and placed on my desk, which probably made a difference in my appearance. They both sat down and looked straight at me. There was no problem with eye contact from either one. I had no intentions of being there until it was dark, so I made no move for the light switch.

Honestly, I thought they recognized me. Apparently, neither one had a very good memory. At this time, these two people were extremely polite.

This man, who identified himself as a lawyer, began with the biggest batch of lies I have ever heard about myself. I did none of those things. The wife supported everything he said. I kept listening.

When I agreed with the man by stating that if the officer had done everything he reported, the officer was in big trouble. His face lit up. I expected him to really cut loose with more lies. I eased back and took a deep and serious breath before saying, "Based on your report, you have a legitimate complaint. The officer will have his chance to tell his story, naturally, and he could possibly be suspended until this matter is resolved. We have an office of Internal Affairs in El Paso, Texas. You don't have to remain here, just leave your names, address, telephone numbers, etc."

Understand, my voice is unique with a heavy nasal tone. I don't know how they failed to recognize me. Then his wife did recognize me and began trying to get her husband's attention. He had begun telling how I kicked his legs at gun point before I searched him. He said that I had a sniffing horse, too. Some officers do their pat downs with a weapon pointed at the suspect. I never do that.

I had apparently held them both at gun point, threatened to kill them, and tried to find their wallets with their money. I cursed at them, called them filthy names, and threatened the husband many times with my fists and gun. Strange behavior for me! Perhaps they were stopped in Mexico or something and had the officers mixed up.

I asked him where and when this took place. He told me exactly. Yep, that was me, all right! The lady still had her hand on his shoulder. She shook him a couple times. Finally, she got his attention. I was still trying to remember if I did any of those things.

"Whaaat?" he asked rudely.

"It's him. He's da one!"

He looked at me rather strangely and asked. "Aw youse da one who pulled us ovah on dat sniffin' hoss?"

I had to grin while nodding affirmatively. He first stood and pointed a finger at me as if I had tricked him or something. But I had heard all I was going to hear from that man. I told him exactly that.

"Sir, all three of us know that I did none of those things. Now then, it's my turn. But you really don't want to hear it. If I were you, I'd leave before you really dig a hole for yourself." I said this with more morality in mind than legality. I was prepared to physically remove him from my office, which would have warranted a legitimate complaint.

Instead, I said, "I apologize if I appeared rude to you in any way, but you are going to have to learn how to tell the truth before you file a complaint against anyone. As it stands, you both can be charged with a violation of 19 USC 1001." *Talk about lying! There isn't a federal judge in the United States that would hear a case against those people for lying to me so harmlessly.*

I think that's the right title. I hadn't used it since 1972 when I was in the U.S. Bodah Patraw. The law is supposed to cover lying or giving false reports to a federal officer.

His wife stopped at the door and looked back to apologize, surprisingly. She mouthed the words silently.

I smiled and nodded approvingly. While I confess that I should have never responded to his insults in any way at all, she had just made everything okay. I felt much better.

As our laws slowly decay into ambiguous statements that creates more room for lawyers to argue their senseless points, this country will surely lose its border search authority. It has lost its right to sovereignty decades ago to a point where Immigration laws are not even enforceable in a court of law due to the enormity of those prosecutable.

But in law enforcement, one must keep the taxpayers out front. Always! "The general public" is the most important key phrase in all situations. If ever an officer never loses sight of his/her enforceable laws, one can seldom go wrong. It's imperative to keep the taxpayers out front. That will carry with the U. S. Constitution in most all questionable situations.

In locking my office for the night, I did admonish myself with this reminder:

We have no need for buffoons on our federal payroll. The federal payroll begins with the lowest paid federal law enforcement officer up to and through each and every member of our U. S. Congress--all the way through the President and his cabinet. When our nation of taxpayers lose their respect for any of the members on our federal payroll, then we will be living in an unhappy country with little respect for one another. Such a country will not and can not endure its alloted time on earth.

Chapter Nine

To Shoot or Not to Shoot

An act was presented before Congress during the mid-1980's that would allow U. S. Customs officers to shoot down aircraft suspected of smuggling drugs into the United States, but only after such aircraft blatantly refused orders to land.

Rumors of the new law drew protests from the left side of our government. The smugglers stood silently behind the protesters. Most U.S. citizens were ignorant of how drugs were affecting our schools, economy, and general welfare, anyhow. Therefore, when the mainstream news media protested, the entire country deemed their words gospel.

Curiously, the law drew a surprising number of murmurs among the liberal-minded Customs Officers. They wanted no part of shooting anyone at anytime for anything. It just wasn't cool to earn one's wages. Nevertheless, it's always imperative to all new bills concerning our fight against smuggling drugs into the United States.

The last part of this chapter concludes with what many Customs officers were accused of prior to the act making the first house. Naturally, the bill never made it through both houses. That bill had more riders from both parties that the act became secondary. Nevertheless, I listened to the accusations before applying my imagination to comfortably react to the charges. What happens in the last portion of this chapter, never happened.

The truth:

Long ago in a city far, far away, Vice President George Herbert Bush promised a group of U. S. Customs pilots that he would attempt to have an extremely important law introduced to Congress.

This particular bill would save the taxpayers billions in the popular new "Drug War."

Many Customs pilots didn't want this law to be passed. They didn't want the responsibility of shooting a suspect smuggler down. Who could blame them? I sure didn't want to shoot anyone. However, we had to consider the circumstances. If the bill had passed, it would have been our duty to respond positively and blow the smugglers out of the air, those that refused to land, of course.

Smuggling drugs is not a capitol offense. According to me, it should be. One life lost to dangerous drugs doesn't make it a capitol offense. No one twists people's arms to force them to do drugs. Some think that just one innocent life lost is sufficient for a capitol offense. The liberal idealists believe a criminal can be reformed by sound reasoning--if he isn't talked to death first.

First, let's consider the implications of such a law. For starters, it wasn't a good bill to present to a liberal Congress.

However, U.S. Customs pilots, through modern radar usage, have been appearing in a sudden formation with a suspected drug smuggler in the air about once a week, night and day all through the 1970's. Then, according to standard procedure, these U. S. officers always signaled the suspect pilot to land. Smugglers seldom responded positively, not to the radio and not to hand signals. Drug smugglers always have all their radios turned on. They were always equipped with the latest technology. They whittled their chances of getting caught down to toothpick thin.

Most smugglers appeared innocent and too dumb to turn on their radios. They were never dumb! They have more radios than anyone else, and not a word is spoken through their monitors that they don't hear and understand. Still, taking the ignorant and dumb route was easier than answering an order to land the airplane full of dangerous drugs. Even a leftist Congressman could figure this out, maybe.

The aircraft to aircraft radio frequency was and is always on in an airplane. Only a suicidal idiot would turn it off and keep it off. After the Customs pilots received no response from the suspect doper, which was added to the list of probable causes to signal the aircraft to land, they flew in close and signaled with hands for the suspect pilot to land his airplane at the first opportunity. At night all the pilots had to do was to turn on their cockpit lights.

After signaling a suspect smuggler to land his aircraft, the Customs pilots have always received one of the three following responses:

1) The suspect returned the signal with the middle finger prominent then peeled away in a 180-ddegree turn in order to fly back to Mexico...in haste.

2) They nodded in agreement. Sometimes they even came up on the air and declared they would land at the first safe opportunity. They do not always tell the truth. They usually remained in the air and attempted to run the Customs aircraft out of fuel.

3) They failed to wave back without the middle finger and peeled away to fly back to Mexico as fast as possible. They have, in fact, regularly, attempted to fly into the Customs aircraft in order to kill everyone on board in both airplanes. None have been successful.

The bill didn't pass. The predicted billions that the bill would have saved was never an issue. Consciences of Congress are never hurt while spending taxpayers' money.

The new bill would have given U. S. Customs Officers in the air the right to shoot down an aircraft containing smuggled drugs if--and only if--the aircraft's pilot refused to land at the first on a reasonably safe runway, or after a suicidal attempt to fly into the Customs aircraft. When this happens, I have never thought that pilots holding federal officer commissions needed Congress's, or anyone else's permission to blow those suckers out of the sky. Complete obliteration. But the Customs pilots take this as a flying challenge and merely out maneuver the aircraft attempting to crash into them. This does not make for a fun ride for the back seaters in a Customs aircraft.

While Congress deliberated on whether to pass the bill or attach a thousand riders to it, they did what they always do best, run like hell! The news media knew how to deal with rogue Congresspersons and were experienced in controlling the public.

Without the news media, there were still myriads of reasons that the bill failed to pass, none of which, were reported by the news media.

Too much false publicity stymied the new bill. The long-since-gone editor of the AOPA (Aircraft owners and Pilots' Assoc.) ran editorials opposing the bill in that monthly magazine. One cartoon in one edition had two scared men in a cockpit. One stated, "Quick, toss out the aspirin, there's U. S. Customs!" Nothing like a rock-dumb cartoon to speak for non-thinking people!

Then comes the question that would never be asked if a little thought was first applied. The public demanded how U. S. Customs was to know if an airplane contained dangerous drugs and what is was that was being smuggled--if anything? Who could know? Do Customs officers have x-ray eyes? Well...? Duh!

Let's deal with it.

First, understand that no officer, federal, state, or local has the slightest desire to murder or injure an innocent pilot in an aircraft. That's a given. Those that do are as rare as medical doctors that want to kill a victim of disease or injury. How do I know this? Simple. I never wear dark sunglasses at Midnight, I have never snorted, swallowed, or smoked dope. My clothes are always clean and pressed. I try to maintain a fair and balanced view for all new concepts. Then, when all else fails, there exists such a thing as common sense. Personal values do make a difference in the thinking process.

Please accept this fact: Anyone in America could be 100 percent certain that a downed aircraft by U.S. Customs would have most definitely been flown by a known drug smuggler, and it would have most definitely contained dangerous drugs that were smuggled into the United States. That's a solid fact. *If there were even the slightest doubt on the part of U. S. Customs pilots and the gunner, the smuggled drugs would be flown free to deliver the illegal cargo.* Another given.

Years of experience have fairly well rooted out the suspect drug smugglers from the innocent flying public, although the innocent flying public will fly the distance in meeting all the symptoms of drug smugglers. The innocents would still have been spared the absolute terror of being shot down. Ordered to land, sure, but no gun would have been pointed at these suspects.

Okay, the question: First, the aircraft would be flying surreptitiously into the United States, which is a simple and common violation. In the southwest, it is probable cause to be ordered to land by radio or hand signals at the first safe airfield. That's one way the sovereignty of our nation is protected. All nations do it.

With our nation swamped with federal judges, and with all of them as liberal as Senator Kennedy's red tie, do you really think that a U. S. Customs officer would want take a chance on accidentally shooting down an innocent aircraft and miss out on those big wages? Think about it. Most federal officers, including those in U. S. Customs, have already gained sufficient experience in the academy classrooms to literally fear anything or anyone that's been to law school. We were told that most all of Congress were lawyers, inept or not.

Federal and state officers won't even shoot pedophiles! You may take this to the bank: "*Regardless of how the news media might express it, there is a vast difference between professional law enforcement officers and evil people.*"

What you can most profoundly believe as a U. S. citizen, sufficient and mandatory guidelines would apply before any airplane would be forced to land.

When a situation grew to the extreme of forcing a suspicious aircraft to land, the pilot would either land his aircraft, fly until he ran out of gas, or simply attempt suicide by suddenly ramming the U. S. Customs aircraft. The latter has been experienced twice in my station inside two years. It has happened to almost every Customs pilot with a couple or three years of experience. This was and still is fairly good evidence that a load of drugs on board...but it still isn't solid proof.

Logic and experience *will* dictate that the first drug smuggler pilot that was forced to land, after his tail rudder was shot full of holes, would make the headlines for weeks. In the meantime, all other drug smugglers would, no doubt, rethink his drug smuggling mission and freely and voluntarily land as ordered. No one wants to attempt to land a crippled aircraft. In other words, after one aircraft tail was shot full of holes, no smuggler would take the chance. Drug smuggling pilots do have brains and are capable of thinking without the aid of a television set and a newspaper.

File cabinets, prior to computers, were and are stuffed full of suspect drug smugglers and their aircraft. All had a record of drug smuggling and smugglers. Consequently, all of the steps necessary were always taken before anyone would ever consider asking a suspect pilot to land at the first safe opportunity. Again, most smugglers were already listening to their radios and law enforcement monitors, as well as using radar detectors. When the suspect's monitors, radios and radar detectors are all blaring "Suspect!" this is when the pilot looks to his left and finds a huge Customs aircraft flying in formation with him!

The faces in the cockpits are readable in the daytime. The little signs to order the suspects to land were plainly written. In the event of possible illiteracy, efforts were made to persuade the blank face of the suspect to turn his radio on, which is only following well-known rules. If there was no indication of a radio and the suspect has not attempted to ram his aircraft into the Customs aircraft, then the suspects were followed until they landed. So—why can't we treat all of them the same way instead of shooting them? Not all of them continued to fly north. They turn around to smuggle another day. The smugglers usually made it to the interior on the second try.

Very few airplanes can elude Customs aircraft. On rare occasions, they have, which is why the bill was introduced. Vice President Bush wanted no smuggler to get away. I agreed with him.

Night time is a different world. Larry the Cable Guy claims night is only an absence of sunshine. There were and are innocent suspects entering our country surreptitiously at night!

This literally thrills Customs air officers. No radio contact, either! Not even Geraldo Rivera would attempt to do this just to prove that he can beat U. S. Customs in view of the public, which he never has.

Many suspect aircraft have entered our country at night, blacked out (no navigational lights) and the planes were never squawking as they crossed the border. Most were picked up by radar prior to entering the United States air space.

The aircraft were always low, seriously attempting to fly under the radar. It is literally flying next to the rocky surface in the southwest. Casting aside all the other steps in determining probable cause, this airplane is about 99 percent certain to be smuggling drugs, or shrimp, or firearms, or cigars from Havana to avoid Mexico's export taxes.

The innocents with legal items for consumers did not fly low and attempt to avoid radar. They landed soon on their own for legal inspection. Most of these were detected by radar, but not always. They never flew blacked out in the United States. Pilots, as a rule, are not stupid.

Blacked out aircraft always thrill Customs pilots. Customs will cut their lights, also. They could never see each other because the Customs aircraft approached from behind and kept the lead suspect aircraft in sight by the exhaust from the engine/s. There is no way suspects could hide their exhausts that shoots orange flames from the reciprocating engines. The exhausts can be spotted miles away at night. The same can be said of a jet. Customs aircraft zoomed in behind the aircraft and flew above them in the event this aircraft was flying on the deck in the moonlight and failed to spot a highline or a windmill, house, barn or haystack.

Smugglers using aircraft flying into our coastal waters were always right over the surface of the water to escape radar detection. This happened often. Their radar detectors were blaring like crazy and they flew low, thinking the radar was inland and not flying above them. Many have been taped by video. This was dangerous flying at night, and these pilots were the exceptions to those generally thought to be smart. The suspect's props, in one case, were inches off the surface of the water in his/her attempt to fly under the radar. On film taken from the camera of a Customs aircraft, the props of a suspect aircraft did hit the flat surface of the water. This one pulled up a foot or so. Then it suddenly disintegrated in a long line of debris, which was depicted on the infa-red video equipment that recorded the whole thing.

One can safely assume the aircraft was smuggling drugs into the United States. Bundles of dangerous drugs did bounce along the surface of the water for a quarter-mile, another good indication of drug smuggling—for the skeptical. These incidents happened several times off the coast of Florida. Debris of dangerous drugs were always found the next day. Floating debris fairly well verifies the suspicion.

In the southwest, Customs pilots always alerted the police and sheriff's offices in all small towns or cities in the path of the aircraft. If it didn't land in any of the prospect city airfields, it landed in a pasture or at a private runway. Car lights on the ground always lighted the crude runway. The suspect aircraft always turned on their landing lights. The Customs aircraft always landed within 100 feet behind the suspect still blacked out. Chances are 100 percent that these aircraft were always smuggling dangerous drugs. Some became aware of the aircraft behind it and became airborne again without unloading. They flew back to Mexico. This is where the bill to shoot it down would come in handy. It has happened many times. Yet—others remained on the ground and were arrested and possibly sent to prison in President Reagan's administration.

In these cases, all hell broke loose seconds after landing! Believe me, I had much rather shoot the aircraft down than to land behind it. I have never met an officer who did not feel this way.

Once, a Customs aircraft literally crashed into the suspect. No one was hurt. Miraculously!

The ground crew always scattered and ran like they were going to be arrested after they discovered that Customs was landing closely behind the suspect. There were instances that the suspect aircraft did attempt to take off and failed on the short runway. They crashed and usually burned with the pilot still on board. Such crashes have been recorded by Customs video equipment.

One time, the ground crew waiting in a remote area in Louisiana, spotted the exhaust of the Customs aircraft and shut off the lights in their vehicles! The suspect pilot, already committed to land, failed to stall properly and literally crashed into the runway. The aircraft burst into flames. The pilot and his dangerous drugs were all burned to crispy ashes. The ground crew saved themselves from arrest but killed the pilot.

In another remote area in Louisiana, U. S. Customs turned its chase over to their station's Blackhawk helicopter crew. The Blackhawk arrived at the runway the same time as the suspect aircraft. The suspect pilot spotted the Blackhawk hovering at the end of his runway. He added throttle to his aircraft and attempted to become airborne again. He deliberately rammed the Blackhawk in a suicidal attempt to kill both aircraft and everyone on board. The Blackhawk pilot failed to move timely. He allowed the suspect to crash into its well armored belly. The suspect crashed into the heavy helicopter and burned with his load of marijuana. The Blackhawk received dents and scorched paint. Its crew received no injury.

Usually, the pilot gave up after discovering Customs behind them. The ground crew always scattered. The smuggler pilots have attempted to run. Their legs, much like those of the Customs air officers on board, are stiff. The air officers worked out and ran almost daily. No smuggler pilot, to my knowledge, has ever escaped by jumping out of a landed aircraft and running.

Terrorists will soon arrive in this country in the same manner as drug smugglers by aircraft. This is when our federal officers must literally shoot first and be accurate. We need to have the bill passed in both houses right now. This is another reason to finish the war in Iraq timely.

Shrimp smuggling is sometimes lucrative. To save the time and effort to draw up papers, possibly bribe a Mexico official or two, or pay a possible export duty on shrimp that day, shrimp dealers sometime turned into shrimp smugglers. In any event, exporting goods from Mexico legally is a timely and costly process that cuts deeply into profits. Shrimp are perishable. No one can blame a shrimp smuggler for dodging the crooked ways of Mexico officials. The shrimp smuggler will land when ordered to do so.

If another government in the world exists that is as dirty as Mexico's, it will be in the dirty little dictatorships south of that country. To fix our immigration problem, our Congress must clean Mexico's government first. We have no right? I beg to differ right after we clean out our own Congress from people like those who bankrupted our country to make chosen people billionaires. Many of our people in D. C. are of the same caliber as those in Mexico City.

Criteria for shooting down a drug smuggling suspect would be the first requirement in a list of guidelines prior to forcing an aircraft to land. The aircraft would be given every opportunity to land, and all of these opportunities would be safe ones. Then, this aircraft would still not be shot down. Those that would suffer bullet holes in the rear section would be attempting to escape into Mexico. Later, Customs aircraft will possibly have to dodge air to air missiles. Drug cartels in Mexico are becoming powerful.

But what if all the criteria could not be met? Heaven forbid! The smuggling aircraft would *not* be shot down! It would go free! It's as simple as that! I'll be leaving the subject now that question is answered.

Remember the hypothetical possibility: What if the pilot didn't really--really!--understand the command to land? Think about it a couple seconds. Got it? You're right! The aircraft would *not* be forced to land. It would be followed to its destination, whether it was Childress, Texas or Bend, Oregon. If it flew to Canada, it would be followed until Canadian authorities took over, and Customs would probably continue in the chase until it was forced to land for fuel. If it flew back to Mexico after all the criteria had been met, its tail section would be shot full of holes and landing would be imperative and extremely difficult. Hopefully, it would be a safe landing.

After a few weeks in the air, the greenest of rookies can spot a real smuggler aircraft. The suspicious ones aren't always smugglers, either, but they're checked out in the air or on the ground. After sufficient probable cause, it's much like a state highway patrol officer flipping on the red lights and siren on a vehicle ahead that's breaking the law. It's best to pull over.

My point is this: No innocent aircraft would have been shot down or damaged had the bill passed through Congress. It was a good plan to help win the war on drugs. No more and no less.

What? You're still arguing that drug smuggling is not a capitol offense? Okay. Perhaps that might be the main reason the bill failed.

One time in New Mexico, a suspect's lesser helicopter was shot full of holes by a Customs pilot for attempting to ram a Blackhawk. This aircraft did attempt to escape by flying between buildings in downtown Albuquerque for several minutes. The Blackhawk is a heavy and clumsy aircraft on the ground. In the air it is a mosquito! When the suspect pilot in the lesser helicopter attempted suicide by trying to ram the Blackhawk, a Customs pilot in the Blackhawk filled the aggressive helicopter full of holes from his AR-15. It was unharmed and well clear of the city.

You didn't hear about this? Why not? F. Lee Bailey flew down from New York and got the man off in a Santa Fe, New Mexico court. The taxpayers didn't have to cough up money to patch this man's helicopter, but the helicopter pilot walked. If he really wants to murder other people and die at the same time, he will try it again. This will be, of course, after he undergoes the expense of paying F. Lee and having his chopper repaired.

Not true:

I lied. The bill passed! The bill is not deader than my Uncle Les, who came home slightly intoxicated one night and quietly sneaked into bed with Aunt Maude without turning on the lights. It was the wrong house, of course. Matilda Jones is much younger and prettier than Aunt Maude, but to err is human. Matilda's husband shot Uncle Les at close range without hesitation. The sound of the blast almost deafened poor Matilda.

Okay--I'll admit it! I had a personal interest in getting that bill passed. I would've been one of the shooters! I could only imagine what a glorious feeling to shoot an airplane and watch it fly to the ground in smoke and flames!

Well...actually, I did shoot an aircraft down from our Blackhawk.

The Grand Jury indicted me! Liberals! Pretrial hearings like "Discoveries" and "Motions to Suppress" were repeated several times due to the prosecution's routine mistakes. The U. S. Attorneys refused to defend me and helped prosecute me, instead. I had shot prematurely. Remember what I said about federal prosecutors all being in the Justice Department and harboring professional jealousy against us good guys in the Treasury Department? The worst part of it was that I had to go out and find myself a lawyer at my own expense! I was flat broke.

No lawyer wanted to take my case for free. So I finally found a cheap one--very cheap.

Okay!--I may as well confess. I went to the ACLU. There was only one free lawyer that agreed to take my case. A woman! Long braids fell on each side of her rather plain face. Dark shades of rainbow lipstick were smeared over her thin lips. She had horn-rimmed glasses, protruding front teeth, and an adam's apple. Her five o'clock shadow and baggy clothing and sneakers told me to run for my life, but then, I thought she might be a good attorney. She returned that extra smile, which excited me. Then I heard her voice. I began to get nauseated over what I had thought earlier. She also turned out to be the sorriest lawyer I have ever seen!

Her smile soon faded, and her last words were that she hated my guts. She had no reason for ill phrases. I simply laughed at her outfit and shouted "Fag!" at the same time I suspected it. I was shocked for having said it aloud, sure! I had to say something fast. The only thing I could think to say was to boldly admit I had only come to the ACLU for help because I hadn't the funds to hire a real lawyer. We talked that one time and no more. She refused to hear my full story and clever phrases in how I planned to humiliate my cross examiner while on the stand. In fact, the little homely-looking lady told me the same thing months later in court when I refused to sit at the same table with her at the trial.

It had taken months, almost a year, before the federal judges stopped drawing lots to try the case against me. They kept cheating. The winner wanted me tried and hung ASAP. He told a U.S. Attorney this: "This guy is a federal officer. No way is he going to make bail. That was a year earlier.

The prosecution's first pick of the twelve were used as jurors. Since he knew he was being grossly unfair, he anticipated a fight from my lawyer and spent all those months in preparation for naught. My lawyer accepted them without one question. Here's what I had for a jury:

Three female reporters from a local television station in Queens, New York. They each gave me one look and mouthed the word "Redneck" at me. Two street walkers from San Francisco, Caucasian males, who totally ignored me and spent time blowing kissy-poohs at my lawyer. There was one protestant minister, a hispanic male from Tucson, whom I definitely remembered stopping near the remote border fence late one night with a load of illegal immigrants. I had given him a little push across the hood of his car before patting him down.

I remember the two pro-abortionists, male and female, from a cushy section of Boston. They had no idea of where they were or what they were doing there. I smiled at them and they returned it.

No one could forget the four professors from the Socialist College of Maryland, a school for the poor, tuition free and federally funded--all for the sole purpose of our federal government leasing another building from the old Senator's family who owns most all of the federally-leased buildings in D.C. All four were indignant but understood the purpose of their subpoenas. Let no one tell you that U. S. Attorneys know how to win when the academics of federal law are on their side. Federal laws are extremely hard to read, ambiguous, and full of atrocious grammar and punctuation. Federal laws, especially Customs laws, are far passed drawing any type of a hard-fast conclusion by any attorney or any group of them. They are written for argument! The best sentences are thirty-five words long with no verbs--all nouns, adjectives and useless adverbs. Some sentences make no sense at all. Lawyers writing laws invent their own words and punctuation and don't know the difference between a preposition and a fly speck.

The trial lasted two hours, hardly long enough for the prosecution to make his opening statements after he had lost his notes and had replaced them with something from a similar case back in the forties. My lawyer stood in front of the jury in a Janet Reno dress and black pumps. In her strongest voice, weak at best, she made history by delivering the world's shortest opening statement:

"Just look at those tears! Any of you fools can tell that he's not guilty!"

You think that's poor courtroom drama? Well, throughout the long line of witnesses for the prosecution, some of whom I've never heard of or seen before, my lawyer had no questions for them.

She called no witnesses for the defense, either, not even me. The judge and a few jurors had nodded off, anyhow. Most of them were playing tennis next door.

Following the prosecution's lengthy summation, my lawyer then delivered the world's shortest Summation:

"Well, there he is, still blubbering! If any or all of you rocket scientists think he's guilty, you're wrong! In fact, you're all even more stupid than you look!"

Then four long hours of intense jury deliberation followed inside a secluded room. When the jury finally emerged, they appeared slightly out of touch with themselves. Their faces were glum and ashen, not from the verdict they had apparently reached, but from the marijuana smoke that had been leaking from all around their locked door. I held my breath and stood up with everyone else as they began leaking into the courtroom, some in slow motion, some keeping time with a silent rhythm in their minds. By the time they were seated, the judge was nodding off again.

His honor jerked to attention after the lady keeping notes discretely elbowed the bench a couple times. He asked the foreman if they had reached a verdict. That's when total chaos erupted.

Everyone in the jury suddenly shouted obscenities and flung their arms. They all yelled at the same time with each one using a different answer. Some yelled for the attention of the judge, others yelled toward the reporters. The judge banged his gavel so hard that it broke and sailed across the courtroom. A deputy rushed to each member of the jury and tried to shush them. Reporters filed passed my chair and tipped over tables trying to capture his/her own particular jury member. No one could understand what they were raving about. The foreman finally shouted above the rest:

"NOT GUILTY! CAN YOU BELIEVE THAT? WE DEMAND JUSTICE! NO ONE SHOULD BE ABLE TO GET AWAY WITH WHAT HE DID! WON'T SOMEBODY PLEASE SUE HIM?"

A reporter stopped and asked another, "Did he just say, 'Not guilty?'"

"Yeah," the other reporter answered. "What a bummer! I'm going back to the office and write about one of Santa's rain deer having a baby on my neighbor's roof."

The judge shouted above everyone else to announce that I could go free, but to never show my face in his courtroom again! One jury member grabbed my arm as I was leaving and spun me around. It was one of the professors from the socialist college:

"You think you're so smart with your crooked lawyer humiliating us, don't you? Well, let me tell you something, Mr. Hotshot! You're going to get sued by all those people! In fact, in just a few short years from now, O. J. Simpson is going to be found innocent in a murder trial by another all-liberal jury. Afterwards, he's going to get his socks sued off! It's going to happen to you in a few more weeks!"

I looked at him, completely bewildered. "I wasn't tried for murder."

"You weren't?"

"No sir."

He turned and ran back to his jury panel and tried to round them up. I hurried out of there.

Now you know what would have happened if the bill had passed. It was a good bill, an effective one, but years too early.

Chapter Ten

Border Bullets

During the earlier times on the border, numerous exchanges of gunfire between mounted Customs officers and bootleggers from Mexico have been recorded. Prior to those rough and tumble days, renegades claiming to ride for "Villa" bought themselves a handful of trouble by thinking they could get away with raids on innocent U. S. citizens immediately north of the border. Only the remote ranchers north of the Mexico border in New Mexico were helpless against the cowardly raiders. The U. S. Army and U. S. Customs corrected this problem promptly. Today, however, in response to taxpayer dollars and sacrifices our U. S. Army made, we see a statue of Poncho Villa in downtown Tucson. There is a state part south of Deming, New Mexico named from the hordes of raiders claiming to ride for Villa. If there is a statue of General Pershing, a genuine hero and American patriot, anywhere, I don't know where it's located. Exactly what the revolutionist bandit, Poncho Villa, contributed to the United States escapes me. Perhaps Villa can receive a Nobel Peace Prize post humusly.

Regardless of misstated issues in our recent history and how it was rewritten, this chapter relates to our contemporary times. The unsettled differences between this country and Mexico are no more than that, unsettled. There have always been shootouts across the border between federal officers and outlaws in Mexico. With this mind, I do testify that the smarter Customs officers never reported shootouts on the border. You read correctly. To report a shooting incident is opening a can of worms. Our in-house politics simply aren't worth the bother. U. S. politics will supersede practicality and representation of the American taxpayer every time. Unfortunately,

Mexico's politics have always superseded U. S. politics every time. Once this is understood, U. S. officers will do what they have to do in order to keep themselves alive on the border. I've never met a federal officer on our side of the border that cared for Mexico's politics.

Are the Mexico officials on the border aware of these infrequent scrapes? Of course they are! Most of the Mexico Customs and Immigration authorities running their ports of entries practice the common sense factors far more than they listen to the politics of Mexico City. They, too, have an obligation to their families and themselves. Consequently, officers on both sides of the border have a mutual respect for the other. More clearly stated, perhaps, no one in Washington, D.C. knows how to deal with foreign authorities at the field level. When D.C. actually starts running things, chaos is in order. Officers must be hired that can think for themselves if our country is to survive. After our officers begin playing the roles of robots, Mexico authorities on our level will walk all over us as they do on a national scale. The capital of Mexico has dictated vigorously to our President almost two years at the time of this writing.

Our State Department operates outside my understanding. Are our federal officers to lie down and allow Congress and the State Department to make the federal officers' individual decisions? It was coming to that during my time, and I'm sure it's here by now. They're in charge of every federal officer in every aspect, except toilet necessities. When our officers lose their right to think through a situation, we will have an extremely weak government. It will be no more effective than what we have presently in Congress. Our field officers are our last line of defense on the border. They are, in fact, our *only* line of defense!

The Mexico officers worked in a lax attitude when I was there. They had little respect for anyone who didn't. They weren't about to give away their store anymore than they wanted us to give away ours. If field officers were to do their jobs on the border, the Mansfield Act and all of our Neutrality treaties were followed as far as possible. After that, our officers either threw up their hands or else handled the situation.

The U. S. Border Patrol claimed many gunfights across the border over a span of several decades, but since drug smuggling grew into a booming business in the late 1960's, Customs officers have had more than their fair share of border skirmishes. The difference, the B.P. reported their incidents, so long it brought them positive publicity. However, when they had shootouts, they won. That's a given. It didn't take long for Mexico's bad guys to learn that one doesn't mix it up with the U. S. Border Patrol with gunfire. If those agents can do anything right, it is found in marksmanship.

Then again, today, however, the U. S. Border Patrol agents are under strict orders to not shoot, not even if they're fired upon! This is our capitol's reasoning. Washington thinks Mexico's shooters might be lost and not know where the border is exactly located! What a crock! This is the mire that our own federal government at the Washington level has slithered inside for a century.

Exactly how they can persuade their officers to follow this type of mandate? Simple. They attempt to hire non-thinking officers. Our defenses in our federal system on the border are weakened. Outside our military, there is no defense in the field and none in Washington. The reason? Any President that fights for the welfare of the United States is going to catch holy hell from the press.

Thus far, I have never heard of a Customs shooting that wasn't justified. One always has to hear about the shootouts by word of mouth because they sure weren't on paper. When we lost Customs officers, the public learned about it but our freedom to use firearms at our discretion was tightened.

Law enforcement officers aren't the only ones that have suffered harassment in the form of bullets from the Mexico side. Snipers from Mexico have been around since the establishment of the border. I don't have access to all the accounts, but I was on duty in Albuquerque when a shooting of innocent tourists happened on the Rio Grand in the late 1980's. River rafters in the Big Bend National Park received sniper fire from a mountain top on the Mexico side. One man was killed and others were wounded. The sniper, a young man, was apprehended on the Mexico side by our helicopter crew. The news of his disposition wasn't provided.

In the remote areas at an international border, there's a natural tendency from both sides to act rationally without political restrictions--thanks to the rule of common sense.

IN 1975, an Act expired that allowed all Mexico law enforcement unrestricted access to the border towns on the U.S. side. In turn, our federal, state, and local law enforcement could visit Mexico without visas within their 15-mile border nexus. We could roam about, shop, and get falling down drunk in their cantinas as guests of their country. Then, in July, when that Act expired, all Mexico officials wanting to walk into our country for a cup of coffee in the small café across the street from our port of entry were denied access. This staggered Mexico and Immigration officials. It was explained to them by Immigration officers. Washington, again, had driven another nail into their Coffin of rationalism. It practically killed relationships on the border between officers on both sides.

Mexico's border officials were allowed inside our port of entry to apply for a U.S. Border Crossing Card. They could travel to Tucson and Phoenix with these cards and remain a reasonable length of time, up to a month or two if they had visible means of support. The officers working across the border fence from us shook their heads in disbelief but played along with our embarrassing U.S. game of politics. They all received their cards within a few days.

Then, the irony of it all showed its ugly face. U. S. Immigration officers at our port who issued the cards were required to see these cards each time an official from Mexico, in uniform, crossed the border for a cup of coffee. The Mexico officials didn't like that. I didn't blame them. Our U. S. Immigration inspectors at the port of entry didn't care if they liked it or not. They had their orders. Common sense was replaced by liberalism and caused them to act like robots without a thinking brain. These Immigration Officers turned back the officials if they didn't have their cards. The officials might walk across the street three times in one day for coffee or lunch on our side. In each of those three times, no matter how many times they've gotten drunk with the Immigration officers, they unbuttoned their uniform shirt pockets and opened their wallets to show the U. S. Immigration inspector their newly-issued cards each time they entered the U. S. on foot to have coffee across the street. They did this because Washington demanded it. It was a sorry sight.

Then, while I was an inspector on the primary lane, after any Mexico officer entered the first time on any particular day, I saw no sense in him having to stop and show this card again for the rest of the day. I knew each one carried it in their wallets. They were honest with us.

During my turn on the primary lane, I allowed three officials to pass for coffee without seeing their card. I knew all three of them. We often chatted if their English was good enough. There were no strangers in Mexico's Customs and Immigration offices across the border from me. I used them as interpreters when the FBI needed help in Mexico. I wanted to keep these channels open. Lives depended upon it. If a child in Phoenix was kidnapped, the FBI knew exactly where to go. Mexico's immigration and Customs officers were there to help. We saw each other across the fence, waved, spoke, chatted, and swapped stories everyday. They patted their shirt pockets when they entered our country to have coffee within a hundred yards of their office. Patting their pockets was their word that the stupid card was on their persons. I believed them. Their town of Sonoyta was two miles south of the border, so getting coffee there was out of the question.

The Immigration officer brought to my attention the fact that I was breaking U. S. laws in allowing the officials to pass without seeing their cards. He was quite right. I did exactly that. I wasn't the only inspector at the port of entry to violate that stupid law. The officials were not strangers! They had their cards on them and they weren't about to remain in the U. S. They all had fine homes in Sonoyta on their monthly incomes. Their *mordida* (bite) on all the tourists from the U. S. and Baja California earned them tens of thousands of dollars above our U. S. yearly salaries.

In time, U.S. Immigration officials from Washington came to visit our port of entry. We discussed this showing of cards business. I explained that we knew those officials for years. They were taking nothing from us by not stopping, taking out their cards, etc. It was a matter of respect at the field level. I felt it was a childish game of a power play in Washington that was totally unnecessary. The two officials agreed with me. The practice was stupid in their own words!

Two weeks later, Customs received a letter that certain Customs inspectors, namely me, plus one other inspector, were breaking U. S. laws by not forcing Mexico officials to show their cards each time they entered the U. S. They didn't have the fortitude to tell me this in person. Their cowardly and hypocritical letter changed nothing.

Immigration inspectors had no idea of the damage they were doing by playing power games from Washington. If their bosses sent them Directives on how to use the bathroom and how to make love to their wives, they'd follow it to the letter. Then again, I probably do everything wrong. What do they know about getting along with neighbors? If Washington wanted to get their acts together with Mexico and treat it like the stupid socialist or communist country it is, then their stupid rules and Directives would be read and respected. Taxpayers would pay less taxes and there would be no immigration problem with Mexico. We owe Mexico and the other socialist nations around the world nothing. At the field level, however, it is important to maintain a working relationship with their officers.

Each and every one of those countries knew how to have a free enterprise system, yet their ruling socialist government officials forbid it. Then our Congress allows them foreign aid and allows their poor into our country for U.S. taxpayers to feed and clothe and provide medical services.

More irony, Mexico's diplomats have free access to anywhere in the U. S. they want without having to undergo routine inspections. *By all the factors of common sense, this practice is undeniably wrong!* There's a reason for it. It's called "Power."

U.S. diplomats have the same privilege in other countries. Prior to electronic banking, they had to have a way or means to transport their money to Switzerland, Lithuania, and other countries that will bank tax-free U. S. currency. Power, Money and Control are the names of the games. Whoever has the most, wins.

One skirmish with guns happened when a New Mexico rancher grew tired of drug smugglers crossing his ranch, according to him. I had been there several times in 1990 and 91 to help him but my efforts were for naught. The smugglers weren't there when I was there. I couldn't hold a continued surveillance without his permission and prior knowledge. This just cannot happen if one expects success. The least amount of people that know about secret surveillances, the better. People love to talk about important items, especially if they're secret.

Getting a surveillance classified is difficult. I've tried. It never works out. Each time I was there on the rancher's place, I saw no smugglers or anyone else. With my office wanting to know every move and detail of the surveillance by radio, the smugglers merely have to monitor our radios in order to know when to lay low.

But we fixed that! Customs bought us hand-held radios with garblers. They cost almost 4,000 dollars each. No drug smuggler could understand our words after that. Our radio traffic was garbled. All the bad guys could hear was a solid stream of static when we transmitted. The smugglers simply laid low each time their monitors buzzed with this unique type of static. When we stopped talking, they smuggled their drugs because we were no longer around. Man, we really larned 'em!

Some day, some time, perhaps in the twenty-second century, Customs will issue a Directive that clearly states, "You shall maintain radio silence during all operations!" After that is tried and proven effective, Customs can go back to cheaper radios and to the business of interdicting drugs.

Finally, the rancher gave up on us and acted on his own. He approached the smugglers as they approached his border fence. They turned back under his threats to blow them out of their shoes. In a little while, hours or minutes, I failed to pin anyone down, Mexican *federales* crossed the border into the United States, took his guns, and called U. S. authorities to control that crazy man.

I wasn't among the Customs officers that arrived, but I did talk with the rancher later. The *federales*, he claimed, took his guns on our side of the border! He would say no more about it. Knowing the man, I would probably have taken his guns, too. He learned the hard way that the smarter practice is to never threaten or attack an officer with a gun, regardless of where he might be, especially on the Mexico border!

That wasn't the problem, however. How and why the *federales* were crossing the border on to this rancher's property is highly suspect. No one received a straight answer from the rancher. He told us what he wanted to tell us. Perhaps the rancher wasn't supposed to be interrogated closely. Perhaps I was supposed to take his word, regardless of how dumb it sounded.

I had met all those *federales.* I wouldn't trust any one of them any further than I'd trust Hillary Clinton to return the White House silverware. I found no evidence of smuggling there. The *federales* rode with us in the Blackhawk one day while we flew over a cornfield in Mexico near the border fence. I could see no marijuana. We landed on our side and the *federales* walked across the border and began pulling up marijuana plants while we watched. I retired within a couple months.

Four years later, the U.S. Border Patrol officers were still working that area of the border like it was going to yield them headline-making marijuana busts!

Then a border incident arose. It seems that the U.S.B.P. crossed into Mexico to seek out some possible marijuana plants that still might be growing in the exact cornfield we found years earlier. They were caught by *federales.* They didn't want to be caught. I don't know what happened. I never read anything. What I personally heard was this:

The assistant chief of the B.P. Sector in El Paso was the guest on a popular radio talk show. The Black Avenger was the host. The Assistant Chief of the U.S. Border Patrol Sector in El Paso lied his lips off.

He said that this section of the border is remote and is a kind of a "No man's land." Whaaat?

He claimed that no one knows exactly where the border might be. Whoa--Nellie!

From El Paso, west across New Mexico's border to Douglas, Arizona and on west across Arizona to the Colorado River, there is a fence! It's a big fence with signs and border markers! Our U.S. ranchers know exactly where and how much land they have next to Mexico. The fence in New Mexico is not only strong and well maintained, it has eight wires in many places! In fact, in that very place, the wires are tight and close. I am a fence crosser, climber and jumper due to a few years of running from half-brama cows.

The only no-man's land between us and Mexico was north of the river in El Paso where there was no fence. Congressman White gave this land to Mexico back in the 1960's. It is no longer a no man's land. It belongs to Mexico. The river hasn't changed its course since that time. It has been fenced high since that time. Now, there are sandy areas on the California border where the sand dunes from the Buttercup Valley might cover the border fence. That's hundreds of miles west of El Paso Sector's jurisdiction. No border fence? B.P. agents got confused and lost? I think not! I had no idea that the American public could be so vulnerable. I wrote the Black Avenger a letter to help straighten the story a bit. He never answered. However, the radio station in Lubbock stopped carrying his program for some reason or another.

Other ranchers on the Texas and New Mexico border, through Rumor Control, have never called upon our federal or state authorities to help them deal with their neighbors south of the border until the 1990's. Then ranchers on the Arizona-Mexico border near Douglas began asking for help from everyone. They're still asking for help. They've yet to receive it from our federal officers. Mexico President Vicente Fox has asked us to open up our welfare system for his people. I don't blame him. Why not milk a stupid government that never questions him or his socialist government's motives?

Ugly or not, I will say this: We are indeed fortunate that ABC's Sam Donaldson's big sheep or cattle ranch in New Mexico is far north of the Mexico border. From the U. S. assistance in dollars this liberal reporter has already received from the U. S. Government for the upkeep of his ranch is guesswork in my point of view. If his ranch were on the border, there'd be a great need for him to ask much more after he was robbed blind two or three times a year. We taxpayers couldn't afford to keep Mr. Donaldson in the ranching business. The same might be said of Ted Turner if his ranch were on the Mexico border.

WHILE horseback, Tilton and I rode by two graves on the U. S. side of the border in a remote area late one afternoon. They were many decades old. They had almost vanished under the sun over a prolonged time. A week later I asked a U. S. officer with better Spanish than I to ask a local school teacher from Sonoyta, Sonora if he knew anything about those two graves.

Indeed, he did! The teacher explained that it was during one of Mexico's national holidays that several men from each country met while horseback in the small but remote basin. There was no border fence. Gunfire erupted between the American Indians that were horseback and the Mexico cowboys. In the Sonoyta, Sonora school teacher's own words, the result of the gunfight was this: "We almost won!"

No doubt, that meant the battle was close and well fought. The two graves were Mexico's and are within U. S. property about twenty feet. The teacher went on to explain that those graves had remained lost for decades, apparently since our border fence was erected sometime in the early 1950's. There had been talk of caring for the graves if they were ever found. I rode by them the last time in 1985. Both grave sites had cement markers and are still remote on the U. S. side where there is no road. People are people, and there's no escaping the fact that boys will be boys.

The U. S. Border Patrol has been on the border thirty years longer than the Customs Patrol and suffered the hazards of cowardly snipers far more often than any other federal service. The eighty miles, more or less, of international border where the U. S. Border Patrol didn't patrol is on the Tohono O'odum Nation--where we in the U. S. Customs Patrol were granted that privilege. No sniping takes place on those eighty miles. However, at least forty miles of the remote area south of the border is still occupied by Indians of the same tribe north of the border. These people do not recognize the border between the U. S. and Mexico, unless, of course, it's convenient to do so.

Drug smugglers never draw attention to themselves, unless it benefits their cause. They practice safety as much, if not more, than U. S. officers. For example, they have no false pride preventing them from running, hiding, and even crying and vomiting when they're caught. Discretion is definitely practiced among all our outlaws. Soldiers of fortune have been hired by some drug cartels and have proven themselves worthy opponents. But even they, those adventurers supposedly addicted to adrenalin and all they can buy on the street, depend upon the odds in their favor. I've never encountered one, but I do know worthy federal officers that have squared off with them in foreign nations with no problem.

Handicap a drug smuggler by taking away his odds usually removes potential threats.

Federal drug officers, on the other hand, always expect the odds to be against them, from laws set up by federal judges to weapons in all situations. They're better officers if they're slightly handicapped. They know this. They have to think during situations. Fortunately, thinking is their best weapon until firearms are necessary, which is when thinking really becomes important!

This is exactly where upper management interferes. Upper management tries to do all the thinking. Therefore, problems arise. Take away an employee's thinking and you have a robot for an officer. Problems will arise that simply aren't covered by Washington's so-called superior intellect. The Immigration officers at the ports of entries read all their Memos and Directives from Washington and try ever so hard to follow them to the letter. Nothing good will come of it and nothing will change this practice--short of common sense.

To be able to think or not, humans naturally compensate for themselves. Thinking will remain an officer's best weapon prior to arrest situations and on raids with warrants. An officer does know how to call for backup prior to entering a "can't win" situation. That's a key to survival. "Back up and wait for backup."

If I were a socialist leader and sitting at the head of a federal law enforcement service in the United States, I'd insist on hiring officers as unintelligent as possible. If an applicant could pass a Civil Service Exam, that applicant would definitely not be hired! I would hire officers who can't pass tests and too dumb to dress themselves properly. I would do their thinking for them. They would carry out my orders. I would limit their ability to use their weapons, for dummies will cause embarrassment. I would also disarm them, for dummies can be replaced. The "lose one—hire one" policy would be in order.

The U. S. Border Patrol agent that went into the home where seven-year old Elio Gonzalez resided is one of the examples where top management control officers' thinking. The Border Patrol agent had no qualms against obeying outrageous orders. Why didn't the liberal Attorney General disarm him first? Was he not expendable? He wasn't disarmed for one reason. This was a power play for the public to witness. Weapons were and are not outlawed yet, and for the officer to be armed was lawful, for he was supporting a socialist cause.

The uncle of Elio was a hair's breath from death as the agent snatched the hysterical child from the uncle's arms.

This is the type of officer I would pin medals on--*if I were a socialist leader.* He would carry out my orders without question. He would be my stereotype of the ideal agent. Janet Reno had exactly what she wanted in him!

Thinking today in the federal services is good for America! It can be used as a weapon against socialist offices of authority like Janet Reno's, who was appeasing Fidel Castro. Thinking is imperative prior to and avoiding a situation. The real point is that thinking, planning, and organization are the basics for confidence. There isn't a thief or coward in the world that cannot read confidence in an opponent, victim or officer. They can also read the absence of confidence. If the crooks can win, those without confidence will be the first targets.

"One must do the best with what one's got." That was Tilton's attitude, even if it has been used for centuries. He always said that before we went into a situation. Personally, I got ticked every time he looked directly at me and mouthed those words! Innuendos and sarcastic remarks are what I detect best. I've never been in a bad situation with Tilton. The situation was always under control before it happened. Dramatically charging a cartridge into the barrel of a shotgun in the dead silence of a dark night is the best confidence breaker in crooks--short of shooting them. They detest that sound. I would, too. In the remoteness, near the border and when it's dark, calling out and identifying one's self as the police before the smugglers are under control can and will get an officer killed. This is why I never allowed an officer we called Gloomy to work with me the second time on the border.

Gloomy and I were in an ambush situation waiting for a group of single file entrants to walk upon us one dark night. There was an overcast, which made everything pitch black. Gloomy understood to keep quiet above everything else. If I moved and he didn't, no problem. Stay low and don't say a word until I called for it. Gloomy thought that he knew better than me. He called out to the group before they were upon us a good twenty feet. "Police! Don't move!"

I thought this: "They may be drug smuggler with guns!" I dived to one side from that loud-mouth as fast as possible and rolled on the ground while waiting for the bullets to strike him--hoping they would strike him and not me. Gloomy should have been filled with bullets. No such luck! I crawled away from him while hearing the group scatter for Mexico. With our flashlights, we found nothing but tricky bags tossed aside. I was rightfully reprimanded for not keeping my trainee under control. I simply countered with: "Don't ever send that man with me again! If he'll listen to another journeyman officer, let that officer train him."

Mad Cat, a rather restless officer and whose stability I've often suspected, took Gloomy to show everyone that he could train a man where Homer had failed. I was the first to wish him luck.

According to U. S. Border Patrol sources in 1984 and the following year, drug lords were offering up to $30,000 for the head of any federal drug officer. I never believed it. However, each time there was a sniper incident involving the USBP, it made national headlines. Two short reasons are behind this fact:

1) The BP likes to think of themselves as narcotics officers instead of immigration officers, which is only human. It's good to have a sense of worthiness. Their job is mostly amounts to stirring the illegal immigrant pot and accomplishing absolutely zero.

2) The BP has always been dependent upon public support. They have a great need to look good for Congress. Unless their agency has positive publicity from the news media, their agency cannot and will not survive. Our Congress's source of information is from our news media. It carries far more weight than statistics.

The best security blanket that our federal services can have in the United States is to have all federal services sing one song entitled: "More money! More manpower!"

Congress has the money. It matters not if the Border Patrol fails year after year and decade after decade. The BP can always blame Congress for not giving them the money and manpower they needed each year.

Congress only has to claim that they were doing as the agency asked by providing them more money and more manpower. In 1971 the U. S. B. P. was logging statistics close to one million apprehensions per year. There were 1,800 B. P. agents then. Today, at the time of this writing, they have 11 thousand officers. Our immigration crises have reached critical levels. More manpower and more money DID NOT work! It has never worked.

Before the immigration problem can be easily solved, Congress must face up to their responsibilities and fix Mexico's socialist government. It's as easy as sending a Tomahawk missile to the steps of their capital. No warhead is necessary. In fact, the space could be loaded with motivational Amway tapes. Of course, fixing Iraq's government is easy in comparison with Mexico's government. Corruption can provide just as many stumbling blocks as cowardly insurgents.

All federal agencies are, indeed, under tight scrutiny of our U. S. Congress. Rightfully so. U. S. voters have a great need to be thinkers prior to going to the polls. It's a good weapon toward keeping our country free of pork spenders and those who believe socialism run by the right kind of people is the only true government.

All nations have a right to sovereignty, all except the United States of America. President G. W. Bush and our Congress did their best to keep Mexico's Vicente Fox happy, who seemed to be unhappy with our handouts to his people. To fix the problem, however, Vicente Fox needed to be forced out of office after being tarred and feathered, along with the entire capital of Mexico. Replacing them with honest people that are anti-socialist will fix Mexico's problem for the first time in 400 years!

I respect Mexico's people. Their leaderships stinks on the same level as our radical socialists in Washington, D.C.

New York's Senator Clinton runs into barriers all the time in fixing our U. S. Government. Her talents and accomplishments still score at the zilch level. Mexico needs her far more than New York. Mexico has poor people that need to be fed. There's a shortage of doctors in Mexico. Many people die without medical aid in Mexico. Why doesn't she move to Mexico and answer the cries of those people? Perhaps she could become President of Mexico for Life! Of course, nothing in Mexico would change with her at the helm.

Border skirmishes depend upon the attitude and the balances of comfort and power on both sides of the border. Borders have been ripe for shootouts for decades, since the smuggling of goods into the U. S. entered the scene. The best defense for federal officers on our side is to carry bigger and better weapons. The old Border

Patrol inspectors were about as mean as the snipers and ten times tougher--when the patrol first began. They were smart, and they were confident. That agency has changed!

BP agents today can still use a handgun as well as the old inspectors, but the old inspectors didn't have to suffer the headlines, scrutiny and investigations that agents have to endure today following a gunfight. This simply should not be. It's devastating to everyone concerned, including the taxpayers. If an officer cannot be trusted, he shouldn't be on the job. It's that simple.

We have psychology tests that pinpoint honest and dedicated people. Thinkers! These people can be trained to uphold our laws with complete confidence. The Equal Opportunity Law, the one first written, was definitely not in opposition to a psychology test. "Qualified" was the key word in the original Equal Opportunity Laws. There was never a need to question their words of honor. They were loyal to our country, honest beyond question, and thorough. Their integrity was always fully intact.

Let's hypothetically assume that a rumor existed in the days of the old Border Patrol inspectors that some drug lord has offered thousands of dollars for the death of a federal officer--any federal officer!

First of all, the officer or source of the rumor would be brought forth to answer a few "Whens" and "Wheres." They wouldn't wait for the FBI to investigate the rumor. The sun would barely have time to set before the drug lord was tried, convicted, and then made so dead that he wouldn't even need burying. He would be fragmented without ceremony. If the rumor proved to be only a rumor, then the source of such information would immediately learn a completely new set of values. No--the old inspectors weren't a judge and jury. They followed the rules. And--so did the judges and court systems of their time.

Up until today, U. S. Customs officers have returned gunfire across the border in the remoteness, or whatever direction is necessary. Politics slowly prevented almost all officers from recording gunfire incidents, regardless of the defensive postures and measures they've taken. It simply isn't worth the hassle to report it and then have to spend years proving their innocence.

Unless one lives and works in our southwest's desert, one would never suspect that the wolf sage compliments the pencil *cholla* (pronounced: cho-ya) and vice versa. No two other opposite plants, not even in the same Order under the classification system, shared their root system's territory in the scorched earth with the other and grew together as partners. The thin limbs of the pencil *cholla* is protected from the harsh sun by the sage's leaves. One mustn't touch a wolf sage bush in the desert, for the hidden cactus will issue a great deal of pain to the fingers. Browsing and grazing animals avoid the wolf sage, for the pencil *cholla* is hidden in practically all of that brush.

I was in the process of explaining this to Gloomy on our first ride together as journeyman officer and trainee. We had stopped and stepped outside the vehicle when I began this short lecture.

While he was listening, or pretending to be listening, he walked straight into a wolf sage, even as I was cautioning him to avoid that same bush! He yelped and stepped aside several feet as if trying to dodge his pain, which caused him to contact another wolf sage! He yelped again and went sideways this time into another wolf sage, yelped again, and ran straight into another while dodging the last one! He finally dodged close enough for me physically stop him. He claimed to be a former supervisor from some police department in southern California. He didn't apply for the U.S. Border Patrol. He told me so after I had asked him why.

I said to him that afternoon as he was filling his legs up with painful needles from pencil *cholla*, "When I say stop, you stop! It's a simple concept. Just...Stop! Don't dodge. Don't do anything but stop! Is that clear enough? Rattlesnakes use the wolf sage to coil under."

That did it! He broke free of me!

"Yikes!" he dodged again and slipped completely out of my grip and hit another wolf sage, which started a brand new series of yelps and dodges all over again. Unbelievable? You bet, but I saw it happen. Twice!

I walked on. He caught up shortly, marveling at how a perfectly normal looking bush had stickers in it and even pointed one out to me. "Incredible!" he said as if I had never spoken a word to him about the plants. That had to be the remotest man I had ever met. He retired a station senior of special agents with incredibly high wages. What he lacked in brains was made up somewhere else, somehow.

I have wished that Customs wasn't so fortunate in its recruiting efforts, as many have said the same about me. I surmised that he would probably step off a high cliff while I was in charge of his safety one day in the near future. It never happened, because he asked our boss for another officer to learn under before I got him killed by cactus needles. This was, however, after he learned that I dropped him with a thumbs down on keeping him after that night he disobeyed me and scattered illegal immigrants all the way back to the border fence. Tilton also refused to train him.

A year later, Tilton and I crouched behind two different wolf sages that were about two feet high one dark night and waited on what we thought were one or two men approaching from the border fence fifty yards south. Before they arrived, while I was getting ready to spring forward to knock both of them to the ground, he wisely whispered, "Let's let 'em pass before we jump 'em!"

That meant putting us between them and the border. "Sure," I said, "let's cut 'em off from the safety of the border. Let's both die in a moment of glory!"

We had successfully dodged the wolf sage brush in the darkness, but I crouched back, ready for my leap. In doing so, I had leaned back into a wolf-sage, jumped, and hit Tilton, who brushed forward against a wolf sage. He cussed, and the approaching people were on the south side of the fence before we could stop each other from dodging into another wolf sage. He chewed on me for moving. I chewed on him for cussing so loud. No more will be said about moving around in the wolf sage thickets.

I can think of only one case where the snipers never had to dodge U. S. bullets. That would be this rarely told story--not one of my favorites.

I have twelve solid years of hard work and loyal service on our most remote region of the Mexico border. Not one single time have the drug smugglers ever fired at me. Tilton had a ready explanation for this fact: An officer has to be a threat to their occupation before they ever feel the need to waste a bullet. I reminded him that he was still alive.

If there were anyone ever destined to be trapped in the less dignified and non-glorious situations, it would be me. It would never happen to Tilton, Weldon, or Garcia. My experience had to be from a lesser element of the criminal forces than drug smugglers. I have absolutely no gunplay or dodging bullets experiences from the highly publicized bad guys. Sure, I'm grateful, if you're asking, but that doesn't ease the rather ego-smashing fact for me.

My jeep was pointed westbound on the remote desert's border fence and stopped with the ignition turned off. This was only a mile west of the Lukeville Port of Entry and on the edge of a sharp hill that would lower me into a shallow basin. It was there that I spotted a neat stack of freshly chopped wood on the south side of the fence, right against it. Something less of a cord, I surmised. Tracks and debris were scattered northward about 100 yards into a grove of ironwood and mesquite trees that were protected by the National Park Service. Animal poachers and wood thieves were another scourge in our remote desert.

The wood poachers from Mexico were constantly taking the prized firewood from the Organ Pipe National Monument and turning it into charcoal. Lots of charcoal is sold in Mexico's border towns in the desert. All their ironwood and mesquite trees on the Mexico side were already chopped and sold. The charcoalers have no other place to get their wood--other than from our national monument and the U. S. Fish and Wildlife Service's Cabeza Prieta Game Range, which begins twenty miles west of the port of entry.

I don't like poachers of any type. A brushy wash was to my left in Mexico, which trailed from the low basin on our side. Everything was perfectly quite on the north side.

Since the poachers were out of sight and would be armed with nothing but chainsaws and axes, I felt no immediate danger. The rightful thing to do would be to toss the wood back over the fence, seize it physically and on paper, then sell it to our public, since they were the ones that were going to buy it as charcoal, anyway.

I disliked seeing our endangered ironwood in the desert fall prey to wood poachers, especially in a national park where respectful tourists aren't even allowed to snatch a small twig from a tree to use as a toothpick.

That's what I was thinking when a sudden noisey bullet approached in the direction of my head and passed my nose within inches. Then, the area around me wasn't silent anymore. The air in the bullet's wake, alone, almost toppled my hat. The retort that followed caused me to reach in five different directions and scramble for safety at the same time. Safety in that situation was on the north side of my open-aired jeep. More bullets followed in quick succession, all of them high, lest I would've died where I stood. I set a new record in getting out of that old army jeep. But first, my hand became entangled in the steering wheel as I reached for my revolver. The other hand slipped on the canvas seat and was forced to the floor among the gear levers. My knees slipped on the seat where I was sitting and my pant leg caught a shifting lever. Other than that, I was out of there in record time!

I fell on my head at the north side of the jeep and rolled over as graceful as a sack of potatoes. Then I waited for more bullets. The bullets I carried do not penetrate the brush well. I had no target. I placed my reload cartridge carriers carefully on the ground. My fingers and hands were calm.

During those long seconds or tenths of one, were thoughts of my being shot between my buttocks while scrambling for the north side of the jeep. That area was the highest and biggest point of my body while I was escaping the danger zone. Given the choice as a second thought, I would've preferred being shot in the head. But the bullets following were all deliberately high. None struck my jeep. The first was too close. The others appeared deliberately high. For that I was grateful, but my love for poachers still hasn't improved.

Even with the bullets passing high with retorts following, I took a stance and looked for a target with my 357 revolver, my choice of hand weapons with the right ammunition. I saw no target and refused to shoot until I spotted one.

My bullets were copper jacketed but had a hollow nose. Brush is all that I saw when I took the fast peeps from behind cover. I didn't envy the poacher if he had showed himself. He didn't show, not from the area where I was looking by scanning fast and ducking! Once my first scare subsided, I figured my bullets would have to penetrate about forty yards of brush before they found their mark. That would be nonsense, shooting into the brush at a hidden target. Wasting even one of my thirty bullets in an upcoming gunfight wasn't a good choice, either. I always needed a few just for range and accuracy, or until I opened my eyes, whichever came first.

I had no earplugs, so after I fired the first round, I would be temporarily deafened. Believe me, when a 357 revolver is fired, there's no crucial hearing for at least five minutes for anyone within a ten-mile range without ear protection. I had six shots to fire, but I didn't expect to need more than one or two, depending upon how many poachers were there. Alone, one needs to be able to hear any and all sounds in every direction.

I waited. My eyes watered and became blurry as I scanned the brush. Nothing. Then the bullets came again! They had to be in sight somewhere and I had failed to spot them! That's scary! There were two rifles, both of them small, .22 calibers. They were about ten yards apart. For sure, they didn't want to kill me. I had apparently provided them a good laugh or something. I began to feel good over being shot at and missed. I think that they missed me purposefully. I didn't see the bullet pass my nose. I have no idea how close it was. I only felt its wake.

I sat with my back against the right front tire, criticizing myself for overlooking my targets. Even though they were missing deliberately, I really would not have missed them. I didn't want to shoot, but duty demanded it the moment I spotted them. My afterthoughts are that I was glad to have overlooked them, for they were still deliberately aiming high. I kept looking with fast glances and saw no one to shoot.

I counted fifteen more shots, about thirty-five or forty in all. The first ones came rather rapid from semi-automatic rifles but I still had a fair guess at how many rounds were fired in my direction for my defense. Some five or ten minutes later I heard a noise north and slightly west of me. My hearing was still acute! Could they be serious enough to try and surround me? The intelligent answer was negative, but the imaginary ones caused another bout of hysteria.

The felt tipped pen recorded the incident on the north side of the jeep, its gas tank, in fact. I wrote while they shot. I carried no paper in my pockets. We feds are programmed to record incidents. I recorded all the counted shots, the time, time lapses, everything. I had spotted no targets, and that was recorded, too. The location was exact, and I wrote where I thought they were. I had to abandon my cover due to the noise north of me. I recorded that, also.

A second after the last message on the gas tank, I was off on my belly to interdict the one/s attempting to get north of me. I would not be surrounded. Serious countermeasures were at hand. If I saw anyone north of me, I would not miss.

The occasional high volley of bullets repeated themselves. The mesquites' top branches danced a few times overhead. I didn't give them the top of my head to shoot at anymore, nor did I lift my rear end. Then, as a last thought before I crawled further north, I scrambled back to the jeep and found the microphone while crouching in my original position. It was time for backup. My station didn't answer, so I had to go through Sector, which was in Los Angeles. No satellite communications were up there in the old days. Instead, the mountains between border stations and Los Angeles had relay (repeater) stations on top of them, which provided a clear radio response between Sector and my station.

I asked Sector to send Tilton and Johnny to rescue me from this most embarrassing situation. I also added for them to use extreme caution as they turned south from the main road to my location on the border, for they were attempting to get north of me. He acknowledged, and I heard Tilton's response within a minute! He was hardly a mile away on the east side of the port.

With Sector knowing that I was taking on harassing gunfire, the whole Customs world west of me learned of it, also. I would suffer many wood poaching jokes from San Luis, San Diego and a few other stations later. Tilton and Johnny's burst through the brush north of me like a stampeding buffalo. Both of them joined me beside my jeep. They were curious why I was still alive and why I hadn't dived into that brush to flush them out. I was curious why they took most of the afternoon before responding. Actually, it was hardly more than a minute.

I explained that they might be trying to get north of us.

"I don't think so," Tilton said while Johnny chuckled. "The only thing north of you is one of Bobby Gray's mares. She's moving east but taking her time. She moves each time there's bullets hitting the ground west of her."

Just my luck! I thought. Then we heard the third vehicle in the area. It was to the south. The wood poachers were driving away after my help arrived. Their pickup was red and approximately 150 yards south, far out of range. The cab of the pickup had been cut away, much like a jeep from the distance. Both of them had rifles pointed straight up as they parked momentarily on top of a small knoll to give us a good look at how bad they were. They were out of range for our handguns and for their small rifles. For me, it was how bad they *could* have been. They had to have missed me deliberately! They were too close to miss me, and they never put one bullet into my vehicle that I hid behind.

I'm not going to tell you that we returned their harassing fire. They had parked on the knoll only briefly--very briefly! Whatever they were driving moved mighty fast in a southern direction across the desert's floor. The dust in their wake rose high. Speeders, one can't escape them!

Tilton got tight lipped because I had not returned the gunfire, mostly because it could be bad for our image, and rightfully so. No one wants to be thought of as cowardly but I stood my ground. I have never shot without a target. Once, when I was about ten years old and had learned to shoot my dad's .22 rifle safely, I walked into the pasture late one night and shot at the moon. A chip didn't fly off its round outline, and it didn't explode, so I must've missed. That was a wasted shot. I couldn't believe that anyone could miss such an easy target, which is why I didn't fire at an unseen target. Never waste bullets!

Sector Communications had notified Internal Affairs in El Paso, according to the rules. I spent the first ten minutes back at the station talking with an IA agent. He was a decent officer but skeptical when I told him that I had no target to shoot at. Consequently, no bullets had been fired into Mexico. Had I been able to get off one shot, I would have hit my target. Each of my bullets were going to hit their marks—providing I could keep my eyes open long enough.

Johnny chuckled again in the background. "It's awful hard to find a target when one's nose is buried in the dirt."

One never has to travel far to find a comedian. I didn't have to repeat myself but once before I.A. was convinced that I wasn't just feeding him a barrel of sour mash in order to avoid the paperwork and to give our illustrious leaders a "Heads up" of an impending international incident. He grasped the concept of not shooting without a target okay but had trouble with why I didn't go seek out the target. That's the part I hated to admit. I deliberately didn't go into Mexico because they had missed me deliberately. I still believe that. However, I was seriously seeking out that noise north of me. The service's reputation might've been resting with my inactions of the report, but it was me in the situation, and given the second chance under the same circumstance, nothing would change. I wrote no paperwork on the incident, although the I.A. asked for a written report. Nonsense!

Nothing was going on paper to give those monkeys a reason to stand me in front of examining boards and possibly fired just to keep on the safe side of Mexico politically. The government of Mexico don't give two toots from a gaseous puppy about border shooting incidents or anything else that doesn't bring them money. That's not so terribly difficult for anyone to understand, but it whooshes over our State Department's head like a meteor.

Under President Reagan's administration or under Presidents Bush, I would have considered crawling south of the border through the brush to seek out my antagonists. Had Tilton's rescue been moments later, I might've crawled north several miles through the brush just to save myself from being surrounded.

A drug smuggler later shot at one of my men, another incident that failed to make the news. Our officer was parked off a north-south highway that led into Mexico a couple miles south. It was a clear, moonlight night.

It was well passed midnight when an old Cadillac passed his position slowly in the remoteness. It had come from south of the border fence, for that's where the small wagon road led.

The officer might've followed it north a short while before stopping it, as would've been the normal procedure. Its lights were out but that isn't unusual on a bright night. If it were driven by a drug smuggler, the car was, in all likelihood, fading heat. Fading heat is driving north first to flush out the officers that might be watching the road. While the officers were after him, the smugglers with the drugs would follow soon after the officers were out of the way. Heat cars drive slow, then at the sight of the officers, they race north exceptionally fast. Our officer was still making the decision to go after it when he heard the truck. As he first suspected, the old Cadillac was trying to fade heat.

A dump truck passed his position. It was a mile behind the old Cadillac. There wasn't another car within fourteen miles of them, which would be on the east-west Tucson highway. They were definitely alone.

With lights out, he fell in behind the truck. The driver spotted him in the moonlight, made a u-turn and merely headed back south. The officer drove off the pavement to provide him room, then made his own u-turn to fall in behind the truck. Of course he knew that he was then temporarily surrounded, and that the Cadillac would soon catch up to him from behind.

As he approached the truck, he saw the driver's face in the rearview mirror in the bright moonlight. He wasn't smiling or making a face of any kind. The truck was moving about fifteen mph. Suddenly a man that was lying down immediately behind the tail gate of the dump truck, raised up with a fully loaded automatic pistol and fired.

The bullets danced their way up in a straight line from the pavement and up passed his windshield, penetrating the radiator, hood, and windshield. The two bullets that passed through his windshield to his right missed him a few inches. The ambusher fell prone behind the dump truck's tailgate again, completely out of sight. The officer calmly stopped and took aim with his .357 magnum revolver at the exact position where he thought the gunman would be lying. In doing so he noted that the truck's deferential was painted red. It was thoroughly exposed beneath the tiny bed atop the frame. He fired three times at the tailgate where the man was probably stretched out prone.

His bullets were also copper-jacketed and hollow-nosed, not for penetrating metal on a dump truck. They could render a human's body severe damage, which is why they're designed in such a manner. One bullet could save an officer's life in the event he had no time to fire the second shot. The bullets dented the heavy metal considerably but failed to penetrate. Had he been thinking more clearly, he admitted later on, he would have shot the red deferential. The inspection plate is a rather soft and thin metal. Then bullets could have rendered the truck useless.

More so, he also admitted, he wanted to shoot the rearview mirror that portrayed the driver's expressionless face. His training under our passed administrations didn't allow such entertainment, so he declined and became very scared. He was shaking as he replaced the three rounds.

His second gun was a snub-nosed Colt, a .38 caliber. He didn't feel well with the fact that the truck might stop and try to finish him. With the old Cadillac speeding toward them, he positioned himself and waited.

The Cadillac roared back south and passed him in close pursuit of the truck without incident. This was under President Reagan's Administration, but shooting the driver of the Cadillac wasn't fully legal. The driver was definitely guilty as a conspirator in smuggling drugs and defending their venture with the attempted murder of an officer, but such arguments could last for years. An officer defending himself in federal courts in southern Arizona was about as chancy as swimming with shark with a bleeding finger.

Mexico's officials confiscated the truck the following day and held it several days before returning it to its owner. They didn't find the drugs, the drivers, the Cadillac, or the shooter.

The slugs that struck his car were .45 caliber. I saw where two pierced the highway in front of the car, one took the radiator out, two tore through the hood, and two got the windshield. Those piercing the windshield were even with the top part of his chest and forehead, just about four inches to his right.

Our best response to the shooting would have been to go after the truck and its shooters. The officer needed help to do this. Help was more than an hour away.

Our head offices forbid us from going into Mexico, especially after the fact. Yet, it was necessary!

I asked for no reports other than a damage report to get his car repaired. He may have written one for District. I never heard about it if he did. Even though Mexico's police told us the .357 slugs almost pierced the tailgate, I advised him to not admit returning fire unless he had a wounded or dead body to explain.

Chapter Eleven

Chapo, a Tragic Tale

Chapo isn't his real name. It was changed to protect his good family's name. They live in southern Arizona. Chapo was born on the western side of the Tohon O'odum Nation near the Mexico border and was raised on both sides of it. He later earned his living trading commodities from each country and eventually turned to smuggling marijuana. He delivered to a place on the highway that led to his village from Tucson and other cities. From the spot on the highway where he delivered it, or stashed it, someone from somewhere north hauled it to parts unknown.

Chapo stood over six feet and weighed well over 300 pounds. He had a lot of muscle and a small amount of fat around his middle. He chose his fate with his eyes wide open, then died before reaching his thirtieth birthday. His living relatives already know the circumstances of his death.

The Customs Patrol Officer that arrested Chapo claimed to have been on the case a year. I'll call this officer Mad Cat, who is the same man who agreed to train Gloomy. The name Mad Cat seemed to fit his hisses and bristles. Sometimes he could be humorous.

Mad Cat was a leader of men, but only to those who followed other men by their nature. He told me about the arrest of Chapo from the very beginning. He swore that he could show me the floor where the bullet struck and the wall where it remains today. It was, of course, an accidental discharge from a government-issued weapon inside a church and was never reported.

In all times of the accidental firing of weapons, this time has to be the most accidental. Such matters are, of course, strictly confidential. Mad Cat knew how to build mountains without materials. By telling as many people as possible that he only confided to his friends, it would eventually become a common story, one that made himself look good and the officer discharging the weapon to appear a blunder head, who was Gloomy.

Gloomy denied the incident vehemently. It doesn't matter if he denied it or not, since all of us chose to favor Mad Cat's version. Furthermore, Gloomy denied everything, good or bad.

Mad Cat, Gloomy, and I are all retired. Many people mourned the loss of Chapo. We remember his friendly personality and his ability to laugh at the blunder during the time of his arrest. His arrest, of course, eventually led to his conviction, not a real common occurrence, you understand, during the mid-1970's. This was when drug smuggling trials were a common occurrence, especially in the highly democratic region of southern Arizona.

Following the arrest caused many of us in the U. S. Customs Patrol to seriously suspect our dubious judicial system; both state and federal, but only with the fact that the number of drug smuggling arrests had overcrowded the courts; however busy they ever were.

The Tohono O'odum Nation borders Mexico for approximately eighty miles. This nation's elevation is higher than the lower regions of the desert that expands west a few hundred miles. It's fairly cool at night on the reservation throughout the summer. To sit alert in a parked vehicle overnight in that remoteness is really quite difficult. The only sounds are a dwarf owl's ghostly whisperings inside the walls of a saguaro and, of course, the snoring of one's partner. The Sandman rides fresh breezes that sift through the open windows of a vehicle. Far too many spells of deep slumber and peaceful dreams have been cast during the all night surveillances in efforts to apprehend drug smugglers.

I can't blame Gloomy for sleeping throughout the shift, if he did. I can't blame the nervous and restless Mad Cat for staying awake. Either way, a sleepy officer will err, especially if awakened during the action. Apparently, Gloomy was anything but fully awake when Chapo entered the United States at that remote gate in the border fence at about 0500 hours that morning. It was the same gate he had used most of his life. Gloomy, of course, was still in his probationary period. Only his partner, Mad Cat, would dare take a probationer on a serious case. New officers, however, could seriously learn from Mad

Cat by paying attention. Gloomy chose to listen to those who could further his career the fastest, and learning was never a factor.

The eastern horizon's rosy tint developed slowly when Mad Cat began to hear the distant sounds of Chapo's old station wagon. He began to shake his snoring partner awake.

Chapo's big station wagon charged into the scene from the south with two backfires as it crashed into a thicket that hid the border fence from Mad Cat. Backfires are common where air filters remain choked from endless miles of dirt roads with ruts containing nothing but fine powder.

Customs Patrol Officer Mad Cat jumped and caused Gloomy to go for his gun before his noisy snore was completed. He missed his gun because it had already fallen to the floor because his holster was unsnapped. Gloomy usually unbuckled his gun belt to ease his paunchy mid-section when he settled for a few hours of a peaceful time out.

Gloomy gained control as Mad Cat began attempting to start the old seized vehicle that Customs brought into service for the patrol's use. He hacked coarsely: "What was that?"

Mad Cat silenced him and pointed to the brushy area a good 100 yards distant. Gloomy jumped again, this time he was going for his rifle. No one crosses the border surreptitiously in his jurisdiction! Not on his watch! Mad Cat cautioned him and pressed for patience.

As soon as Chapo gunned his engine to continue his trek northward, Mad Cat, once again, began pumping the gas feed of their dilapidated old pickup that drug smugglers had once used when they were arrested. Smugglers wised up during the mid-seventies and used vehicles too old and worn out to be used against them in the event they were seized. They had lost too many new ones to the Customs Patrol. However, the dilapidated old clunker was the best transportation that the U. S. Customs Service was going to afford, so we took turns driving it if we weren't on the horses.

Mad Cat waited while Gloomy was itching to nab the suspect right on the border. Why wait? They had him! All they had to do was charge forth yelling: "Police--police! Don't move! You're busted!" Something like that was Gloomy's planned m.o. in any circumstance.

Mad Cat explained: "The suspect is just going to naturally freeze in his tracks where the safety of Mexico is only a step away?" Mad Cat usually saved his sarcasm for those not likely to counter. According to Gloomy, they could always finish driving the car across the border if it wasn't already in the United States.

Mad Cat hissed and ignored him until the time was right before stomping the gas pedal several more times and hitting the noisy starter. This was part of the ritual that only Mad Cat could perform.

"Hope it cranks this time, Gloomy. You got a twenty-mile walk over the pass if it don't."

"I ain't walking nowhere!" Gloomy informed him. "That's what this radio is for."

Gloomy was still new, an optimistic role from his character when he patrolled as a city policeman. He walked a beat among sidewalk vendors and street vermin selling drugs and weapons to kids. Gloomy didn't really take to the desert--not even a little bit. Once he saw that he hadn't improved his life by making a change from city to federal, he wished he was back walking a beat. He liked the action in the crowded streets. He had seen no roads and absolutely zilch for action during his indoctrination with Customs. He was bored beyond measure and claimed that all those stories of chasing dopers through the desert had originated and died in barrooms. He was about to learn better.

Mad Cat pumped the accelerator frantically. The engine hadn't yet caught and the battery was getting weaker. "Come on! Don't just sit there, Gloomy. Talk to it!"

The battery was always good for about thirty seconds before it died and had to be jump started. Sometimes the eleven-year old pickup fired half of its cylinders before sputtering into action. Sometimes not. This time it caught just as the battery fizzled. Gloomy said nothing. He despised the transportation the richest federal agency in the world afforded him.

"Atta girl!" Mad Cat cried out in delight. "And that's Chapo, all right! See that old white station wagon?"

Gloomy rubbed both eyes and yawned. "I don't see nothin'!"

Chapo drove passed without spotting the officers. He followed an old wagon road that had washed deeply over the decades, which made it barely passable for self-propelled vehicles. Some of the deeper ruts had rocks piled in them to prevent the vehicles from high-centering in many places. Ten mph was a speedy ride. Late smuggling entries happened no later than sunup, when officers would be at their sleepiest time, and when many of them changed shifts. They could hear Chapo's engine sputtering over their own.

Chapo drove without lights as the predawn light began to cause the starlight to fade. Mad Cat swung slowly in behind him from his hidden position under the ironwood tree.

"Hot damn!" Mad Cat yelled. Chapo had glanced behind him and gunned his station wagon over the rough road. He would be encountering a smoother dirt road within 100 yards. Mad Cat spun the steering wheel frantically in both directions as he dodged the deep ruts, trees and saguaros. The road waiting for them would be a picnic. The flat surface between the two mountain ranges was full of washes. Some were a few inches deep, others a foot or so. Chapo was building his speed with no regard to the rough surface. The chase was on! Both vehicles leaped into the air often. They were at an extremely high speed at twenty mph!

Gloomy yelled often from pain and a pleading request to slow down. After finding the dirt road, they had a half-mile to go before reaching the south end of a north-south highway, which was slightly over a mile north of the border fence. Dust rose behind both vehicles in the early sunrise. Angry cactus wrens scolded as both vehicles raced passed at high speeds from five to twenty miles per hour.

The vehicles bounced into the air several times before covering the short distance to the highway. Mad Cat was scared that the station wagon would outrun them once they reached the highway. No one could get speed out of the Customs pickup. All four wheels of the large station wagon went high into the air frequently. Its heavy front end always came down first, exposing its bare belly to the pursuing officers. Its muffler and driveshaft seemed intact each time they saw them. Mad Cat braked their truck each time the station wagon went airborne in order not to suffer the same consequence.

Many vehicles have wrecked at those speeds in the desert. Tree stumps are completely unforgiving, and one of the many two-foot deep washes that are several feet wide will smash a front end of a vehicle into permanent ruin. When the lead vehicle exposed its belly to the pursuers, the front end was sometimes waist high. One still has to remember that these vehicles are not specially equipped as those in the movies. Those in the movies are reinforced underneath in order to safely race over carefully organized paths and the constructed obstacles always carefully engineered. The real life chases chanced boulders, washes, stumps, and many saguaros. When axles snag a large boulder or an ironwood stump at ten to twenty miles per hour, something always gives and scatters the vehicle's under parts in heart-wrenching sounds.

Chapo reached the highway first and roared away. Both officers cussed. They thought they could see his large hand waving at them as the distance between them grew. Mad Cat slapped the steering wheel and gunned the old clunker to its top speed. No one knew how fast it would go on a level highway, providing no cows were on it. Some claimed it would reach sixty-five, but its speedometer was always jumping to ninety and falling back to zero.

Chapo's exhaust thickened. His top speed was also around sixty mph. Mad Cat, to his amazement, gradually closed the distance between them as the miles slowly rolled by. Eventually, Chapo's white and blue exhuast began to strike and dissipate against Mad Cat's windshield.

"We got 'im! We got 'im!" he yelled and glanced down at his speedometer. Their speed: an estimated sixty-three miles per hour!

They raced over the highway at that speed for five more miles with Chapo ignoring the Kojak redlight perched askew on the dented top of the old clunker pickup behind him. Saguaros and greasewood bushes whipped passed them.

Gloomy tried frantically to make the siren work. It wouldn't respond because it was one of the old manuals that had broken its hinges during a prior chase in the desert and was permanently lost there. All remaining of the siren was its broken mounts under the hood and dangling wires serving no purpose except to short out occasionally against the manifold. He tried the radio: "Mayday! Mayday!"

"Cut it out!" Mad Cat yelled. "We ain't crashed, and we ain't going to! Besides, we don't have radio contact out here!"

Gloomy looked both hurt and confused. "Then what are we doing out here? We're not ever supposed to be out of radio contact!"

"Just shut up and ride!" Mad Cat yelled. He snatched his badge and I.D. and held it against the windshield. Chapo couldn't see it, and if he had, he would have ignored it.

Gloomy stuck his AR-15 out the window and followed it with his head. He screamed as loud as he could. "Pull over, you son of a b...!"

Mad Cat yelled at him. "Gloomy, get your head back in here and put that damned piece away before Chapo stops and teaches you a new way to use it!"

Gloomy stuck his head out the window and finished his sentence.

"Hey!" Mad Cat yelled at him. "I know this man's family. He comes from good people."

Gloomy slid back inside. "Sorry. I was just trying to make him stop. Yikes!"

Chapo had suddenly braked hard and slid sideways to a dirt road. They bounced again for a mile or so to a tiny village in the desert. Chapo's car was overheating and had slowed considerably. Steam gushed from under the hood and mixed with the exhaust. He slid sideways and stopped in a cloud of dust next to a tiny, one-room chapel, the village's only church. Its steeple had a bell. He raced inside before Mad Cat and Gloomy bailed out in hot pursuit.

They followed him through the only door. There were only a few pews, yet they filled the tiny room. At the front was a room-wide curtain behind the pulpit. It bulged forward considerably at one spot. Large toes of work boots protruded from under it. Both officers leveled their AR-15's at the huge bulge above the toes.

Mad Cat's voice held more humor than firmness. "Come on out, Chapo. We see you."

Chapo emerged from behind the curtain, grinning. "I ain't done nothing."

Mad Cat continued to grin. "Come on out here and lay belly down on the floor so we can handcuff ya."

Chapo obeyed. But getting his hands behind him was a physical impossibility. Mad Cat managed to fit one handcuff over Chapo's huge wrist. The handcuff was about half the size it needed to be. Meanwhile, Gloomy was trying to help Chapo get his other hand behind him. He huffed and puffed and braced his feet against the pews for support, which only slid away. He failed to lift the other huge hand up toward the man's back. Chapo wasn't resisting. However, he wasn't helping, either. He simply suggested that they handcuff his hands in front.

Gloomy ignored him. Years of police work had taught him to trust no arrestee, so he continued to huff and puff and grunt and strain. He could use only one hand. His other one held the fully prepared AR-15.

Both men grunted and heaved. Finally Mad Cat gave up. He would have to be handcuffed in front. Gloomy, however, continued struggling. His rifle barrel was dancing in the air and actually came down toward Mad Cat's rear end. That's when Gloomy's trigger finger accidentally tightened, causing the weapon to fire.

Mad Cat jumped straight up and dropped everything to clutch his bottom. There was no blood. The fire from the rifle's nose had merely burned him. The bullet ricocheted off the floor and imbedded into the thick adobe wall of the church. Gloomy ceased his struggling. His ears seemed to have exploded inside his head, causing him to feel terrible. Firing a gun inside an enclosure causes temporary deafness.

In the meantime, Chapo, who didn't know what was happening, suddenly changed his attitude: "All right! I did it! I did it!" He turned and sat straight up, and in doing so, accidentally spilled Gloomy, who tumbled backward into more pews that were, by now, all oblique.

Gloomy held the rifle straight up but his finger was still posed within a micrometer of the trigger. "No harm done."

Chapo held his hands in front of him while Mad Cat cuffed him. All three of the men's ears were ringing so loud that they could barely hear above a shout. Outside, Mad Cat talked the loudest.

"We wasn't trying to scare you, Chapo." he explained. "This officer's gun just went off! We're sorry!"

Chapo studied the slowly stabilizing Gloomy for a good sixty seconds, then said, "It's okay. We had better get out of here before the priest comes."

Dogs had met them moments earlier and were barking excitedly and running around both vehicles before anyone stepped out. After the rifle discharged, they seemed to have dispersed, but only momentarily. They returned with new vigor. Sleepy faces peeked from windows among the houses but no one stepped outside. A half-mile down the road from the village, Gloomy stopped and added water and oil to the station wagon from Chapo's ready supply. He was driving, and if he wasn't mistaken, U. S. Customs would claim this proud vehicle for its own. Chapo rode in the cab of the pickup with Mad Cat. Chapo's vehicle, did, of course, contain 500 pounds of smuggled marijuana.

They heard nothing later from the villagers about the discharge of a weapon. The hole in the wall matched those made from nails, according to Mad Cat. The bullet's scuff mark in the cement floor blended but was slightly deeper and a great deal newer. Its mark was quietly dismissed or tolerated as it blended with the times.

Chapo cooled off in the holding tank at the Lukeville Port of Entry and did, in fact, caught a cold. His t-shirt wasn't enough to keep him warm. Someone had tossed him a blanket by the time I arrived. He was sneezing when I brought him a hamburger and coke that afternoon.

Even though it was well into the hot season, the air conditioning in the brand spanking new port of entry that cost several million U. S. dollars, didn't work. It was uncontrollably cold in the holding cell and uncontrollably hot in other offices. Today, if the air conditioning has been repaired, I haven't heard about it. How GSA inspectors approved such an atrocity is still up for grabs. They claimed to have won most of their money at Las Vegas. Chapo, was, in fact, the second arrestee to be held in the new building's Holding Cell. He needed to be arraigned before the judge in Tucson closed his office, if he opened it in the afternoon.

The DEA arrived shortly thereafter and mercifully hauled Chapo away to Tucson. He was beginning to cough. The reason DEA agents took custody of him was that the Customs special agents, who filed our prosecution papers, were all busy. All the dope had to be turned over to the DEA, anyway, unless we burned it. If the DEA took the case, they'd need the drugs for evidence. We tried to give them Chapo's vehicle, but they refused it. We could do the paperwork and sell it.

The judge liked Chapo, especially since it was Chapo's "First time" to smuggle marijuana. Chapo had attested to that under oath. Mad Cat threw his hands up in disgust. He had been trying to catch Chapo more than a year. Chapo had been bragging to a local service station worker, an informer, according to Mad Cat, that he was making a small fortune in smuggling dope. Since the judge knew where Chapo lived, he released him "O.R." his own recognizance. Chapo had that type of charisma!

Chapo obtained another vehicle and continued to smuggle drugs, according to Mad Cat's informant, he was boasting about it. Again, no one could catch Chapo. We were a great deal busier at other portions of the border. Anywhere from 100 to 500 pounds of marijuana were seized once and twice a week, which kept us buried in our giant portion of paperwork. We worked seven days a week and slept whenever the opportunity arrived, anywhere.

I didn't feel like working on our west side of the reservation, anyway. The Customs Service had already hired Indian patrol officers to take care of the reservation. They, too, were buried in paperwork with at least 500 pounds of seized marijuana per week. Mad Cat was the only officer at our station that thought the Indian officers needed our assistance. We had eighty miles of remote border fence to patrol, and there were less of us than there were Indian officers in the patrol.

Even though Chapo had given the judge his word that he would be a good citizen, we all heard Mad Cat's hissing and complaining about Chapo's renewed smuggling while released on his "Own Recognizance!"

Mad Cat was taking it personally. He had grown tired of Chapo's boasting to the informant at the local service station. I knew a little about Chapo, and I believed Mad Cat's ravings. The trial wasn't coming up until late June, which was probably why Mad Cat related the accidental discharge of a weapon to me. He needed assistance to nab Chapo. Everyone else had turned him down.

May rolled around. Someone called the federal judge about Chapo's continued drug smuggling, but he only scoffed at such absurd information. No one had the courage to smuggle drugs while released on his own recognizance, not in that judge's jurisdiction, anyway!

Chapo finally went to court, but only after a two-week *Continuous* granted to him due to family problems. Naturally, according to Mad Cat, Chapo used the time to smuggle more drugs. His family was poor. The judge understood that. Later, during Chapo's hasty trial, the judge asked him if he had, indeed, smuggled drugs during his release from jail as per Rumor Control.

Chapo surprised everyone by calmly replying: "Once or twice a week, maybe. Why do you ask, Your Honor?"

No one doubted Chapo's honesty after that. He had thought that the judge was on the side of law enforcement and that he already knew about his smuggling.

The judge slammed his gavel down at the end of the trial and issued the harshest sentence he had ever handed down to any drug smuggler in his jurisdiction: "Seven years!"

Officers breathed sighs of relief for weeks afterward. Our bitter attitude toward our Mickey Mouse judicial system had finally dissipated. That particularly federal judge had his pride!

Chapo was flown immediately to a federal prison in California. That Christmas, a grueling five months later, he was released on a ten-day furlough. The warden liked Chapo. That's understandable. The man only smuggled dope. Dope smugglers in the mid-seventies were personable, for they had little to fear from the judicial system in those pre-Reagan days. Lots of college grads from the sixties practically worshipped drug smugglers and pushers during the seventies.

Instead of returning home for Christmas, however, as Chapo had promised the good warden, he hiked into the Mojave Desert, which was a military proving ground. It was a remote desert, much like the one where he was raised, so he spent the Christmas holidays hiding out there. The military police spotted signs of the trespasser's presence several times but failed to catch him. He slept in tin shacks and in the open desert. Rumor Control claimed he left the military reservation several times to break into a local store for provisions. Chapo never took more than necessary; that is, what he could carry, including binoculars and some of the more needful things in order to eat and drink and stay warm. He wasn't a bad burglar; that is, if he did those things.

The military police didn't put two and two together until news of the nearby burglaries reached them. That was, of course, after the ten days of leave had expired and the good warden began spreading the word that one of his trustees had forgotten to return. It was a rare happening.

The ten-day furlough grew to thirty. Chapo was identified as the trespasser and burglar by a partner in crime that had grown tired of him. Everyone but the warden felt as if there had been a terrible mistake in granting the man a Christmas furlough; the military police were downright furious. They went after Chapo in full force.

Chapo traveled much easier without a partner. He remained well ahead of the military but had to leave the proving grounds. When local law enforcement authorities asked the military police, "Which way did he go?" they had no idea.

Rumor Control also reached the U. S. Customs Patrol at Lukeville, Arizona that the prisoner had not only broken his word to the warden but had escaped into parts unknown.

This was early February, 1978. A warrant had been issued for his arrest, according to Mad Cat. Intelligence sources claimed he was hiding out on the reservation. It was my understanding that the Customs Patrol at Lukeville was to simply drive to the house where everyone suspected he was hiding and give him a lift to the local U. S. Marshal's office.

I wasn't one to shirk my duties, but the Indian Customs Patrol on the reservation had the same authority as the U. S. Marshals.

I related my more true feelings to Mad Cat, "If the warden wants Chapo returned to his prison, he can come and get him. Otherwise, Chapo is a free man as far as I'm concerned."

In other words, no one in Customs paid heed to the hissing of Mad Cat. They figured if Mad Cat wanted him, he could go after him. It wasn't due to fear, it was from the disgust we had for our judicial system. If Chapo hadn't admitted to smuggling drugs while released on his own recognizance, he wouldn't have served time in the first place!

When we first received the word by telephone from Mad Cat (who was off duty), I was on the evening shift. By the time the instructions were given by the local supervisor, Tilton, I understood that my partner and I were to drive to the suspected house and arrest him. Actually, I didn't think we would find him there, and to locate him in the desert would be like locating a specific rabbit. I didn't go. My partner, a trainee, agreed.

I told Tilton the next morning that I didn't do that little chore on the grounds that Chapo was released from prison, and that was that.

Besides, I had never seen the warrant for his arrest, which makes a difference prior to arresting anyone. If there was a warrant, let the U. S. Marshals serve it. The Dept. of Justice paid them to do that sort of thing.

Mad Cat was thoroughly disgusted at me for not going after Chapo. After all, his informant had told him where Chapo was hiding out. Mad Cat was back on duty two days later and drove to Chapo's house, then to his parents' house, leaving specific instructions for Chapo to surrender himself to the nearest U. S. Marshal's office in Tucson, immediately! He wasn't to smuggle anymore drugs, either. So Mad Cat took care of that little chore, himself. For all I knew and cared, Chapo could've been hiding behind the door, and probably was.

A little girl had approached him and solicited Mad Cat's help in retrieving her cat from a thorny mesquite bush near her yard. He retrieved the cat, so the trip wasn't a total waste.

A week later, after we all decided that Chapo preferred not to give himself up to the nearest Marshal's office. I had no idea where it was located and could care less. It might have been next door to our own Customs offices in the Federal Building in Tucson. Mad Cat became even more furious and blamed our entire station for having no enthusiasm to go after the man. True enough.

I am easy going so I was blasted the hardest by Mad Cat. That led to a private understanding with Mad Cat, which left him humming loudly to himself in order to shut out my choice words. At any rate, he understood that I wasn't about to arrest Chapo, but he was free to do so, even though no other law enforcement officer cared about Chapo until they caught him smuggling. Mad Cat's rage failed to subside.

So we met in an empty room at the Lukeville Station, just the two of us, and had a second understanding. I thought that would be the end of it, but according to the supervisors, who waived a written complaint under my nose stating that I had gotten verbally abusive with Mad Cat.

The complaint was true. I attested to the fact that Mad Cat never exaggerated one word. Both supervisors shook my hand and congratulated me. Later, when Mad Cat learned that he wasn't chosen for a local promotion, he resigned from the Customs Patrol without ever seeing Chapo again.

Mad Cat was always at liberty to arrest Chapo anytime he wanted, but he, too, lacked one important item, a warrant. No warrant, to my knowledge, ever existed for Chapo. The marshals probably thought it wasn't worth the effort. If the judge sent him to prison, the warden would release him.

February came and went. Then word arrived sometime in March or April that Chapo was somehow back into the secure arms of our federal prison system in California. The news reached us through Rumor Control. Chapo might've given himself up, perhaps not.

Chapo returned home again during Christmas of 1978!

On his own recognizance! Another ten day furlough. One might wonder how a criminal can repent so fast. Oh--well! The sixties, according to me, was the dumbest decade in U. S. history. However, the decade of the seventies tried hard to claim that title for itself.

Someone at the service station had seen Chapo. His ten-day furlough from prison expired the second time. Chapo kept a low profile. If there were a warrant on him, and had I seen it, I think that I would have still found a way to avoid it. Chapo wasn't smuggling drugs, according to the informant, who, by the way, was not an informant. He simply did his civic duty.

Another warrant was, indeed, issued for his arrest, as Rumor Control depicted, but no one had the interest to pursue the rumor from the Marshal's Service. Had I caught him smuggling, I would have arrested him and followed through with the correct paperwork, but I never believed in helping the system poison itself.

Customs and the local U. S. Border Patrol promised one another that they would keep a sharp eye out for him.

It happened well into 1979. A local sheriff's deputy called the Customs Patrol Office in Lukeville by telephone. It was late on a Saturday night. Chapo was dead.

He had been partying with a group of young people in an automobile that Saturday night on the east-west highway about thirty miles north of the Lukeville station. He had become obnoxious, so the rumor had it. When Chapo's friends let him out on the highway to relieve himself, they quickly drove away, leaving him alone on the dark highway at 0130 hours.

This was between Why and Ajo, Arizona. At that hour, the road was relatively empty. Chapo laid himself down on the highway for a nap. One has to remember that a highway retains its heat and provides warmth for snakes, cattle, and, believe it or not, a number of people! A car came along about 0200 hours and ran over him. In doing so, the car was almost wrecked. Its clearance, naturally, didn't clear Chapo's huge body. His skull was crushed.

No one knows if anyone ever notified the good warden at the federal penitentiary in California that Chapo had passed on. The warrant may still be good. Chapo was given a local funeral and buried in a family plot on the reservation. Many people attended. Mad Cat did not.

Chapter Twelve

Rattlesnakes

Of all the species of rattlesnakes, none are more dangerous than the sidewinders. They can remain coiled in perfect camouflage and strike from that position as fast as any other snake in the world. They can then crawl as fast as any other snake its size can move while striking at the same time. To make them even more of a threat, they can strike backward or forward or to either side while moving forward at an incredible speed. Still unbelievable, they can reverse directions 180 degrees without slowing down. What they can't do is strike much higher than a few inches. While driving at walking speed on a sandy road one afternoon on the border fence, one appeared out of nowhere and began striking my left front tire repeatedly as we moved along. I speeded up slightly and it kept up without slowing its repeated strikes. This happened over a distance of about twenty feet. I stopped and it kept moving.

Of course, science tells us pit vipers only strike at heat from warm blooded creatures. Science knows far more than I on all things, but science is still far from being all inclusive when it comes to sidewinders. I wouldn't hold my favorite teddy bear close to a sidewinder if I didn't want it bitten.

Southern Arizona has dangerous species of pit vipers but no copperheads or cottonmouths, which are of the eastern side of America. The little coral snake is our only poisonous asp in Arizona and the whole nation. The coral snakes in southern Arizona like to enter dwellings. Housecats, natural enemies of these snakes in the desert, are valuable house pets.

In the southwest's rugged terrain and harsh environment where people are scarce, a big old western diamondback might be coiled under each rocky ledge or bush right where you're standing, whether on the side of a mountain or in the flat surface of brush country. Your nose might pass within a foot of his while ascending or descending a mountain. The black tail rattlesnake loves the mountains, and he might watch you pass within inches without singing out. What one must keep in mind about the western diamondback is that it isn't there to bite anyone. It's hunting. It hunts twenty-four/seven outside the winter months when it's time to go underground.

Diamondbacks hunt just like the sportsmen using a blind to hunt deer. When the deer enter an open area to lick the salt bait or eat some rare corn kernels--Pow!--the hunt is over. If a mouse or rat strolls within striking distance of a diamondback—thunk!--the hunt is over. The rattlesnake, however, is more of a sportsman. It uses no bait.

If there's evidence of small rodents anywhere in a brushy, sandy, or rocky habitat in the southwest, that's where western diamondbacks are found. Sidewinders do not like rocky surfaces, but they will pass through them.

The western diamondback, the most common snake found on the western side of the Great Plains is probably the most sensitive to its environment. That is, it doesn't do well on the Great Plains, but it will be found in the rocky ledges on both sides of the giant mesa called the Great Plains and further east all the way across Texas. The western diamondback probably grows larger in south Texas than in any other area in North America. Its habitat will stretch east until it reaches a damper climate and higher trees. As its species keep moving into the higher and cooler mountains, it grows larger and meaner. It changes color. In doing so, science finds it necessary to place it in another species, the eastern diamondback, not to be confused with a timber rattler.

The western diamondback has a white tail with black rings around it, and there's even more species within this particular marking of a western diamondback. It's known in Texas (east of the plains) as a diamondback. In the southwest it's known as a ringtail rattler or a coontail. Sizes, shapes, and the white and black bands of the western diamondback vary with the particular species, each claiming its favorite habitat that it shares with a few to no other species of western diamondback.

The western diamondback in the more populated areas where it's hunted, harassed, and killed, will appear to be anything but docile. In less populated areas, one can easily understand my reasoning. In the wild they appear as someone's pet, a species without an enemy unless it's the turkey vulture. Then, if it lives long enough, it will learn quickly to fight for its life. Roadrunners, in my limited experience, eat more lizards than anything else. If a roadrunner eats a snake, it will, indeed, be a small one. In most times of the year where snakes aren't hunted or killed on sight, they actually have to be harassed or startled before they'll rattle or strike.

In fact, a majority of snakebite victims from the Organ Pipe National Monument are those who misinterpreted the docility of a western diamondback. It doesn't like to coil or defend itself by biting. It only likes to bite a rodent, something that it knows is going to be half digested before it's swallowed. It likes for its poison to start dissolving the rodent right away. A human being is too large to swallow, so it really doesn't want to bite us. Step on it or pick it up without proper training, and its docility rapidly changes into an attitude. In other words, if its harasser wishes to have part of his hand or arm digested from harmful acid, the diamondback will be accommodating.

On the Organ Pipe National Monument, western diamondbacks seldom coil or rattle when first encountered (not startled). The victims of snakebites usually decide they are gifted snake charmers, friends of wildlife, one with nature, or any of the other imaginative misnomers these environmental tree huggers create for themselves. When one decides to physically put his hands on the snake (harassment), he always claimed the bite was painful. One doesn't have to consider the source to believe it. The poison is pure protein, a harsh acid, and it's designed to dissolve skin cells, which makes flesh all mushy for easy digesting in the stomach.

If a tourist at this monument wishes to not be bitten, then the snakes must be passed, or allowed to pass, without giving it problems. Western diamondbacks are slow to strike where the people population is low, and they never rattle a warning without a reason. This has been my decades of experience with them.

Outside the spacious desert, a rattle is a warning signal, not a bluff. The buzz is designed to frighten potential foes and predators. It will strike. There have been instances when people have been bitten without a warning. Never count on hearing the rattles first because they can strike fast if they think they have to defend themselves. They will sound the warning later.

If one will notice any species of snake, poisonous or not, vipers or asps, you'll find the end of the tail is quivering quite radically. The bull snake (of the harmless asp group) will shake its tail and hiss like it has rattlers, often causing people to claim it's a rattle-less rattlesnake. The only rattle-less vipers in the United States, to my knowledge, are the cottonmouth and copperhead. Then, there's the extremely bad news viper in Mexico that will bite humans for practice. It's called the "Bushmaster." The cottonmouth and copperheads can very well kill a human. The bushmaster, on the other hand, as in Rumor Control, will not only kill a human in a matter of hours, it will eat his lunch first, shoot all of his dogs, and then burn his house down. One doesn't mess with a bushmaster, the rattlesnake without rattles.

In the Organ Pipe National Monument in southern Arizona, the western diamondback's only predators are U. S. Border Patrol agents, turkey vultures, Tilton, and poachers who wish to sell them to pet stores. I've stepped off my horse many times to kick sand and tiny gravel in the face of western diamondbacks that don't crawl away. I want them wild. I was also curious to see how long it would take to make any of them sound a warning. The small pebbles were harmless but harassing. They had to hit each snake's head area before they retreated into a coil and finally sounded off. Otherwise, I could've visited for hours at a distance without experiencing enmity with any of them. I would never rub any of their heads or allow them to sniff my hand. No one outside a clearly-marked air head would attempt to pat a docile rattlesnake's nose and say, "Nice doggie."

Reptiles have no friends. Believe it! People have no friends that are reptiles. None! Such pets are members of a one-sided love affair. The pet python you read or hear about living in some rocket scientist's house on the block will someday swallow the piano, the children and the Mustang convertible. There should be a law against these mental giants from keeping large reptiles for pets, and another law that would forbid them from marrying, voting and reproducing.

Among the western diamondback species are the black tails and mojave greens. The black tail has pastel grays, blacks, and browns that have more contrast than the lower level snakes. If ever there was a pretty snake, it is the black tail rattlesnake. In certain times of the year its eyes are turquoise in color. Its head and neck are also black. If I were ever to call Tilton over to view such a pretty snake, he'd barely have time to shoot it before he fainted.

The mojave green is almost identical to a plain old diamondback. I can't tell the difference. The difference is supposed to be the tiny scale at the end of the Mojave green's nose. I asked a national park ranger, who was a naturalist, to explain the difference. He tried, but he really didn't know, either. The nose scale and distance between the black bands around the tail differ. The Mojave green has an extra hash mark across its face, also. Maybe. A good rule of thumb is to believe every western diamondback is a Mojave green.

I studied one Mojave green in great detail that was under glass in the Arizona-Sonora Desert Museum. I could detect no difference in that snake and a plain old western diamondback, and I've seen a trainload of plain diamondbacks. It isn't green nor is it necessarily greenish. If the determinable difference is a scale high on the nose of a Mojave green, who will notice it?

Where ever one might go in the southwest, west of the Great Plains, the western diamondback's size, bands on its tail, and body shape are going to vary. I've seen bands reach all the way around the tail perfectly. Some, however, reach all the way around but the ends of the bands are offset and don't come together at the bottom of the tail evenly as do the others. Some of the bands taper to points and never meet. This is rumored to be a marking of the Mojave green..

Of all the species of rattlesnakes one doesn't want to encounter, it's the Mojave green. Whether it's aggressive or not, I don't know. Rumor Control says the Mojave green is aggressive. I doubt that. I've never seen a western diamondback that was aggressive in the desert.

Many fellow customs officers have asked me if some particular diamondback we were looking at was a Mojave green. I always answered affirmatively, for that's the way to treat all diamondbacks: We humans, the great thinkers of our time, need to put space between us and the snake then *leave it alone!* If I had a favorite way to spot any snake in the wild, harmless or otherwise, it would be from the back of a horse or from an airplane at 30,000 ft. But we were paid to be out there to live and survive among the rattlesnakes, the pesky ants, and zillions and triple zillions of arachnids and honey bees. We have a need to know them as well as possible at a distance.

What makes the Mojave green so rare and frightening? Its venom. The venom actually contains the two types of toxin from both the asp and viper. The asp's poison, if you recall, attacks the nervous system. The viper's toxin attacks the skin cells and turns flesh into mush. Thus far, no other species of snake is known to have both venoms. When a snakebite victim is rushed to a hospital in the southwest, the doctor will, no doubt, treat the bite accordingly in which type of poison was injected into the victim. Never both, unless he's told that the bite came from a Mojave green. Otherwise, the bite either came from a viper or an asp. If the report is from a viper, and it usually is, which will be a rattlesnake in the desert, then the doctor treats the victim accordingly. The same treatment if it were a copperhead, lyre, or cottonmouth.

This has been the norm for years, doctors in the southwest treating rattlesnake bites with anti-venom for vipers. However, some of the victims died following treatment. Years passed before researchers found the nerve-killing poison in this pit viper's venom. That amazed the scientific community. The rattlesnake victim died from paralysis or whatever kills the victims from asps.

Then, as in most tales concerning environmentalists and nature lovers that love animals above human beings, there lies a touch of irony: *The rare Mojave green was placed on the endangered species list!*

Then, and only then, did I begin to kill rattlesnakes that I suspected of being a Mojave green. If everyone would kill them on sight, then they would become even more endangered.

If we had bunches of poisonous asps in our deserts, such as cobras, then I, among many other patriots, would help put them on the endangered list and keep them there until they were completely extinct.

I'm not a careless person. Yet I've found my boots within striking distance of rattlesnakes on several occasions throughout my lifetime. These are times when they didn't sound off before I was in striking distance. I've never been bitten. There's no cause to credit myself with any special ability, keen eyes, or anything that would set me apart from those who have been accidentally bitten. I've learned to step around places where I can't see the complete ground in front of me; that is, a small bush that can easily conceal a snake coiled underneath it. Stepping out of vehicles and walking trails at night are when one will get within striking distance before the snake sounds off.

During the fall and spring seasons of my years on the border in the desert, I usually rode a bicycle up the highway a few miles for exercise instead of jogging. These are the two times of the year when rattlesnakes will either go into a winter's location or leave winter dens and then go searching for food in the springtime. The twilight hours, or the cooling off stages of the summer's days, will bring out the snakes, which is not the time for jogging. While riding my bicycle on the desert's highway during the fall season, I've accidentally ran over the backs of many western diamondbacks. In the twilight and darker times, the snakes simply weren't spotted in time for me to brake or dodge them. I did have time to lift my feet. There were two fast bumps as the wheels passed over them. I left them unhappy but unharmed. They always sounded off loudly behind me. On one night, I ran over four rattlesnakes within two miles, all moving in one direction and in my pathway. I saw others moving. An apology to the snakes is not in order. I never stopped and rendered aid, and I do hope each and everyone was a Mojave green.

Through this day I still remain alert for snakes in the grassy areas on my five acres south of Lubbock, Texas. There isn't a rattlesnake within thirty miles of me. The nearest would be in the rocky ledges on the eastern side of the caprock (the borderline of the Great Plains). Would they spread out here if not for the cotton farmers consistently stirring the ground? Of course! The rattlers occupying the plains prior to farmers were the common prairie rattlers, similar in color, perhaps, to the pacific coast rattlesnake.

Please bear this in mind the next time you hike in the desert or in the southwest's back country. Rattlesnakes do not like to sound off. If the snake is under a ledge or a bush, or for that matter, occupying a shady area, it's there for a reason, which is either to hunt or to hide from predators, perhaps both. Their food is little mice and desert rats. Both of these rodents have keen ears. When they hear that sound, the snake automatically knows that it's going to have to change its hunting spot, for no mouse is going to enter that particular area for days. A rattlesnake may go days between meals, anyhow. They need all the food they can swallow for the coming winter months when they won't eat at all. Leave them as you find them. They are contented to be in that particular place of its choosing to find food. Mice are crucial to their survival. In the barn, however, if you can't poison your mice and rats, you'd better be prepared to deal with a rodent-eating snake.

The coral snake has a particular color pattern. Its bands, red on yellow, will kill a fellow. Those with different color schemes are harmless--so I'm told.

What to do if one hears a buzzing noise while hiking in grassy and brushy areas? Beats me! Here's what I've done: If the buzzing was more than three feet away, I stopped to locate the source of the sound and stood perfectly still. If I couldn't locate it, I backed away 180 degrees from the sound--as fast as possible. I've also had them to sound off directly under me. Whether the rules are to freeze or not, I don't know. What I do know is that my feet always moved first, and all I had to do to avoid a bite was to follow them. Chances are you're no different. I thought about nothing other than hopefully landing where there was no other snake. In sidewinder country, where this particular species thrive, are monogamous. One can easily dodge one snake and step on another in any direction. Depending upon the hunting, sidewinders can be found within feet or yards of each other.

Rumor Control says people never completely recover from a pit viper's bite. That person will live and die with a certain change where the bite occurred. The poison will eat part of the tissue where it was injected. The skin or muscle cells where the poison congested won't reproduce or regenerate. Where the poison has thinned, the cells will reproduce.

While hiking through the desert, if you enter low underbrush and can't see the ground, back up and walk around it. If the grassy area or underbrush can't be avoided, then you have no other choice. Study the brush closely. If a snake can avoid you without having to sound off, it will, especially in the brush. It's there waiting on food, not to bite people. The elements are on your side, but don't stake your life on it. Avoid brushy and grassy areas where you can't see the ground.

There's no specific pattern, rule, or guideline other than avoidance and the ability to move fast.

On the plains in cattle country, I've been struck at by prairie rattlers, even out of range. This was in the open and before they sounded off. I was always horseback on the prairies of the Llano Estacado. I'm told that's when they're blind and shedding their skin they strike first and sound off later. Actually, I don't know what the agitated snake was doing within moments of my arrival or passage, shedding its skin or having survived a vulture attack. I could see their eyes, and if I can see theirs, they can see mine. If the eyes are showing, there's an excellent chance that the snake can see. If there's loose skin over its eyes, chances are it can still see. Forget the folklore, the wives tales, stories, and rumors. Avoid closing the distance between you and a snake. Never walk at night in the desert without a flashlight. Better yet, never walk in the desert at night. In addition to rattlesnakes, there are myriads of scorpions and centipedes scurrying about twigs in search of insects.

Early mornings and late evenings in the warm spring and summer are excellent times to encounter a diamondback. Otherwise, it's coiled under a rock or around a bush in order to keep out of the sun. It will be well camouflaged. If you're in the open, look before getting within a snake's entire length before walking near a ledge or brush where a snake can hide. How do you know what the snake's length is before you see it? Easy! The snake that you are about to encounter is at least six feet long. Measure it with your mind. That's the distance to bear from an overhang or brush if at all possible. I've probably seen, perhaps, two rattlers in my lifetime that were as long as six feet. Nevertheless, it's a good rule to follow. Ten feet is even a better distance.

In the early spring when snakes move from their dens, they can be seen almost any time of day or night. The same thing applies in the fall when it's time to return to their dens. I've watched the "Discovery Channel" a lot since retirement. I've found this channel quite correct in their reports on southwestern snakes--for the most part.

Sidewinders are also adept in the art of camouflage. I hauled pea gravel from a local wash in order to discourage sidewinders from taking up residence in my native-surfaced yard in Why, Arizona. I made the gravel thick across my front and back yard. It would also discourage little desert mice against burrowing holes in the yard where there's fine gravel to spill into them. Little mice attract rattlesnakes of all species.

Our little girls always had two pet cats. Cats are excellent pets that can keep rattlesnakes at bay and will discourage them from taking up residency. The same can be said for coral snakes. I found one coral snake in my yard quite dead. Its front half had been eaten. Little girls; excellent pets are hunters and a good barrier against rattlesnakes smaller than them. Pea gravel or not, one Saturday afternoon, immediately after sundown, I saw one of the half-grown cats acting like it was stalking something near my truck. The other kitten was acting much like a snow leopard stalking a goat, also. Sure enough, they had cornered a sidewinder that was apparently passing through. It had struck one kitten on the padded spot near its nose before I could do anything.

Cats, so I've heard, are impervious to small snake bites so long it strikes where the whiskers grow. I didn't tell my daughters or wife about it and saved myself a huge vet bill. The cat never stopped eating but it did swell a little around the nose. For a couple days it didn't play much. The swelling was never too noticeable. My wife kept telling me that a snake had bitten one cat and to get it to a vet. I assured her that if a poisonous snake had bitten one of the kittens, it would be dead. She finally settled for a scorpion sting. If a scorpion pops a cat where the whiskers grow, it won't hurt the cat, either. Instead, the scorpion will be eaten. The cat was fine. I watched it closely for fever and any type of congestion or infection. It did have a slight fever but only for three full days..

I've always believed that sidewinders are monogamous, but I never found that snake's mate. Neither did the cats. During the same week, the gophers came and dug in close to our storage shed far from the pea gravel. Soon enough, along came a big old diamondback and sounded off by our screen door as I opened it. The snake measured four feet. It didn't stay with us long enough to get the gophers. The gophers didn't stay with us long enough to bring in another diamondback.

In the sand and loose surfaces, a sidewinder will coil and burrow down flat while remaining coiled. They have different muscles than most snakes. It'll cease burrowing down after a fine surface of sand covers its back, then it lies perfectly still with only its eyes and little horns above the sand. You can spot them clearly in the open, for there won't be any weeds nearby. Roots get in their way. Its coil appears like a round saucer has been placed on the sand and lifted, with only the indention remaining. Looking close, you'll find the horns and nose immediately above or even with the sandy surface.

Strange, but no big secret, a sidewinder cannot close its eyes. Its eyelids are a clear dish of plastic like material covering the eyes. These lenses are never removed and the eyes are never closed from seeing. So how does it sleep? The same way, probably, that people sleep while surrounded by noise. People don't close their ears while they sleep. (I have a cousin that can.) The noise skips the conscious portion of the brain and goes directly to the subconscious. If nothing in the subconscious tells the person to wake up, sleep won't be interrupted. In the processing of sound, certain noises are supposed to wake the listener. The same applies to the snake, what it sees during sleeping probably doesn't disturb the conscious portion of its brain.

On the other hand, the sidewinder may never sleep. That could be the reason that it's so cranky all the time.

Illegal immigrants have victimized themselves many times by walking over the small, round, saucer-shaped print in the sand. The sidewinder will strike and smell later, and perhaps even rattle. If any snake doctor or scientist wishes to claim they only strike at body heat, that's fine. I've killed rattlesnakes while working as a cowboy in New Mexico, all with ropes. If I missed the snake with the first swat, the rope was bitten. A rope has no body heat. The tire of a pickup has no body heat, but it may have heat.

An illegal immigrant pulled out of the desert by SCPO Walker had been bitten on his sandaled foot slightly lower than his instep. He described the sidewinder to Walker. Since he had been bitten hours before he found help, he lost his leg near the knee joint. That's how much muscle tissue had been completely destroyed by the toxin, which also causes a serious type of infection.

During the evening shift at the Lukeville, Arizona Port of Entry in 1985, I jerked the tourniquet off a Mexico Customs Inspector that had been bitten on his ankle by a sidewinder. I just happened to be there at the time the man and his wife sped through the primary lane and stopped in the secondary. They were on their way to Tucson in a major hurry. His left leg was swollen all the way to his knee, and his ankle appeared to be on the verge of exploding. The ends of the tourniquet were protruding from his swollen calf.

When I pulled it out of there, I did hear a painful expletive from the victim. I thought he was going to bite through his bottom lip. The tourniquet was buried beneath the swelling!

His English was excellent, thank goodness. He said he had been bitten in his backyard only a half-hour ago. He applied the tourniquet and waited around for the local doctor. Too bad. I know that doctor, who was also the local mayor and a very good friend of the governor of Arizona. I think he contributes to their campaigns--for some reason or other. On busy Saturdays his police have road blocks for a Red Cross Drive. All tourists are encouraged to participate by dropping money into the buckets the police shake under the drivers' noses. It's best to contribute. This Mexico Customs Inspector that waited around for a doctor-politician longer than two minutes almost cost him his leg and life.

I knew that he didn't have time for the three-hour trip to Tucson by car, but there was no choice. The local doctor in Ajo, Arizona might help with an anti-venom, but he wasn't equipped to deal with the man's leg. It was in bad shape. He was going to lose it, for sure, thanks to the tourniquet. I sent them on their way with a customs escort, which was equipped with a red light and faster than the speed limit, then called the emergency number for an Air-Vac at Tucson. A helicopter picked him up at Ajo in due time and flew him to Tucson for treatment.

His leg was saved. Doctors quibbled daily almost two weeks while the man lay on his back in the hospital. One wanted to amputate, the other wanted to wait, and so it went for several days. When he returned home, he told me that tourniquets were out of his life forever. He claimed they hurt like hell when they're removed.

I'm no medical researcher, so tourniquets may have their place for certain things under certain conditions. Whether I would ever apply one above a viper's bite depends upon the circumstances. One is almost certain to lose a limb if a tourniquet is used on a viper's bite. My knowledge is limited to sucking the poison out with a special syringe without cutting or puncturing the area in any way. I kept one handy while raising my children in southern Arizona.

It's still in my bathroom. I used it once on a mosquito bite. Didn't work.

There are annual roundups of western diamondbacks in the Snyder and Sweetwater, Texas areas. There's no protection for the wildlife there, so the divine enmity between humans and snakes remains alive and well. The poisonous snakes are milked . Some are skinned for hat bands and its flesh was probably eaten.

For all the beautiful young women out there, such behavior among men is macho and very brave. They're tough without doubt. Personally, I'm a full-blooded and 100% redneck, yet I don't associate with men wearing a snakeskin hat band with a hawk's feather stuck in it. The same goes for the women who associate with such men.

Hand to hand, *mano a mano*, I've yet to hear about one snake hunter that can handle a sidewinder without special equipment. No sidewinder resides east of the caprock in Texas. They're mostly in the desert areas far west of the Pecos. Although I'm sure there are a few men who are fast enough to handle a sidewinder. Under normal circumstances, that little snake would not only bite a west Texas snake hunter at least a dozen times before he could withdraw, it would chase him all the way to his pickup, rip his hat band to shreds, swallow every can of snuff within the cab, then drink every beer in his ice chest.

Two Horse Patrol officers were in the open bed of a speeding pickup holding on to their hats and squinting from the wind whipping around them. Two more Horse Patrol officers were up front. One was supposed to be driving instead of talking with both hands and looking out toward the Jonses. Suddenly, in broad daylight without a cloud in sight, except for the big one surrounding a mountain top two miles east, they were suddenly broad-sided by a three-foot wall of rushing water. The pickup swapped ends and was pinned against the bank of the wash twenty yards down stream. The two officers up front sat still and immediately rolled the windows down while the water filled the cab. They complained about it being cold or something. They lifted their feet up the seat and yelled while dirty water covered the truck's seat. The water level reached no higher than the small truck's open windows. They looked back at the other two officers in the bed and later wrote this in the incident report:

"As the water filled the open pickup's bed, both officers were frantically trying to open the tailgate so they could escape. It was stuck. With no choice, they sat quietly as the water spilled over the truck's bed. The water filled the bed of the truck and reached no higher level than its sides. Both officers eventually crawled over the sides of the pickup bed after the water had lowered itself sufficiently."

It was a lie, of course! The tailgate was never stuck. We both sat on top of the cab during this time, and, for goodness sakes, we certainly made no attempt to open that tailgate!

The significance of this is that many snakes were spotted in this turbulent river of water rushing passed us. Some bumped the sides of the truck. Others floated precautious close to the open window of the cab while the driver tried to roll up the glass. We were on top of the cab to escape the snakes as well as escape the brown, ice-cold water. The driver said the windows had to stay down because the passenger was smoking.

Four of us mounted fresh horses one morning before sunup. It was the beginning of a five-day ride on the border in the desert. As usual, I was out front, and, consequently, the most alert. SCPO's Weldon and Tilton rode closely behind me with Garcia bringing up the rear. The usual chatter among the three had slowed after about an hour after the sun climbed into the warm air. I glanced back.

Tilton was frantically searching the ground but not for tracks as we paralleled the border fence. That meant some reaction from his bag of anxiety disorders was acting up. Weldon glanced at me, grinning. No doubt about it, Tilton had developed an extreme case of panic from simply thinking about encountering a rattlesnake. His face was growing pale, sweating, rapid with shallow breathing. He probably had a high pulse, too. Sure panic was underway, so I watched him closely in case of hyperventilation or if his pulse got too high. I don't know what I could have done with his hypertension, but I could stretch him out in a shade.

No matter how much we confronted him in the past few days about his extreme fear of snakes, he just seemed to get worse. The sound of one of us blowing our noses unexpectedly would cause him to jerk both feet into the seat of his saddle and start yelling and cussing. He rode Buck, the shortest of all our horses. No snake could bite as high as Buck's knees, far less of the stirrups.

A nearby grasshopper or a dry weather locust flying up suddenly will definitely get any horse's attention, but there's no cause for alarm. Tilton always panicked every single time his horse jumped from a grasshopper's buzz. Buck, however, seldom shied at Tilton's reactions. When Tilton started firing his sidearm at the snake or at the sound of one, or at the wake of a grasshopper, Buck would protest, somewhat. He never liked for anyone to fire a loud .357 from his back. To make his point, he would suddenly jump sideways and spin around in order to unload his totally irresponsible rider.

Through the first few months that Buck was ridden in the patrol, he learned an English word from me: "Snake!" He could and would jump and shy at that word as fast as Tilton! Gunfire was almost certain to erupt. This was what the horse was attempting to avoid. He never expected a snake in the area unless he, himself, spotted it.

I've never fired my weapon from the back of my big palomino because it would be senseless. He was going to buck at the first round that anyone fired, anyway. It was all I could do to maintain my claim to the saddle's seat, far less of drawing my weapon to join the shooting spree at a dumb snake. After several years of riding out front, I finally learned to not yell "Snake!" simply for the entertainment value. Watching Tiltopn's feet stay planted in the seat of his saddle while he did a balancing act was remarkable, for Buck jumped sideways and spun at an incredible speed.

In fact, all of our horses would go crazy at the word, "Snake!" My horse would start bucking sometime before the first shot. Buck would start spinning, and Weldon would start shooting. Garcia, like myself, after my storm subsided, always stuck his fingers in his ears. After Tilton gathered up the reins enough to stop Buck from spinning, he, too, would start shooting on both sides of the horse. This happened when he didn't even know where the snake was located! If there ever was one! Sometimes I just said the word because the atmosphere was growing a little lax. This happened at least once each day. Perhaps we saw one snake inside a week. They were already coiled under the brush next to the road or some distance from it.

Most of us bore our psychotic disorders silently. We never grew into a catatonic fixation or practiced any of the occupational or trauma mentalities. Not so with Tilton. He suffered aloud with the worst case of phobia against snakes that I've ever seen.

My wife and his were friends. His wife once stated that she had to warn him before she could use an aerosol can in the house. He was apt to jump through a closed window.

The sun was growing higher. The weather was gradually warming. Humidity was in the air, which tended to slow us down. The time was definitely NOT ripe to encounter a rattlesnake near the trail. They would be moving during the cooler times.

Tilton knew that if the crew got too quiet that someone would point to the ground and yell, "Snake! "It was usually a crooked mesquite limb, which would cause fits of spasms similar or a cardiac arrest. So he talked quite a bit and told us a lot of jokes. He sensed that we could grow bored without consistent entertainment.

Both Weldon and Garcia could shoot their side arms like sideshow artists. Very little fancy shooting has ever been seen in the cowboy movies with revolvers that these two men couldn't do better. Tilton was no slouch, either, with a sidearm. Drawing and firing to behead a snake yards distant was fairly commonplace. That's from the hip and plenty fast. They could do the same at long distances but it might require a second bullet. That would just be the beginning. All the horses except Chola, Weldon's horse, would be jumping and spinning with mine trying to buck the white out of its mane. If either of them missed, which was seldom, they fired carefully amidst the spinning, jumping and cussing until the snake was not only beheaded, but divided into equal lengths. A distant listener would swear that war with Mexico had broken out again. Tilton would be firing and cussing while pulling back on the reins of his spinning horse. Both his feet would be out of the stirrups and in the seat of his saddle, naturally. After my horse had placed a sufficient distance from them, he would buck until I could talk him out of it. He really wasn't an easy horse to ride as Garcia often claimed.

As stated earlier, we all attempted to help Tilton conquer his fear of snakes. In spite of our repeatedly miserable failures, we kept trying. Any old stick would do when the time was right. I simply had to look back at Tilton and point to the ground as I rode safely passed. Without even looking, he would jerk his feet into the seat of the saddle and frantically gather all the slack from his reins, cussing and demanding I shoot it before his horse came even with it.

"Just a stick!" I would explain.

"Then why in the hell did you point at a damned stick for?" he'd scream.

This was almost daily! Buck would always wonder the same thing by pointing his ears and looking directly at me. Weldon's blue roan, Chola, would also point her ears at me after the brief hysteria subsided, so would Garica's big sorrel. *"What did you do that for?"* they seemed to ask.

It wasn't easy trying to explain to the horses. If I said, "Snake," Buck would start spinning wildly. My horse would jump forward and duck his head to prove his capability of unloading me at will. The horses just couldn't figure it out. The blue roan of Weldon would point her ears in my direction and continue to ask why I had acted like a snake was there when nothing resembling a snake was about. I've said it before: Horses have absolutely no appreciation for good, sensible humor, and are rather slow when attempting to grasp things explained to them. But--like the U. S. Border Patrol--if they're playing or making a joke, the world needs to laugh and applaud.

It's true. They'd never point accusing ears at me if there was actually a snake in the vicinity. I suppose horses aren't so smart after all. It's a free country, and I can point when and where I want to point, except at horse auctions. Those innocent stares from those horses asking me why I had caused an uproar was the reason I stopped pointing the ground as I rode by a stick.

Tilton was always good for at least one good scare each day. During the spring and fall seasons, we'd sometimes spot one or two diamondbacks daily, so pointing to a stick wasn't necessary. One time when things got slow, Weldon suddenly yelled, "Homer, wake the hell up! You just walked your horse over a snake!"

Tilton lost all control. That meant his horse was directly on top of a snake, even after he had spurred poor old Buck out of the trail, who'd wonder what the heck was going on. Fearing and suspecting gunfire, Clyde, my big palomino, ran sideways and fought for slack in the reins in order to bury his head between his front legs. Weldon and Garcia laughed at me and my horse more than they laughed at

Tilton. If anyone ever needs a comedian, the U. S. Customs Service is still listed in the local directory.

An apology never seemed to appease Tilton, especially if his face had lost all its color during a panic attack. Neither Weldon nor Garcia could calm him at times. Tilton would just rave on with vile threats against all our lives and accuse us of the most unlikely sexual perversions. Garcia didn't worry about it. He claimed that Tilton was mad all the time, anyhow.

Tilton never believed his chances of a snake bite was little to none. This man had survived the dense jungles of Viet Nam where all the snakes were poisonous and just as numerous in a square yard as they are anywhere in the world. That was okay. Viet Nam wasn't home.

Weldon thought he could help by talking to Tilton. "A snakebite is really nothing, Tilton. A western diamondback's fangs aren't as long as regular hypodermic needles and they're much smaller around at the tips. The penetration of the sharp fangs isn't painful at all. It's the injection of the venom that sets your flesh afire with excruciating pain. One just has to imagine that it's really two fangs serving the cause instead of just one needle providing a means for the injection.

"What you don't realize, Tilton, that all this poisonous venom ain't really poison as we know it. It's just another form of excruciating and burning acid. Acid burns the hell out of us warm blooded animals, sometimes, to the intensity of suicide. You see, some humans are allergic to foreign substances like proteins, especially if it's injected into our flesh. It's for this fact that we can die from an allergic reaction, which is why we call it poison. Hell, a snake can't manufacture real poison. Even if it could, it would have to carry it around in its salivary glands, which would kill the snake! Anybody should know that!"

"Okay!" Tilton said after he could find his voice. "I've heard all of that before! Now--why don't you just *shut-the-hell-up?*"

Weldon was agreeable. "All right! But you have to admit that just because a snake slithers or crawls on the ground like some old rusty water pipe that has suddenly turned magic is no reason to fear it. Besides, it really ain't normal for a man to be scared of snakes. God gave that curse to women. Women are supposed to be scared of snakes, Tilton, not men. I just hope that some of this will help clear things up for you."

Like Garcia explained later, Tilton sounded mad. "It don't clear a damned thing up for me! Now just shut the hell up! Is that clear enough for you?"

"Sure," Weldon said with hurt feelings. "I wish I hadn't said anything at all, now."

I had to hear Weldon's lecture several times before I could memorize it. Tilton's response was always fairly easy to remember.

"Homer, maybe you can talk some sense into Tilton," Weldon called.

"Sure!" I said. "Most people with snake phobias will go to a shrink and admit their mental handicaps."

He just sat grim and stared straight ahead, like Garcia said he did all the time.

I continued: "Those who don't usually have cancer of the brain after a few decades will get over their fear of snakes."

He refused to respond, so I continued. "You don't have to worry about copperheads out here in the desert. Lyres are numerous here but you'd have to stick your finger in its mouth before you could suffer its poison. The lyre's fangs are in the back of its mouth, not the front. Their prey is first injected with protein while they're being swallowed. They don't bite with the fangs, understand."

"I really don't want to hear it," Tilton interrupted. But he really did. We all knew that. We could save him a great expense from the shrink, if it ever came to that, if he'd only listen.

"Okay!" I agreed. I won't say anything else about it. You can be bitter. Its your life!"

"I want to hear it!" Weldon said.

"So do I!" Garcia added.

Tilton tried to rein up and let those two ride next to me while he lagged behind. No way! That was Garcia's place. He and his big sorrel wouldn't allow him to pass. I went on to explain the two types of poisons and how the protein from a bite would literally break the flesh down to liquid.

"Rattlesnakes seldom excrete bones unless they're too large to completely dissolve," I said. "Bird bones are hollow, making them easy to digest, but their feathers are sometime passed through the complete digestive track without dissolving.

"The toxin doesn't have to travel in the bloodstream, but it most certainly can if it's injected there. It travels through the skin cells for the most damage and does what it's supposed to do, break down the flesh. I've never heard of the toxin traveling through to the bloodstream fast and stopping anyone's heart. But I don't know much about it. The longer the prey lives, especially up to being completely swallowed, the better the viper likes it. If their prey gets cold before it's swallowed, then it's abandoned. Bull snakes, on the other hand, will squeeze the life out of a rodent before swallowing it. The mouse is dead by the time it's licked and ready for swallowing.

"Bites from the asps will cause a man's lungs to paralyze. The victim just lies there red-faced with his eyes growing wider and wider by the minute until he suffocates. Their toxin attacks nerve cells, you see, and causes paralysis in the victim. Their lungs stop receiving messages from the brain to function. Paralysis. Do you have any questions? Damn it, Tilton, are you listening or what?"

"Yeah--I'm listening!" he growled. "Why don't you just shut the hell up like Weldon did?"

"Yeah!" Garcia yelled from far behind. "Shut up, Homer!" He knew that I had exhausted my short expertise on the subject. "You give me the creeps! Is Homer weird or what, Tilton?"

No one said much after that. Tilton needed a lot of help with his problem but he was too proud to ask for it. He had a way of making his friends feel completely useless.

Shortly before noon we stopped at the top of a hill and studied the terrain below us. A low, brushy area about a quarter-mile wide extended north out of Mexico about a mile. I pondered whether to ride north of it or straight through. Tilton was all for riding around it, as we all were, but one has to remember the horses needed no extra steps.

On the suggestion from Tilton to ride around it, I said, "We'll ride through it."

"Hell-yes!" Weldon and Garcia agreed simultaneously. We all knew that Tilton would keep his position in the group with his feet in the saddle's seat..

Upon entering the brushy area where the grass was almost high as our stirrups, Weldon could keep quiet no longer.

"Damn it, Homer! I wish we hadn't come this way! I'll bet my horse gets snakebit!"

"Mine, too!" Garcia said. "I don't like this at all!"

They were now agreeing with Tilton.

I reined up and searched the tall grass. "Listen up!" I said back over my shoulder in my best boy scout leader voice. "I can't hear any slithering, can you?"

"What's that?" Weldon asked.

"What's what?" Tilton wanted to know. He was getting pale and breathing shallow again.

"Oh--it's nothing," Weldon said.

I rode on bent over and watching closely. Chances were that we were actually riding through snakes. It was a perfect habitat, plenty of mice and predators couldn't see the snakes. My horse had his nose as close to the surface as possible, listening and watching for any sign of a snake. I glanced back and found the other three horses moving the same way. I suggested that Tilton get his feet down and into the stirrups, that Buck might actually shy to one side at any second. If he did, he would dump Tilton into the lap of the snake. Tilton responded positively but answered negatively:

"Okay, but if I get bit, I'm shooting you right between the shoulder blades!"

"Don't let 'im do that, Weldon," I said without turning back.

"To hell with you!" he growled. "I'm damned sure going to shoot you if my horse gets bit!"

I called out without looking back, "Garcia?"

"Ditto, Homer!"

They weren't cutting Tilton any slack by pretending that they were scared.

Moments later, while watching the grassy surface closely, I saw a giant, brown tarantula fight its way through the mass of grass stems. My entire body jerked into a tight spasm, and the big spider was gone. My heart beat faster than normal, for that spider was larger than the palm of my hand! It was probably as big around as a baseball, or soccer ball. I know it would have filled the track of my horse. It had eight legs! I hate the sight of those things. I wanted to ride faster.

I didn't feel too good. It was hot and my hands were shaking. My knees felt weak. This definitely wasn't such a good idea. One isn't supposed to ride where there's spiders!

The last half of the grassy patch was slow and meticulous. I didn't know if I could ride or not through the last half of the grassy flat. A grasshopper jumped and buzzed as we passed near it but that was all. It had six legs! That's too many. I hate those things, too! The horses ignored it. I'm glad there's nothing to report, except that I just saw a tarantula as big as a catcher's mitt.

I've heard that they taste like shrimp! Good lord! My slight dizziness didn't seem to let up. I felt my heart beating more rapidly. Breathing became more difficult. We would be in safe ground in just a few more yards. I was extremely weak by the time my horse reached the edge of the tall grass.

I stepped down in the first open space and my left leg gave way at the knee. I sat with my head between my knees. I breathed deeply and slowly, consciously using my stomach muscles. I remained that way several minutes.

When feeling normal again, I looked up to see all three men sitting quietly on their horses, staring curiously at me. None of them knew, thank goodness, what spiders could do to me.

I said, "Well, are you going to get down for a lunch break or you just sitting there until Thanksgiving rolls around?"

Tilton grinned the broadest. "I saw the same spider you saw. If you ever mention a snake to me again I'll catch one of them and slip it down your collar. Are you listening or what?"

Chapter Thirteen

Jesse Fernandez, Entrepreneur

For years, Jesse Fernandez (not his real name) of Sonoyta, Sonora, Mexico legally imported burnt adobe bricks through the Lukeville, Arizona Port of Entry. Once each week or ten days he would arrive with his old stake bed in the primary lane to present his import papers. Then, without instructions, he knew to drive straight to the secondary lane for a thorough search of his truck and bricks. The tax or import duty on the consistent number of bricks was $15.30, which he always presented in the exact amount. No Customs inspector could expect better organization, cooperation, and friendliness in an informal entry.

I was a Customs Inspector at the time.

Jesse's destination with his bricks was always Gila Bend, Arizona, the second town north of Lukeville through some eighty miles of scorching desert. The road to Gila Bend was and is a super-heated asphalt highway that cuts through the National Park Service's Organ Pipe National Monument from Lukeville to Ajo, Arizona (pronounced Ah-ho). North of Ajo the area flattens into the remaining leg of forty miles that painfully stretches through a desolate Air Force bombing range, which, somehow, falls short of Gila Bend. The point being the intensely hot pavement in southern Arizona was a trial for loaded tires. Jesse consistently kept expensive new tires on his truck. His tires and fuel costs cut into his profits considerably. With this fact, alone, Jesse topped the list of all drug smuggling profiles. There was simply not that much profit showing.

Jesse was the most congenial of our nation's importers. He smiled, nodded, shook hands, and never wore his hat inside our port of entry, a sign of respect still practiced in Mexico. Our small, two-roomed adobe building that used to be a gas station during the 1940's appeared to be anything but a place of respect. Its old second-hand furniture from a GSA warehouse full of obsolete goods had witnessed drunks, drug smuggler interrogations, protests from trinket smugglers, heated arguments among federal troops, and brawls with arrestees. Yet Jesse entered our tiny room of business with hat in hand. Then, late in the afternoon of the same day, he would return to Mexico through the same gate he entered to be received by the Mexican officials with an empty truck. Mexico Customs also taxed commercial exporters from their country and charged them again when they returned, more dips into his profits. While returning, he would always honk his horn and wave to the U. S. inspectors.

"Highly suspicious," I muttered one afternoon in my best skeptical voice. I was set upon instantly by every inspector within earshot, both of them. I had wrongly assumed that no one else had ever suspected him.

The U. S. Customs Patrol came to Lukeville in 1972. The new officers occasionally followed Jesse every step of the eighty miles and watched him unload the burnt adobe bricks. This was long before I arrived at Lukeville in the spring of 1974. No evidence of smuggling was ever detected.

The two DEA agents that had been at the port of entry for years thought we inspectors were too inept to find the drugs. Well taken but they would say anything to break the boredom of their cushioned jobs. The next time I was on duty when an agent was there, I invited him to do the searching or else keep his lips zipped. He searched the truck and found nothing. A moment later he was back at it, claiming that he was no inspector, but if he were, he could find the drugs. Small and never overly busy was our port of entry with that old DEA agent. He was far passed being ready for retirement, probably overlooked by head offices.

Jesse worked hard. Loading and unloading those heavy bricks for years had put muscles on his arms that I could hardly believe. He didn't have an ounce of fat on his entire body. He was the same age as myself, but twice as muscled. I know hard work but muscles always eluded me. He was, by all appearances, just what he presented himself to be, an honest, hardworking individual with no time for afternoon *siestas*.

One would normally believe a smuggler with a modest education would sooner or later blunder somehow, or, at least, appear not so perfect and proper. It didn't happen with Jesse. This perfection had us scratching our heads with bewilderment. I have unloaded his bricks, searched the bed of his truck, and been through that old truck inside and out. I found nothing in or about that truck that would conceal drugs. His old truck was kept immaculately clean. Jesse was beating us hands down.

Throughout those years, every visiting U. S. officer, state highway patrol, and local deputy sheriff, plus every U. S. Border Patrol agent that had ever met Jesse were suspicious of him. The truth was they had a gut feeling about the man but nothing further to confirm their feelings.

One of Phoenix's top FBI agents visited our port of entry once a month for a report of laws violated outside Customs authority. He said to me once, "I don't know if you guys that see this man all the time can feel it or not, but he is probably smuggling drugs. Have you ever searched his load of bricks?"

That's the FBI, the smartest officers in the business with the world's most stupid questions.

I transferred to Lukeville as an inspector from the U. S. Border Patrol in California in the spring of 1974. Since that time, I had climbed aboard that load of bricks, looked between them, under them, and even broke some of them at Jesse's expense. I knew that truck fore and aft, how many boards were in the bed, and recognized the ends of the bolts that held metal together. There were no drugs in Jesse's truck, nor was there evidence of drugs ever being in his truck. All the old inspectors had already told me that, but what did they know? Regardless of who said what, all suspect vehicles are searched at that port of entry.

Then, as time passed, the newer inspectors that I trained on the job told me that if Jesse were smuggling drugs, they'd find it. What a relief! About time Customs hired inspectors that could find drugs where the older hands failed for years. They, too, searched Jesse and found nothing. That old truck had been scrutinized and taken apart more times than a third generation set of tinker toys. It had been torn down and rebuilt more times than President Johnson's first State of the Union Speech. Jesse was not smuggling drugs through the port of entry, and that was that, but we searched him, anyway. Please don't ask if we looked in the tires and gas tanks. That's reserved for the FBI.

The Customs Patrol officers followed Jesse to Gila Bend so many times that they no longer got lost on that eighty miles of straight and empty highway. Customs Patrol aircraft have flown high over Jesse's truck many times through the duration of his trips to and from Gila Bend. Zilch! After the third year of senseless and useless searching, I gave up and told the port director. "Jesse ain't smugglin' nothin'!"

"Yes, he is," the still smart and honest director responded. He had been the port director at Lukeville almost twenty years and had searched Jesse more times than he could count. Nevertheless, he was always ready to help search Jesse's truck again and again.

Why did everyone say the same thing about Jesse for years when there was no physical evidence outside a very thin line of profit? Gut feelings. I don't care what the courts say or what the law states. Gut feelings are as natural to mankind as breathing. I knew Jesse as well as my own mirrored image. I knew his shabby clothes were always clean. He was always well shaven. His skin texture and muscle tone were that of a well-trained athlete. He was too different! His straw and felt hats, however, were dirty from too much sweat and dust.

Too much sweat and dust! That fact always brought me back to his making the bricks and loading them on his truck. I could think no further than that.

After all those searches for years, he was still friendly. He knew that we were only doing our jobs, but that was no longer true. It was personal. Everyone wanted to find his drugs. If an officer ever found them, he might as well have won the lottery. As you know, people outside mothers and grandmothers do not normally like Customs and Immigration inspectors. Jesse treated us like brothers. That was another in the *"Gimme"* profile, a free one.

The bricks were manufactured in Jesse's backyard and were widely known in southern Arizona for their consistency and durability. Many expensive homes in Phoenix were built with them, plus many in surrounding communities over the western half of southern Arizona. Jesse's humble business was, in fact, a legitimate commercial enterprise. The profit, however, after all of his expenses, just didn't seem all that great after the bribes he paid in Mexico, the expensive tires, import duties, and gasoline.

If Jesse were smuggling drugs for years, he would have been wealthy. The wealthy officers in that area of Mexico, and most all of them were, would have grown far wealthier. Someone would've eventually slipped up and exposed such wealth, which is human nature. Jesse wore the same type of clean work clothing for years, drove the same truck, lived in the same house, and attended mass regularly. Exactly why U. S. officials continued to suspect him explains why we love to be challenged, which invariably leads to total frustration.

If you think a truck with its home based Sonoyta isn't suspect because its engine is clean and hums like a Rolls, you don't know your vehicles on the northern frontier of Mexico. Any truck registered there burning Mexico gas has to be kicked and spurred, cussed and threatened. Their engines misfire, sputter, clatter, and often stall in the middle of the road. Their socialist government only allows one oil company, to my knowledge, so there's no competition and really no reason to manufacture a decent grade of gasoline. It's extremely low in octane. It's also dirty and expensive.

One day he wore a felt hat, a wide-brimmed floppy. I had seen it before and knew something was amiss. Its color used to be brown. The sun had faded it into gray, rust colors, and charcoal splashes. *Why?* Not many people driving a truck will wear a wide-brimmed hat. Very strange! I couldn't put my finger on what I knew was the key to his smuggling. I asked him about that hat.

A nosey immigration inspector standing next to me quickly took up Jesse's defense and explained that most all felt hats manufactured in Mexico were wide-brimmed and floppy. The sun faded all of them and had obviously done something to that inspector's brain. Jesse didn't have to say anything. Even he knew the Immigration inspector was full of spoiled cabbage. That hat was telling me something that I didn't understand!

I could not help myself. I suspected him even more. The immigration inspector has probably never owned a hat and wouldn't know a Guanajuato Straw from a Five-X Beaver by Stetson. I've worn hats all my life and I do know something of their quality and endurance. I also know something about people who wear western hats--I think. Their crease and how they treat their hats tells much of their character and what they really know of western culture or tradition. Jesse's hat was manufactured in the U. S. I didn't bother to tell the inspector this fact. It was faded because he worked outside making adobe bricks and loading them on his truck. That's what I knew.

My slow speech with a heavy nasal tone usually keeps me listening more than talking. I had to later correct that inspector from interrupting my short sentences once I managed to get the words rolling. He was offended and hasn't spoken to me since unless it was on a professional basis. At any rate, Jesse wore that hat only once during the time I was on duty when he made his entries. It came to me almost three years later!

Gila Bend, Arizona is a small town. No one smuggles to that small town consistently over the years without being exposed. If that tourist trap was more attractive, it might have been taken for any of Death Valley's tourist stops. As it stands today, it's not even a national monument, but give Congress time.

Jesse said he liked Gila Bend. That remark waved more of the irritating yellow-flags in front of my nose. No out of town people liked Gila Bend! Whether it's a prosperous business community or not, an outsider liking Gila Bend makes about as much sense as a termite liking a Brazilian anteater. I say this because most people are as fond of their wallets.

Our Bill of Rights' clever amendments protect drug smugglers better than a White House staff member until enough evidence is gathered for a prosecution. In southern Arizona during the 1970's, finding a prosecutor willing to accept a marijuana case with less than 500 or 1,000 pounds was harder than a Republican sub-committee convincing Janet Reno to accept a case against Bill Clinton. I could think of nothing that would expose Jesse's underhanded smuggling schemes.

I need to emphasize that all Immigration officers check the Border Crossing Cards for authenticity and tampering, even though they, themselves, sometime typed, laminated, and issued the very card they inspected. They picked it up, folded it, smelled it, held it up to the light and checked numbers. Getting a false card passed one of those guys would require the talents of David Blaine, the

Street Magician. Jesse always had his card ready as instructed. After passing the secondary inspection with flying colors and having his card thoroughly scrutinized, he gunned the smooth engine and drove straight to Gila Bend to unload his bricks.

All right--okay! I know! You're going to tell me that the drugs were inside the bricks, aren't you? I only broke a few of them. The remainder built people's homes, whether drugs were inside them or not.

The port director would always set his crossword puzzle aside when Jesse entered. Each time he would say, "Let's find the dope this time, Homer."

Occasionally, the fuel tanks were drained in order to count the gallons. No hidden drugs there. The tires were deflated and taken off their rims. Nothing. By the way, a new tire with solids taking up valuable air space in tires on that hot pavement would have exploded. He's had a dozen sniffing dogs called on his truck. Zilch!

My wife forced me to resign from the Inspections Division of the U. S.

Customs Service at Lukeville after three years. She got tired of me coming home every night and going through the cabinets and canisters, feeling under and behind the sink, mattresses, and emptying her purse and our baby's diaper bag on the kitchen table in search of illegal drugs. She argued that she never set foot in Mexico unless I was with her, but that's what they all say. I'd just smile and say, "Yes--ma'am."

Then she'd throw her arms up in despair. I'd always add the clincher with an empathetic smile. "Have a nice day, ma'm." That really gets 'em! How I loved to watch the real wise butts drive away red-faced with their lower lips protruding. I liked it even more when I was challenged by a lawyer prior to his secondary inspection. In court we played in their ball park. We lost. In the Customs inspection lanes, we played in our ball park. They lost.

To save my marriage, I transferred into the Customs Patrol. SCPO Tilton hired me and saved my wife from shooting me. He issued me an old clunker Blazer for transportation to and from the corrals in order to feed the horses, my collateral duty twice daily. The corrals were five miles north of the port of entry. The Blazer and the corrals north of the border were responsible for Jesse's undoing.

It was an exceptionally rare accident that I stumbled upon Jesse in the desert; that is, he stumbled upon me. I was returning from the horse corrals late one afternoon and turned east on a small road that led to a windmill two miles distant. The small road I was on paralleled the east-west border fence but was a half-mile north of the border in that area. I did it to cut sign for the southbound backpackers, the smugglers that delivered their loads to a pre-planned destination anywhere alongside the north-south highway to Gila Bend.

I drove slow over that east-west road in search of the southbound tracks. Suddenly, and with no warning whatsoever, the southbound Jesse, jogging from the north in that late and hot afternoon, almost bumped into my left front fender! He popped right out of the nowhere. However, it was brushy in that area. Believe me, the friendly Jesse Fernandez possessed an entirely different demeanor! He wore his wide-brimmed felt hat as he was jogging south across my east-west road with the impressive agility of a professional football player. Two more men were jogging briskly to his left, east of him. This was why his hat was faded. He wore it in the afternoon sun as he jogged back to Mexico from delivering his drugs to a predestined area on the northbound highway! Hats don't become sun-bleached in any other way than being exposed to the sun for long hours. Jesse wore the wide-brimmed hats for protection from the sun while he smuggled drugs on his back and jogged back to the border! *That was what the hats were trying to tell me! Jesse was a boss of mules! He smuggled his own drugs and only did the adobe brick thing once a week as a cover!*

We were about a half-mile north of the border. Instead of finding their southbound tracks in the desert, I had found the people making them!

Jesse and two other mules had delivered their loads of marijuana somewhere north and hid it close to the highway. When they reached my small, east-west road, they had suddenly leaped in front of me from the brush and almost collided with my old Blazer, which would've fallen to pieces had they hit it. They had neither seen nor heard me until they glanced my way for about a tenth of a second. They wore t-shirts, trousers, and good gym shoes. I'd recognize Jesse's faded brown hat anywhere. It floated in the air behind him on the road in front of me. Jesse was 10-8 for Mexico in the Code 3 mode, down and out with pedal to the medal! He was twenty feet south before that hat touched the surface in front of me.

Backpackers usually travel the highway at night, or in the daytime, and simply hide in the brush to the side of the road when a vehicle approached from either direction. They left no tracks on the highway. Exactly why they used the desert to travel back was the reason that they hurried, and running tracks were hard to follow in the rocks. Many of them jogged south on the highway at night, which is why the Customs Patrol in vehicles seldom used their headlamps, unless they shared the road with another vehicle. Customs Patrol Officers have had joggers to almost run over their patrol vehicles on their return trip south, but it was always on the highway.

Why we back-tracked the southbound mules that preferred the desert instead of the highway was to locate their favorite stashing places near the highway. Sometimes we found their drugs before being picked up by the car that came for them. Sometimes we sat on the stashed load and ambushed the smuggler from Tucson or Phoenix. It was a simple method that worked well for a short time. Using horses to back track them never raised their suspicions.

Upon spotting me, Jesse and the other two mules scattered like three, ground-fast quail, southbound, of course. All three carried nothing, not even water. Being a backpacker for years explained Jesse's muscles! Backpackers are tough people. They pack fifty or sixty pounds of marijuana from three to fifteen miles north of the border then jog back to the border in the summer as well as winter. Do this two and three times a week for a little while and muscles soon replaces fat. They were running hard in the hottest part of the afternoon!

I quickly scanned the area south while they sounded like runway horses. If they reached the fence, they were home free. I stepped out and twisted the two hub switches on the Blazer's front wheels. After that simple task, I jerked its grinding transmission into four-wheel drive to bounce cross-country in order to catch up with the nearest of the three fleeing bodies. I would be catching one of them.

What a solo officer doesn't want to do is physically lay hands on a backpacker when he's fresh!--not unless he possessed the rare ability to kick Chuck Norris in the rear and make him like it. *Had I been a professional football player and suddenly faced with the unfortunate chore of tackling the great Earl Campbell, I would have allowed him to run at least 100 yards to tire a bit before attempting to bring him down. As the famous Inspector Clouseau might say, "There is a time to be brave and a time to run. This was not the time for either!" No one manhandles those guys!*

I drove behind the runners in my bouncing Blazer over the rising mounds and shallow washes. They were almost as fast as my Blazer. One passed through a mesquite thicket to the left. The thicket's line ran north and south, meaning he had crossed a wash, so that one was home free even before reaching Mexico. I now had two to choose from. The washes south of the mountains meander south. We were paralleling them. The backpacker on the far right crossed a deep wash to his right, so he was suddenly home free. The middle body ran like a deer straight in front of me, who just happened to be Jesse Fernandez. I still wasn't ready to catch him until he showed signs of tiring. As it was, the old Blazer was nearing its top speed on that rough surface! The fence that used to be a half-mile south was closing in fast.

My plans were to almost reach the border before bailing out and tackling him. That way, if he were tired enough, I just might live to see another sunrise. I definitely needed a horse and a long rope in this situation.

He looked back and quickly figured what I had in mind. He leaped to his right and landed on the far right bank of the wash that he paralleled. He wasn't even breathing hard. I was and I was riding! I gunned the engine to keep even with him on the opposite side of the wash. The border was growing too near to keep this up.

Actually, I was a jogger, of sorts, but not in this man's class. Unknown at the time, he had just jogged from eleven miles north! He was jogging at least five times each week when he wasn't selling adobe bricks north and collecting money at some opportune time. I had planned to stay fresh and enjoy the race from my clunker as long as possible. I felt weak and out of breath, and my feet weren't even on the ground!

Then the wash bent sharply to the left, directly in front of me! We were within a hundred yards of the fence. My quarry knew what was happening and peeled off to his right. I braked short of the wash and snatched the keys at the same time. I would have to hustle!

Fresh, I easily jumped the wash, almost, and belly-flopped on the far bank. No problem. I was up and after the man about twenty yards distant.

He was tiring as the border fence closed in. Realizing that he wasn't going to make it, he skidded to a stop. He was going to fight. *Just my luck!* They always do that if they think they have a chance at winning while that close to the border. I did not want to tangle with Jesse! I ducked his swing still running and plowed into him with my left elbow forward and hit the strongest oak tree in my entire life!

He rolled on his way down and I rolled to my right. I was on my feet and too close to him, thinking I had plenty of time because the elbow connected with his breast bone. It hurt my elbow. Several places on my body hurt but there was no time to check for broken bones and fill out the proper forms. I was preparing defensively and waited for his charge. I planned to use his strength to my advantage. He sprang up like the handle of a rake when the business end is stepped on.

I fought against panic. If that man hit me, there'd be more forms to fill out. Today, not then, we have a self-defense law that will allow an officer to shoot an attacker with the greatest physical strength, under attack, of course. The best law to follow while working under a liberal administration, as we were then, was to run like hell or die! Shooting a drug smuggler, in top physical condition or not, would get a federal officer hung on Jimmy Carter's front lawn. Of all times to daydream, I suddenly remembered a lady that once encouraged me to study hair styling for a career.

I quickly jumped back a step and glanced both ways. I didn't need his two *compadres* surprising me. They had both cleared the border fence and were still southbound. I panicked and rushed Jesse, going under his right swing again and felt his left as we went down. Nothing ever went as planned, but the angels were with me. I was up and he was down, but only temporarily. He appeared angry. I had to do something different.

I was reasonably sure that he was too tired to fight, so it was imperative to restore the man's dignity as fast as possible, lest he rested for a moment and tore me apart. I did not want to use my gun, but good sense was telling me to save my life and shoot him between the eyes. Kneecapping him would only tick him off. An officer is supposed to be killed before he has legal authority to even lift a gun from its holster under this administration. I'm just grateful that we were allowed to carry guns with real bullets!

I shouted in Spanish. "Jesse--no more fighting! I will use my gun!" No. I had not drawn my weapon. But I could and would, however, and it would have been fast and sure. Jesse would have two in his chest and one in his face as soon as I drew the gun--if he had moved the slightest toward me. Then I could watch my small children grow up from prison. I practiced those shots regularly. Copper-jacketed and hollow-nosed .357 caliber bullets were my choice. I also planned to use the other three bullets on myself in case shooting him merely ticked him off.

That did it. He froze like a huge mountain gorilla with his arms spread and legs ready to spring. He turned around according to instructions and I pushed him to his knees, not easily done. I cuffed, attempted to cuff, his wrists. They were too big! Too bad. I forced them, which was possible since his wrists were oily from sweating too much for a long period of time. He was dehydrated and didn't even know it. After one uses up his body moisture, he will sweat oil with only a bit of water.

He protested but I never sympathized until he was under control. While driving back to the small road with the Blazer, I stopped and retrieved his big felt hat from the road, well worn and faded from the sun.

I said, "This is what I've been looking for, Jesse, exactly when and where you were using this hat."

He turned his head silently. Only God and Jesse know how many hundreds or thousands of pounds of marijuana he had smuggled into the United States.

Finally, like all good criminals, he asked me why he was arrested. An insult always opens the door for a deserving response from an officer without witnesses.

"Already, I told you, Jesse, *Cabron!* It is against the law to wear this hat in our desert!"

I think that he called me a dirty name in English, which was going to get his butt kicked before we made it back to the port of entry. On the other hand, I like to make jokes sometime. It takes the sting out of insults.

"Silence yourself!" I warned. "I will not hear your words again!"

He obeyed, thankfully. He might have gotten mad and snapped those cuffs off his wrists. Besides, we had to hurry. If those cuffs weren't off him in just a few minutes, his wrists and hands would be in trouble.

A moment later he complained that the cuffs were too tight. I agreed and speeded up the last quarter-mile. This was before we heeded the new law to use seat belts had reached us in the remoteness. Jesse's hands were cuffed behind him and his head bounced off the ceiling when we hit the highway. I braked hard and his head hit the windshield. He came back down against his hands. We hurried!

Smith and Wesson, by that time, had never increased the size of their handcuffs, which were made from molds when mankind was only four feet high and hunted toads for lunch with spears. Nevertheless, S&W has never admitted to manufacturing handcuffs too small for some people. As I perceived, S&W always seemed confident that the federal government was going to buy their products by the trainload. I liked their revolvers but the love ended there. Jesse didn't understand it, either. He told me that the handcuffs were too tight again. I told him in English to write Smith and Wesson a nasty letter. That would work, right after they sold the federal government another 50 million pairs of handcuffs too small and had cleaned out all of their old warehouses.

At the port of entry I gently coaxed him inside the holding cell. I didn't want him to get mad and run through the walls of the brand new port of entry building that was no more than five months old. It was May, 1978.

At this point, I'd like to explain that the new 8 million-dollar plus structure still had a few defects that needed to be corrected. The super big air conditioners for the huge building didn't work properly. All the thermostats on the walls were for show and to fool GSA inspectors. GSA inspectors approved the building suitable for federal use, so the saying goes, so that could easily include a faulty air conditioning system. The clever contractors passed the final inspection, eventually got paid, then retired in Alaska after declaring bankruptcy with millions in the bank.

In short, the air conditioning system only worked in two rooms. It worked at full blast in the coldest mode in the holding cell where Jesse was going. My office couldn't be hotter if it were in the open air without a shade. I removed the cuffs. His wrists had already swollen but not seriously.

The holding cell was far too cold, of course. I cooled off inside the door while Jesse glared at me from his cement perch in the cell. We could have hung a beef in that room. Poor Jesse, he was still hot and sweaty. It would have been better to simply cut the electricity off to the air conditioner, which we did after the sun went down. Being sweaty, I didn't linger long in the artic-like air. Jesse didn't mind, at first. He was still breathing hard and too bewildered to believe that he had been caught after all those years! I found a blanket and brought him a plastic pitcher of water. He drank most of it.

What I didn't tell him was that I had no hard evidence against him, just darned good probable cause to hold him for questioning. I couldn't back track him that night, but I'd be on his tracks by sunlight. He really wasn't in trouble until we found his stash. Then, if his load weighed over 500 pounds, we might find a state or federal prosecutor who would believe me when I claimed to be an expert tracker, which would tie him to the load. But we needed to hold him overnight or until we found the drugs he smuggled. According to law, we could only hold him until Midnight, which is when the port of entry and border gate closed. This was the seventies. Our country had only begun to tumble downhill.

Jesse knew his guilt, that he was caught, and had accepted it. Crying wasn't his and most other Mexicans' way of expressing their grief when caught. That was a learned thing we developed in this country during the 1960's. And we developed it into a fine art.

The port director, my former boss, left his crossword and could hardly believe that the wild man in the holding tank was Jesse. Jesse's dirty t-shirt was saturated with sweat and mud, and he wasn't smiling or holding his hat in his hand as he had for the past years while facing the port director. The blanket was draped across his shoulders.

The director turned to me, "Don't you think you ought to get 'im another blanket or a coat or something? He's apt to freeze to death in there!"

I said, "He hasn't said anything about being cold." The remark fell on deaf ears. The port director had already conversed far too much for such a short period of time.

I found another blanket and filled the pitcher again. Then I sat down to collect my thoughts. Tilton would be arriving soon. By law, I'd have to turn Jesse loose at Midnight. People track people in the dark all the time, but only for short distances. In rocks, for miles, we needed the sun's brightness.

Regardless of the blankets, Jesse was soon shaking uncontrollably. He had the sniffles. He also began to cough. I removed him from the refrigerated room. It was probably forty degrees in there. I had to have help in order to watch him. That was obvious, even if he was too stiff to move. His cough worsened.

One of the Immigration inspectors came into our room where Jesse was beating Tilton and myself hands down during the interrogation proceeding. He said in Spanish, "Jesse, do you have your Border Crossing Card?"

Jesse didn't break out laughing like we did. He answered humbly, "No, sir."

"Well, in the morning I want you to bring me that card because I am going to take it from you. Do you understand me?"

Jesse nodded affirmatively. "*Si, senor!*"

I thanked the inspector and apologized for laughing at his question. After all, the small threat to lift his card was all the punishment Jesse was going to ever receive. The chances of his returning it to the inspector were about as great as Massachusetts' senators converting to conservatism.

Suddenly, a burned plastic stench reached us. Someone across the huge building was smoking a filtered tip cigarette. Jesse coughed and remarked about the stench in our house, one of the building's defects yet to be repaired through this date, twenty-five years later. No problem, smoking is no longer allowed in the building.

We talked with Jesse until Midnight before turning him loose. His cough was deep. I think the stinking cigarettes from the thoughtless inspector had hurt his lungs. My lungs were also stinging a bit.

At first light Tilton and I were horseback and on their tracks from the east-west road. The tracks crisscrossed and mixed with many other tracks. Tracks last for weeks in the desert. Our progress was slow but correct. We back tracked Jesse and his two mules eleven miles before finding the stash at 11:30 AM. Three packs weighing sixty pounds each gave us 180 pounds. We balanced it over our saddles and rode back to the station.

The first chore upon returning was to ask the Immigration inspector if Jesse had showed up that morning to surrender his Border Crossing Card. He had not. No one this side of the border at Lukeville has seen Jesse since that time. He still has that card if it hasn't been sold to someone else.

The backpacking didn't stop for another few months. At one stash sight nine miles north of the border and within ten yards of the highway, we planted sensors that would pick up footsteps in the area. Tilton and I sat up all night waiting for the stash to be picked up from the north. He was about a quarter-mile north and I was hidden in the brush that far south. Both of us had sensor monitors. The first sounds would bring us to the site, at the same time, hopefully.

The sensor monitors failed to sound off. The transmitter's battery apparently failed during the night. The transmitter, itself, was dug up by men during the night and carried back to Mexico with what remained of the stash. That hurt.

A DEA agent from Yuma knew one of the *federales* south of us. He drove there and located the officer. Together they drove straight to Jesse Fernandez's residence and arrested him. While the DEA agent waited outside, Jesse was interrogated inside the Mexico holding cell. Within minutes they retrieved our sensor transmitter from Jesse's shed. Jesse wanted to talk voluntarily. Confession must have felt good to him. Mexico's interrogation processes are creative but rather primitive. He did not take the sensor, personally, and had not been to the United States since his arrest long ago. He said that he had four mules working for him. His confession gained him a night in a Mexico jail, and I'm reasonably sure that he was in pain during the night and several thereafter. The disposition of his case, however, has not been revealed to us. Jesse had money, then, lots of it. Well, until his arrest in Mexico, he *had* a lot of money.

Rumor Control had Jesse working 120 miles east of us in the Sasabe, Arizona area. If this is true, Jesse is, at this time, a very rich man if none of the Mexico authorities have decided to simply take his money from him at their discretion.

Chapter Fourteen

My Cloud

SCPO Tilton is still adamant in claiming that it never happened, the miracle that saved both our lives. He's wrong. I remember it well. I had looked up intermittently for fifteen miles over that supposedly straight road, and it remained between us and the sun regardless of our speed and slight shifts in direction. It was there, although at times we crowded the edge of its shadow. Our eyesight was not playing tricks on us as we suffered from heat exhaustion for almost two hours. Without that cloud, our bodies would have shut down and we would have crashed. Neither of us had the strength to walk. This is why I constantly looked up, hoping that cloud wouldn't leave us.

Decades later, he still denies it. But that's Tilton. He'd argue with a rock. I have seen people pass out with less symptoms of heat exhaustion than we had that afternoon. His mouth was clenched shut and, his eyes were barely opened as he stared straight ahead. No color tinted his face. His hands and knees shook uncontrollably, the same as mine. My body had already shut down once that afternoon, and without that cloud protecting us from the direct sun, it would have shut down again. Without sudden help, which was most unlikely, it would have been permanent. Neither of us could have possibly lasted another five minutes in the direct sunlight.

Tilton is still a man of sound quality, intelligent and God-fearing. He was always honest to work with, always doing his part and someone else's if he thought they were too slow. He made sense of mountains of worthless paperwork. Each report was correct to the letter. However, if he thought he could add one gray hair to my head or one ounce of stress, I think he'd lie until his lips fell off.

Nevertheless, he was a good friend for all the years we worked together. If I ever frowned or complained due to something he had done, he'd find it hilariously funny.

He stood opposite of my side of this story the first time he heard me tell it. Today, there's still no way to know whether he believes the truth of that miracle or not. It never mattered which side of the argument he took, just as long as it was an argument. I half believe that he thinks it never happened. That leaves me without a witness to the miracle that saved our lives.

This leaves you, the reader, to believe him or me. You are within your right to say the story is unbelievable or else a mere coincidence. It's not a problem for me. I know that it happened as it's depicted.

Most miracles can be interpreted as coincidences. Let me tell you before I start, this story was definitely *no coincidence!* I know heat exhaustion symptoms better than the common cold. I've seen dozens of cases, perhaps more than most doctors. Heat exhaustion requires no physician to diagnose it and the victim will die without first aid and protection from the sun.

That cloud formed right over us among many other thunderheads scattered across the blurry sky that afternoon. It followed us a moment and was replaced by another that stayed with us for thirty minutes. Although part of the dialogue is forgotten and omitted, what's depicted here is exact.

We both suffered from heat exhaustion that hot August day, and, at one time, we were in a bit of a fix. Lukeville, Arizona is one of the two hottest spots in the nation on television's daily weather reports. The other hot spot is Death Valley. Garcia claimed if he ever wanted to cool off, he'd just drive up to Death Valley in the middle of summer.

No breeze that day. The soft blue sky was a bright, cloudless, eye-watering blur for six long hours. The air was as still as the lifeless, scorching earth surrounding us, miles of practically colorless surfaces reflecting the sun's rays and blocking our vision with silvery waves that offered no relief or escape. It was early August, a week or so prior to the afternoon showers that would fall on the mountains. It was no more than 108 degrees f. that morning when I checked our thermometer, about average in August of 1978. But it had warmed up considerably by that afternoon, especially where we were, some sixty miles west of Lukeville on the border. We were right in the middle of the 120 straight border miles between Lukeville and San Luis, Arizona

The western boundary of our border jurisdiction, about half-way between Lukeville and San Luis had to be checked regularly. In order to get to the western side of our area of the desert, we used whatever transportation suitable for the time and circumstance. An airplane was good but too fast for sign cutting and intricate details.

An airplane could not be requisitioned that day. We had no time for horses, three days of slow travel would get us to our west side, then three more on the return trip. I kept a twenty-mile limit on our horses for a good reason, although they were capable of twice that distance and more. We needed them fresh at all times in case of an emergency.

Our vehicles simply weren't reliable. They could break down faster than any vehicles I've seen in my lifetime. Our vehicles spent more time in some money-grubbing mechanic's garage than we used them.

The desert lent us an uneven surface at the border that day. It was rocky and full of shallow washes that ran ninety degrees to our westward travel near the border fence. We were reduced to using dirt bikes, but they were new, not seized. At least we got that much from our budget before the remainder of the money went for new furniture in some remote office in D.C.

We could make it to the west side and back inside eight hours on dirt bikes--if everything went smoothly. This was with reasonable riding in order to catch anything amiss at the border fence. We used Honda 175's.

"I want to get back in time for you to feed the horses," Tilton announced as we were leaving that morning. That meant he wanted to set our pace, which was always too fast over those blistering rocks lying loosely on the fence road. After securing our water, we fastened our helmets.

"If you're going to speed," I said, "go by yourself." Both of us knew that no one goes into the desert alone unless it's with plenty of provisions or with a good horse. The dirt bikes might carry a good brand name, but they're only machines.

"Oh--you can keep up just fine," he said, which, after being translated into truth, meant I was going to be narrowly escaping death every few seconds. "You can outrun me on these bikes anytime."

That positive stroke meant that I was going to spend the day eating dust, cussing, praying, crying, and yelling obscenities at him each time we stopped. It wasn't going to be a good day. If I were going to set the pace, I'd have to race him for it.

Now, believe me, I tied the canteen behind the seat of my bike extra tight and made sure he did the same. I have experience as a mule packer at Grand Canyon, Arizona and I know how to tie knots suitable for specific occasions. Tilton, on the other hand, is a capable outdoorsman but he could only tie one knot, a grandma type that would come loose with the least amount of pull. He only wore boots because he couldn't tie a shoestring. I also did a lot of jogging to keep in shape lest I would've stayed in the air conditioned office that day and tried to listen to a radio. Television was lousy that far from Tucson and Phoenix.

The first fifteen miles of our western border road is maintained by the NPS for tourist travel to an oasis called Quitobaquito.

Quitobaquito, the oasis, is also a hot spot for narcotics smuggling. It is right on the border. Some say it is the reason that our surveyors cut the Arizona border back north from Sasabe, Arizona instead of running it straight west all the way past the northern tip of the Gulf of California. It had a fresh water spring and a pond that was suitable for swimming if one didn't mind the filthy water from wild ducks and loons.

The border road further west of that point has always been closed to tourists without special permits. Anyone entering that stretch of desert did so at their peril and would be sought out by rescue units if they didn't return within a specified time. We weren't tourists. *We didn't need no stinking permits!*

The surface used as a border road is up and down through hundreds of rocky washes knee deep to ten feet and usually about as wide as they are deep. Some of the rocky banks are straight up. Even the professional bike racers avoided places like that.

We were on our brakes, skidding sideways and spinning our back tires to maintain a snail's pace ninety percent of the time. At least one foot was down through those rocks that rolled under our tires like marbles. It was anything but enjoyable. Each time that I had a free hand it would shoot behind me for a split second to check the position of my canteen. I never lose things that I pack with my own knots.

Tilton stopped for a drink of water every half-hour after we passed the oasis. The first time he stopped he eyed me skeptically, waiting for me to bombard him with obscenities. That would have pleased him to know he was getting to me. I asked him, "Is this as fast as you can go?"

"No. I'm trying to cut you some slack, but apparently you don't appreciate it!"

I took a long pull on my canteen, then gave him a fair warning. "If you don't pick up the pace up a bit, I'm going to leave you here to grandma your way back home."

That got a chuckle out of him. Our top speed was about fifteen mph, and we were on our brakes half the time and lifting the front wheels over the steepest banks. I knew he was getting tired. If we went any faster, we'd only exhaust ourselves. I had already resolved for a miserable day. It was unwinding as predicted.

He tried to go faster and crashed inside the first five minutes. I saw his bike sail in one direction without him while he skidded face down. I had to brake fast to keep from running over him. He frowned at me as if it were my fault.

I was laughing but managed to say evenly, "Don't try to kill yourself. If we don't get back before midnight, the horses won't starve."

No wheels were bent, only the clutch handle had to be straightened. We were at another maniacal speed inside a valuable minute.

Thirty miles of stifling heat later I was tired. I was ready for a rest each time he stopped for water. It was passed noon and exceptionally hot. Except for an occasional ironwood tree and cacti, all the vegetation was behind us in the heated, rocky surfaces provided no shade. Not a cloud was in the sky. The bright blue dome engulfing us was so harsh that we had to squint. We had never heard of glasses with ultra violet ray protection. I reached for my canteen. *It was gone!* I had left it at the last break!

I was already losing moisture from physical exertion, not that it was collecting anywhere, except inside my helmet. Without water to replace it, dehydration was certain within an hour or so. I had to make a decision. We had fifteen miles to go further west. At that point we could cross the fence into Mexico and ride back home on Mexico's highway that paralleled the border with a great speed. I could survive that long without water. I had no problem with that plan.

I knew that serious heat exhaustion would happen in about a half hour for myself, and I was in good shape. I had tended hundreds of heat exhaustion victims at Grand Canyon while working as a mule guide there. At least two women in my party would faint each day from the heat, sometimes five or six. Tilton had water and faced no risk. I wasn't about to let him know that I had no canteen.

Also, I wasn't about to mention this extremely important philosophy that we always practiced: One doesn't challenge nature unless the odds are in one's favor. Losing one's water is strictly forbidden, a pilot error, a price to pay dearly. With anyone else, I would've stepped forward, announced my mistake, openly admitted losing it, and suggested we turn back at that point. Even then, we would have had to use the highway in Mexico that paralleled the border a couple miles south of us.

That Mexico asphalt road paralleling the border between Sonoyta, Sonora and Tijuana, Baja California is called Highway Two. It's definitely not designed for American comfort. It was barely wide enough for two burros to pass safely. It was built up above the desert floor without shoulders. Over thirty cruiser buses a day raced over that highway between Tijuana and Sonoyta. Sometimes the unregulated drivers are sleepy and use the middle of the road. Tourists and natives alike have left the highway many times and wrecked as a result. That happens where there are no shoulders. The road is dangerous at its best. Many of the crashed victims died from dodging the buses. It happened once or twice each year over the 130 miles of emptiness between Sonoyta, Sonora and San Luis, R.C., Sonora.

Anyone riding a motorcycle on that highway would be challenging that robed skeleton that sulks around with a sickle. Tilton wasn't going to like the news that was about to be broken.

"Ain't you going to drink?" he asked.

I was drumming my fingers on the handlebars. "Hell no! I just had a drink a minute ago while we were riding. I'd like to get back sometime before next Christmas."

I shouldn't have said that, not in that harsh tone, anyway. But Tilton had a way of bringing out the best out in people. I was already too tired and dehydrated, making myself ripe for mistakes. A gate in the border fence was our destination. We had to see if tracks led through it or not. I told myself that I could last that long.

During the next fifteen minutes I was forgetting which was the clutch and brake, even after using them hundreds of times that day with hours of consistently stopping and starting. My fingers trembled. Both elbows felt rubbery when I tried to steer fast. Putting my foot down didn't help. My knee bent too fast. This wasn't good. Those half-hour drinks were more important than I had realized, and I had only missed one. I thought that I could see tiny beads of water under the crystal of my watch, making it blurry and hard to read.

I knew more about heat exhaustion than Tilton. Being strong and knowing how to conserve energy were also in my favor. Then the inevitable happened. I squeezed the front end brake handle for no reason at all and did a swan dive over the handlebars into the rocky wash below. I could hear the dreaded sounds of the bike tumbling somewhere in the distance. My foremost thoughts were contacting those hot rocks. Falling had to be done correctly. For some reason or other, my leather gloves were in my hip pocket!

My hands, palms down with my elbows locked immediately under my armpits. The helmet would take care of my head. The idea was to not let the ribs, knees or backbone contact those hot rocks. This all happened at a low speed. The rocks rolled under my palms and boots at the far end of my prone body. Miraculously, no other part of my body touched the ground. I lifted my hips and jerked my knees and was on my feet before coming to a full stop. My hands were on fire!

Those rocks are hot enough to burn one's hand if they're picked up during the heat of the day. Tilton had his gloves on when he went down, so he wasn't burned. The slight abrasions in the palms removed enough dirt to let the heat in. The sweat did the rest. I danced around trying to fan them at my waist. "Ouch--ouch--ouch!"

Tilton angrily stooped and recovered my bike while I danced around and tried hard to think of a way to cool my hands.

"Where in the hell is your canteen?" he yelled, dead serious.

I confessed. My hands suddenly didn't burn anymore. I would never live this down. I sat down on the bare rocks but quickly got up, wishing that Tilton would go away. But he said and did a remarkable thing:

"Hell, Homer. Accidents happen. There's a big ironwood over there with a lot of shade. Get under it and I'll ride on to the gate. We'll have to ride back on Highway Two. There's no time left for you, though. You're already loosing it. I wondered why you hit your front brake like that!"

"You were watching?" I asked, getting overly skeptical about him sparing my ego so eloquently. This wasn't the Tilton I knew.

Then he said it: "What a dumbut!"

"I asked if you were watching or not!"

"Yeah, I was looking back to see if you were still with me when you suddenly went airborne over perfectly level ground. You've lost your coordination. Get in the shade!"

Tilton was a fast learner. I had taught him all I knew about heat exhaustion, however much that might be.

That ironwood looked familiar as well as inviting. Sure enough, as soon as Tilton sat down nearby under the shade, he told me that we had made it to the gate. I was shaking from what I thought was embarrassment but I was actually shivering, getting cold. The blood was already collecting around my stomach. I would be vomiting in minutes.

"Better have some more water," he said and shoved his canteen toward me.

I refused. We'd be needing it if either of us went down between there and Quitobaquito.

He insisted. Of course he was right. I would've went down as soon as we hit the sunshine without it. Revived and saved, we crossed into Mexico through the wire gate and found the notorious Highway Two somewhere south of us. When we turned east we opened the throttles on those bikes in their highest speed. We had about forty-five miles between us and water, Quitobaquito!

There wasn't a car or bus in sight. We did occasionally pass a few tourists during those miles--but no buses.

We glanced behind us regularly. Even though we were doing seventy mph, one of those cruiser buses that were built like aircraft carriers, two stories high, could and would overtake us like we were sitting still. They had no speed limit out there. If we spotted one, we would slow down and leave the highway.

No doubt about it. I was living righteous enough for both of us, which is what I frequently pointed out to Tilton. We made the gate that was three miles west of Quitobaquito in about a half-hour without encountering a bus from either direction. The angels were with us. We peeled off the highway right at the gate where the Organ Pipe National Monument borders the Cabaza Prieta Game Refuge. That gate in the border fence had to be opened. I sat straddled my bike with my feet on the ground.

I tried to dismount to open the gate but couldn't lift either of my legs. I was about to go down. I could only sit there. Tilton let us through and didn't seem too wobbly to me. I couldn't see my watch, so I don't know what time it was. We had covered those forty miles in due time without water.

When the temperature reaches 108 degrees, the wind loses its ability to cool. It actually acts as a heater, like a house furnace. The only way it can cool is to strike a cooler or wet surface first. Our helmets and clothes actually saved us from permanent dehydration during that fast ride. Tilton probably didn't realize that, and I could not talk to tell him, not that he would've listened.

The amazing part of going bonkers in the heat is the fact that the discomfort of thirst isn't all that bad. A dry mouth will only cause so much discomfort, then it reaches a plateau. Freight trains were racing inside my head at full steam. The blood was being pumped to my brain at an extremely rapid rate to keep my head cool. There's very little blood remaining in the arm and leg muscles, which explains why the legs failed to function.

Once complete shock sets in, the blood collects around the stomach and flattens it. Regurgitation is unavoidable. Anything digesting there is definitely coming back up to make room for the body's blood being placed there temporarily. Without blood, the muscles won't function. The body won't move without muscles, and no further energy is used to move about. Without water, the victim reaching this stage is going to fall asleep permanently. We found dead men each year out here in the desert.

I wasn't that far along, neither was Tilton. But the warning alarms were sounding fast. Our bodies were telling us to use what muscles we had remaining to find shade, lest they would stop functioning altogether. We had, perhaps, ten minutes. That was sufficient time to get us to Quitobaquito, about three miles further east.

We have found the remains of many men and a few women that have died painlessly with the exact symptoms that had fallen upon us. People do strange things once the blood to their brains cease to cool the cells properly: They strip off their clothes, drop their pants as if intending to void their bowels as they regurgitated their stomach's contents. I've seen some men that died with their naked buttocks raised high, their stronger thigh muscles propped the ends of their trunks permanently. Their heads rested peacefully on weed stems, cacti, rocks, whatever it fell upon.

Finding people like that changed our whole political and social views. Today our government is doing something about this. Mexico's Vicente Fox will sue us for sure if he loses many more people that could send precious dollars into his fat, communist wallet.

It is difficult to realize that the President of Mexico is the most obnoxious man in the world, more so than Osuma Bin Lauden, could be friends with a straight man like George W. Bush. A lot about politics failed to reach my level of understanding.

My point is that they were no longer illegal immigrants or narcotics smugglers once they were dead. They were human beings without fault that had served as a host for their spirits. Their empty shells were as innocent in death as it was when they were born. If one has the urge to hug a newborn baby, the same applies to those exact dead bodies that have died in the desert. I've never hugged one of those stinking carcasses yet, but I wanted to when we found the dead El Salvadorian women one year. I always hid my tears for the dead in the presence of Tilton and Garcia.

When I was a youngster and read of such things, it was called thirst madness. Thirst seldom kills anyone directly. Of course they die from a lack of water, true enough, but if one actually dies of thirst, it takes a long time. About 90 percent of deaths in the desert are from heat exhaustion, which takes only a few hours, a half day, perhaps, a little longer or less for some. The discomfort of thirst is only an alarm bell. An overwhelming need for sleep is another alarm. The sun's victims mercifully die during this fatal sleep. It doesn't require a pathologist or any type of rocket scientist to determine what had happened. They paid no attention to the alarm bells and spent their strength by continuing to walk in the sun instead of seeking shelter.

Three years later from that time I did learn the difference between people dying of thirst and heat exhaustion by personal experience. There is no similarity. Tilton and I found one woman still alive that was dying of thirst, or dehydration, which is in another chapter. The sun had not killed her as it had her companions. She had made it to a shade.

We pushed the top speed of the motorcycles toward the safety of Quitobaquito on the border fence road. I didn't look up but I would've sworn a cloud's shadow accompanied us to Quitobaquito those last three miles to safety. That's the way I truthfully remember it, but I never mentioned that part to Tilton. But the amazing part was yet to come.

We stopped by the large pond at Quitobaquito. It was surrounded by wolf sage and other underbrush. When my bike stopped, it fell to the right side with me still on it. No problem. I sort of chuckled. I could pull my thighs up but my arms from the elbows down were paralyzed. Tilton went down the same way and was about twenty feet west of me. He could still walk awkwardly with his arms hanging straight down. I remember being grateful for no mosquitoes to swat during those heated hours, for my arms were completely useless. Swimmers could be heard on the far side of the muddy pond.

My numbed knees met the ground in whatever manner they chose as I managed to roll over. My ankles and knees were still attached, but numb, and following the thighs as I began to crawl.

Tilton didn't talk, so I know he was thinking something serious. When he was serious, trouble was imminent.

I managed to get to my feet after pausing a moment. Water to cool our bodies was only a short distance away. We walked to the western side of that waist deep pond of black, brackish water and fell to our knees at the muddy edge. Two college-aged males stopped their merriment and stared at us with arms spread and mouths open. The pond's loons were hidden under a tall growth of cane near the water's edge at the far side. Had it not been for those two air heads nastying up the pond, I probably would've drunk that water and died from amoebic dysentery. I knew Tilton had sense enough to not drink it.

"We can't drink with those bastards in there!" Tilton grumbled.

.

"We don't need to drink," I said. "Just splash water all over yourself. We're suffering from heat exhaustion, not dying of thirst." I was right.

We did exactly that. In a few minutes we were soaking wet and as good as new, strong and revived. Of course we dried out within minutes and sat down in the shade of one of the giant ironwoods to get wet again. We splashed more water on our bodies. Our wet clothes were drying in about ten to fifteen minutes. Our mouths were as dry as bleached flour.

"Where did you get your medical degree?" Tilton asked. "You seem to be a real expert on this heat exhaustion business."

I've never passed an opening to agree with a compliment in my direction, for they are rare. "I have no medical degree, but you are quite correct in assuming that I'm an expert."

I was a professional cowboy a few years before I went to college. A well-known cow boss once explained this expert business during one of his moments in deep, philosophic inspiration--if I can remember correctly:

"You know something?" he stated instead of meaning it to be a question. "If a cowboy knew anything at all, he would have to be an expert at it. He has an opinion on just about everything in the universe plus the universe itself. With all that combined knowledge from all those opinions, he has to be, therefore, an expert on something or other."

Tilton eyed me skeptically. "So--what's your point?"

"Later," I explained, "I'm an expert over this entire matter of heat exhaustion. I can't see any sense in questioning facts, nor do I fully appreciate your senseless sarcasm."

Tilton had already stopped pretending to hear. "I wonder if those swimmers have any water? Got any opinions about that?"

"I do and I'm sure they have water to drink."

The men in their early twenties had resumed their feminine squealing and jumping up and down and splashing dirty water in the other's face.

"Hey!" Tilton shouted. His tone was exceptionally hardnosed, as usual. Those guys froze in mid-action and slowly looked in his direction.

"You got any water to drink?"

"Yeah! We have water in our car over there in the parking lot!"

We both said, "Thank you!" and wet ourselves down again. I felt as strong as a horse.

We rode up to the parking lot about 200 yards away. Neither one of us didn't know where the spring was located that fed the pond. The NPS kept this a secret for good reason. Vandals would have destroyed it years ago. Of course we could've followed the line of vegetation toward the mountain and located the spring. I never thought of that.

We parked our bikes in the sunshine and walked to the car of the swimmers, the only one in the parking lot. It was locked tightly. Windows up. Completely burglar proof. It was fifteen miles home over a good road. The swimmers were having a delightful time. We could hear their squeals of delight.

I considered riding back down there and shooting both of them. For whatever good they were, it didn't show. But what the heck? If someone had shot me each time I failed to think, I would've been completely ventilated by the time I was sixteen.

"Can you make it home?" Tilton asked.

No time to waste. We were in the sunshine and our clothes would be completely dry in another few minutes. That's when I did glance up. I did see a cloud gathering directly overhead. Thunderheads gather over the mountains first in the desert. Quitobaquito is in the foothills of a small range of mountains. It was a small cumulus cloud and I noticed others moving in the winds aloft, swelling in a fast stream of air high above us.

No sooner did we start eastward for the fifteen-mile journey home when that cloud posed itself between us and the sun. That was our good fortune. I believe it kept us from getting too hot again and falling down. In the hot sun it's hard to realize that such a shade can make such a difference. It does! I hoped that we could stay in it just a few seconds before it left us. That few seconds would provide our energy supply a few moments longer. It left us as we turned slightly south of east. It was replaced by another one immediately. Of course we still had water in Tilton's canteen, but that had to be saved in case one of us wrecked.

I saw the line of shade ahead of us. Our speedometers read 30 mph on the winding road, dodging deep washes and circling smaller hills, etc. I expected to lose the cloud's shade that was keeping up with us and still blocking out our sun. I have never--in my life--ever stayed within one cloud's shadow over a minute! Miraculously, we didn't lose it. It wasn't a large cloud. I glanced up and saw that it was small but it floated in a straight line while we wound around a lot on the crooked road. Its line of shade remained with us the entire fifteen miles! I looked up many times, desperately hoping that it would remain between us and the sun. It did! I looked aside several times and saw its shadow line in plain view. So we did border its shade, occasionally. I was amazed, and how grateful I was!

Our speed had to slow to ten mph at times just to cross the washes before we regained our 30 mph. Each time we slowed we managed to stay within that cloud's shady area. It took us slightly more than a half-hour to cover that fifteen miles and we never lost it's shade one time!

When we reached the north-south highway leading from the port of entry at Lukeville, we turned south and rode the highway the last mile at an exceptionally high speed in the direct sunlight. Our cloud kept going east. We split in the housing lot where we lived at the time and parked in our respective yards.

Tilton said later that he drank water and gorged himself with iced tea and didn't upchuck any of it. I took a shower and cooled down awhile before I drank water slowly from the shower head. Once revived, there was a lot of energy left. I could've ridden back to the gate on the western side of our jurisdiction that afternoon but didn't.

Days or weeks later, whenever we talked about me losing the canteen, I told him that I would never forget that little cloud that kept us shaded during that entire ride from Quitobaquito. He looked at me as if I were crazy.

"You're kidding me!"

"No. If it weren't for that cloud, we may not have made it."

"There was no cloud, Homer."

The argument that ensued through the years remains through this day. I've warned him several times about not giving a divine miracle its due respect. Blasphemy isn't in Tilton, yet denying the cloud sent by God borders blasphemy. Tilton jerks people around a lot but that's his limit. He swears that he saw no clouds in the sky that day and that we rode in direct sunlight the entire day. That's his stand, and, three decades later, he's still wrong. I didn't mention the cloud that stayed with us from the gate three miles west of Quitobaquito. He was already in enough trouble for denying the cloud that stayed with us for the last half-hour of our journey.

Were there tracks from Mexico through the gate out there in the remoteness? I really don't remember looking.

That's my story of our miracle that day, which saved our lives. In fact, we couldn't have made it without the cloud.

Chapter 15

Buck

This spooky little buckskin stood at fourteen hands and weighed a thousand pounds while rolling fat. His head was shaped intelligently, yet it was too long for his thin neck and long mane. His tail drug the ground before it was thinned. He possessed no large forearms like fine-blooded quarter-horses. In general, his confirmation just wasn't all that great, but he was heavy-boned, strong and fast for his size. Furthermore, he was willing to work once he was mounted. He worked for the Customs Patrol many years but never learned to quiet down while he was led by anyone on the ground. Rollers were in his nose. He crouched backwards while saddled, snorting, threatening to go Code 3 at the drop of pin head. Stating this little horse sensed danger at every sight would be an understatement.

Leading him to the water trough following a twenty-mile trek through the heat was a story in itself. Even though he saw the water truck far ahead and smelled the water with the other horses, he was wary of a white man's trick and extremely concerned for his safety. Even while unsaddling, he watched for cougars, bears, insurgents and long-ranged missiles with nuclear warheads. We filled a half-barrel from the big water tank on wheels that the Army gave us. All the horses waited anxiously for their turns.

Yet—Buck remained a zebra at an African waterhole surrounded by hungry lions. He snatched a fast mouthful and raised his head, immediately prepared to run for his life. He snorted and would jerk backwards at the slightest sound while he drank. It didn't matter if another horse was drinking at the trough or not. It was his habit to remain alert. In the water trough at the corral, he was the same way. I watched him from a distance. Even if no lion was going to jump him while he drank, he pulled a mouthful and jerked his nose up, looking and smelling all around while swallowing. Another mouthful and the same thing happened. He spent twice as long in watering as the other horses. This horse could teach a textbook paranoid new symptoms.

The rule was that all the horses watered first, then we drank. The rest of us had our horses tied in a shade and wearing their oat bags while standing next to chips of alfalfa. Tilton, who rode Buck all the time we patrolled, patiently held the lead rope and waited for Buck to finish drinking. He learned to take a drink from his canteen at the sight of the water wagon. If he didn't, he'd almost die of thirst while waiting for Buck to drink first.

When arrested for smuggling narcotics back in the early seventies, Buck copped his plea and reluctantly agreed to work with the U. S. Customs Service. For his work, he would receive free medical benefits, footwear, and room and board for the rest of his life--or until we turned him over to GSA for property disposal, which is exactly what happened years later. The Saguaro National Monument in Tucson, Arizona was the lucky recipient. Buck died shortly thereafter.

He was at least 16 years of age when we first began using him in the patrol. No more than light duty would be asked of him for several years. Yet, shortly after his arrest and while he was recuperating from starvation, I was asked by the local rancher to help gather his mares that had not been corralled in five years. Since Buck was born and raised a cow horse, I chose him over Clyde and Speck to ride that day. Not that these two were not larger, thereby appearing much stronger, I didn't think they had the heart to perform what was about to be asked of a horse when chasing mares that were too wise to be corralled. None of them were gentle.

This local rancher, Bobby Gray, wanted all his mares gathered off the Organ Pipe National Monument. The NPS was taking his ranch without paying for it whether he liked it or not. That meant all of his horses and cattle would be taken, also. If he didn't have them off the national monument in thirty days, the NPS would serve papers on him and hire cowboys to trap all of his cattle and horses. He would receive no money. It was legal robbery from an extreme socialist part of our federal government.

Mr. Gray, who was nearing seventy at the time, could no longer ride. He had about fifteen head of mares and colts that ran wild in the desert. The NPS superintendent had determined that horses with colts were unsightly for tourists. Since the National Park Service failed to live up to the bargain the senior Gray had made in person with Franklin D. Roosevelt, the sons were to move off the property. The senior Mr. Gray and his family settled this ranch long before the ranch was made into a national monument. The senior Mr. Gray struck a bargain with FDR, on paper and in good faith, that he and his sons would be able to raise cattle and horses on that national monument until all the sons died or left voluntarily.

Well, about thirty-five years later, the superintendent of that national monument decided that all three living sons were to leave voluntarily. Otherwise, heavy fines would be levied against them.

The last living son, Bobby Gray, didn't want his mares trapped and sold for killer prices. By selling them, himself, he would, at least, get a little money after his livelihood was stolen from him. The NPS wanted the ranch and it was going to have it long before Bobby Gray was dead. Within the last three years, two of his brothers, also partial owners of the ranch, had died. One passed from suicide, the other from a heart attack. Bobby Gray's life style was already in jeopardy. Lawsuits were filed against him by the NPS, the very service his dad had given to the National Park Service as a free gift in the early 1940's.

The National Park Service had no time for sentimental values or, for that matter, what was legal. The superintendent wanted him gone. True, he was burning natural wood from what used to be his ranch. That was his violation. His brother that committed suicide in1974 burned firewood for branding and heating his house. Illegal immigrants crossing the ranch burned more wood at their campsites than the Grays. Ranchers could hardly appreciate facing huge lawsuits for burning wood gathered from their own ranch. In spite of what President Roosevelt promised his dad in writing that their ranch would be secure inside the monument until he and all his children were dead, the NPS filed lawsuits to move the brothers out. The monument was about 22 miles deep and 27 miles wide, and with the exception of a few scattered ranch sites and the city of Lukeville, Arizona, pop. 36, it was solid desert.

Somewhere within these 380 thousand acres were his fifteen head of mares. All the mares' needs had been met in the wild. The wild burro had bred some of the mares for years, evidenced by several sleek mules a mule colts running with them whenever they were spotted at the waterholes, which was only a few times each year. The sleek mule colts were wild from birth and never roped or corralled. The oldest mule colt was probably four years old, fully mature. Thank goodness this mule was a jenny. If he were a jack, I'm not so sure he would have been gathered, except by a rifle, which the NPS rangers were willing to do. The baby mule colts tagged close to their mares. A horse, female (mare) bred by a stud donkey (jackass), will produce a mule.

In fact, all the siblings were still running with the mares. To save confusion, please understand that these off springs of mares all stopped nursing at the mother's decision. She had to save her milk for the next offspring. Three colts followed one mare, and there were several mares. The four-year olds followed closely to a lead mare.

Mares, domesticated or otherwise, never run with wild burros, unless they have an overwhelming need to be productive. Then, and only then, will they settle for the first male that comes along. The romance doesn't last but minutes after the mares realize their conception.

There were no wild stallions on the ranch. Mr. Gray's last stud was sold years earlier. Mules don't run with wild burros, either, not when they have a choice to run with horses. Nevertheless, a single donkey will run with horses but they prefer their own species.

The mares were never ridden. Before the NPS began imposing strenuous rules against his ranching methods, he had rounded up the mares annually to wean their colts, doctor them, brand them, and trim their feet, etc. It was difficult for a rancher to tolerate the NPS.

Why was the NPS so interested in this ranch in the first place? It held what the Department of Interior's naturalists wanted, the organ pipe cactus. It grew there and in no other place in the United States. What's so unique and great about the Organ Pipe Cactus? It's a dinosaur among plants. *The irony of this immoral debacle from the NPS, this cactus was/is slowly fading away!* I saw several dying cacti. Was it a bug or a disease? Probably both, but the NPS never interferes with nature. Nothing was/is being done to save this species. If it died of diseases imposed by a cactus fly from Africa, that's only natural. The senior Mr. Gray, who gave his ranch to the NPS could have waited and sold it for millions today, but patriotism conquered greed in those days.

Bobby Gray and his brothers lived to see the promises made to their dad fade by the wayside. Thousands of dollars in penalties were imposed upon them by the NPS by 1974.

When the first brother committed suicide, he left a widow in her fifties to pay more than 50,000 dollars in fines. She was broke and told the NPS to go straight to hell. She worked in local cafes to earn her living after the NPS moved her out of her house on her ranch. The irony of this? Her husband and her names would soon be on an iron plaque near their home site that virtually sang praises of their pioneer bravery and hardships! Nothing will be recorded in history of the NPS breaking its contract with the Grays and literally stealing it with the law supposedly on its side. Moral issues? You never discuss morality with a socialist government. The NPS is, in fact, a government of its own, yet it answers to the Sec. of Interior for accomplishments. Outside Stuart Udall, this country has never seen a Sec. of Interior that knew the difference between a national park and the state of Texas.

In the meantime, the widow of the first Gray brother to die worked as a cleaning lady and a waitress to earn her living not twenty miles from where she had lived for decades on the ranch.

Not possible in the United States? Tell it to the Gray family survivors.

If you don't know socialism, find yourself a national park and live in it a few weeks. Become acquainted with its rules and regulations, etc. You'll find that the superintendent has all the authority on his realm as a Duke had in the properties of the King in old England. The part about personal marriages has changed for couples living on the park or monument. Couples no longer need the consent of the King to marry and consummate the marriage. Other than that, I can imagine that it's close to the same.

Stewart Udall, the Secretary of Interior under President L.B. Johnson, acquired millions of acres in Alaska and in the continental United States by mid-1965. This is actually when the Gray family began to have problems on their own ranch.

The NPS had decided to break its contract with the Gray brothers and asked them to leave. This was after the senior Gray had gone to

Washington at his own expense and willed the ranch to the NPS. A most grave error against his children! The senior Gray had no idea that three decades would change the morals of the people of this nation and its government.

The Gray brothers were remaining on the ranch until their deaths, for sure, but their ranching methods were stifled. Their deaths were coming earlier and earlier. They could build no modern corrals. The corrals had to remain as they were originally built decades ago.

The oldest brother died two years before Bobby Gray was being forcibly moved. He was left alone to defend his rights and fight the NPS at his own expense.

He had no freedom to work his cattle or horses. They were running loose. Many of the steers were ten to fifteen years old and weighed up to 1,700 pounds. They were wild and dangerous if cornered. The NPS wanted them out. These big steers were trapped and, in my personal opinion, shot in the corrals. They were 100% wild and too dangerous for tourists and illegal aliens. Jumping one of these steers in the wild, if it didn't run away, would kill a human as fast or faster than a grizzly. The steers could very well die from stress if they were hauled away in a truck or trailer. None of these wild animals died naturally.

Bobby Gray, continued living on his ranch without affording hired hands. In doing so, he had no choice but to ignore the NPS. Another Customs Patrol Officer, Will Williams, and I delivered the message of one of his brother's death two years earlier. He said, "Oh--Lord, I'm next!"

I don't know if he meant he was the last of the brothers to die or whether the NPS would double its lawsuits and efforts to add more stress to his life.

It didn't matter. He had to trap his cattle and sell them without the NPS's knowledge. This was due to the penalties levied against him by the NPS. His mares needed to be trapped without the knowledge of the NPS, also. His wife and children had to live in another city to save harassment. Bobby was pushed, virtually, into the corner of his home. He lived on one-quarter section of deeded land. The NPS wanted that deeded land! Since they owned the land surrounding it on three sides, they had a right to claim it. This is made possible by a legal flaw within our system. It has been on law books since our founding fathers made it a rule in the event there was ever a national emergency when the land was needed.

The NPS merely used the law without an emergency in existence, and they have been doing it since 1965. Bobby Gray sold his deeded section of land to a rich man who had little use for the NPS. This man owned Lukeville, Arizona, which is surrounded by the NPS land, also, but the NPS would never attempt to acquire it. This man had money to fight the NPS in court. The NPS, like any other socialist cancer in our world, has no fear of the little man, but will fear the rich man until the Second Coming of Jesus Christ.

When the NPS arrived to bulldoze the house down with Bobby still living in it, he showed the new ownership papers to the rangers, who backed away apologetically.

Nevertheless, Bobby Gray was scared and tired. He wanted his cattle gathered, along with his mares. Then he would have to haul them away at night to sell them. The NPS had liens on all of his animals. He trapped his cattle by waterholes and sold all but the wild steers, a mere handful too wary to be trapped.

The mares watered at night, as did the wild burro and the remaining steers. The burro herds were wild but could be easily spotted by tourists. No one spotted the mares or steers.

A small boy, then living with his parents who had a mobile home on Bobby Gray's ranch yard, made a pet of one of the wild burros. This was a no-no, according to NPS regs. But for years, even while the kid was in college, the burro would stand near the north-south highway between Mexico and Ajo, Arizona and beg for handouts.

I saw this domesticated wild burro many times before all the wild burro on the national monument were trapped and shipped to the dog food companies.

I lived twelve years on the Organ Pipe National Monument and spent most of them checking its border with Mexico, mountaintops, trails, roads, and waterholes. I know its southern border fence quite well. Not once have I ever seen any of the wild burro or horses close to the border. The wild burro had only five watering places on the entire monument. (Some BP agent is going to write the publisher claiming there's only two or three watering places.) There are five! Four of them are man made by the NPS. They are man-made to accommodate the bighorn sheep and varmints like fox, coyotes, and bobcats. A domestic species, wild or not, was not allowed to drink water from these sacred waterholes.

Bobby Gray's fifteen head of mares were the last horses on the Organ Pipe National Monument. History will not depict this fact. I conversed with both Bobby Gray and the NPS rangers. From these conversations, I firmly believe that what NPS officials put on paper--especially contracts!--aren't always worth the paper it's written on. Without question, the NPS was illegally pushing the last son off his land contrary to the contract many decades prior.

The National Park Service could not be more socialistic if it were controlled by Fidel Castro. It is the exact opposite of the democratic federal government that supports it. The NPS has zero respect for individual rights. All goals must point toward the good of the people; to wit: future generations.

Contrary, also, to what the NPS may depict, ranchers Henry and Bobby Gray did, indeed, die on their land prior to their moving away. After Bobby's death, a few months after we rounded up the mares, the NPS dropped all their lawsuits. In other words, now that they had the monument to themselves, they didn't need to wave phony lawsuits under the noses of the survivors. Bobby Gray's widow and sons were left alone without their ranching heritage for support. They, too, will have plaques permanently erected on some wall of the NPS to commemorate their bravery and hardships for the future generations to view in awe.

Bobby Gray's house and most of the outbuildings were immediately sold to the NPS by the rich man at a sizeable profit and bulldozed away within a week After the valuables were properly disposed, which was in short order after his death. Cactus plants were planted in the wake of the bulldozers within the week. Bobby's home and corrals were on the border fence a half-mile west of the Lukeville port of entry. As far as the NPS is concerned today, this once beautiful ranch setting never existed. But it did! The ranch house and corrals had a mountain on its western side that shielded it from the harsh, afternoon sun. Plants and trees by the pond that was fed by a windmill are no longer there.

The few outbuildings were allowed to remain on the other brothers' individual ranch sites. They are maintained by the NPS with signs commemorating the handiwork of the pioneers who settled that portion of desert.

The relevance of these reports is that no other federal service can be so openly hypocritical!

Bobby Gray asked the kid, who made the pet of the wild donkey, to help gather his mares for the last time. The kid was in college, so his time was limited. The NPS were apparently going to hire contractors to trap them while Bobby was still alive.

I knew the NPS rangers, and I knew the superintendent of the monument. With the exception of one ranger, Thompson, the lot of them would poison their grandmothers if higher offices ordered it. This is where the weakness in our federal government lies, in the non-thinking category. There's nothing wrong with being loyal to an employer, but lying down and rolling over without question doesn't support a democracy, nor can a democracy remain strong with this type of hired help.

The border rider for the Agriculture Department's agency called APHIS (Animal, Plant, and Health Inspection Service) dropped by the Lukeville Port of Entry often. Rufus Allen was his name, the late brother of the late, famous singer, actor, and documentary narrator for Walt Disney, Rex Allen, of Wilcox, Arizona. Rufus Allen hauled a fat, overly pampered appaloosa in his horse trailer. He used the horse to rope Mexico's cattle that strayed over the border. Rufus didn't feel well in his twilight years, either. Some old cowboys like Rufus Allen and Bobby Gray lived in pain but never complained. He retired a couple years later and died shortly thereafter. In other words, Rufus wasn't physically fit to chase any of Bobby Gray's crazy mares. No one blamed him.

Rufus loaned the kid his fat appaloosa. The horse needed a good workout, anyhow. Rufus always said that. I had Buck, who was still thin, recuperating slowly from his skin and bones state at the time of his arrest a few months earlier.

The kid, whom I will call "Harry," and I rode north of Bobby's corrals on the border, approximately eight miles before finding the band of mares. Harry had located them at Tiger Tank the day before. Harry held fast in order to relieve me after I circled them from the north side, so I had the first run. They allowed me to get within a half-mile of them. I was a U. S. Customs Inspector, never qualified as a wild horse runner. The academy just doesn't teach it, but I had heard stories growing up in how easy it was to get in trouble chasing wild horses without enough manpower. Two or three extra saddle horses need to be on standby, fresh. Backups are needed when the ones being ridden got ready to drop from exhaustion.

The mares headed for Tiger Tank, which was south of us about two miles. They were running fast over the rough country. They knew their antagonists' horses would tire just the same as they would, so they were getting down to business.

I was on their eastern side as they ran. The nearest other watering would be six miles south of Tiger Tank at Bobby Gray's home corrals. That's where the mares were always corralled. I assumed they would head for that watering as we pushed them past Tiger Tank. They beat us to Tiger Tank and waited for us. They didn't head directly south but southeast to another watering on the border two miles east of the port of entry on the border. This watering is roughly eight miles across country. That was on my side. Buck was in bad shape, not having been ridden since his near starvation ordeal with the drug smugglers. He was already blowing hard but our job was to turn them back southwest.

The mares were smart. They knew where to go and were merely testing us for speed and durability. Harvey hadn't held back as much I did on the way to Tiger Tank, so the mares suspected he was the greatest threat. I had no idea that Buck still had the wind to catch the mares and turn them from their southeastern direction. I didn't urge him to do it. I didn't have the heart to ask him, but it was unnecessary. Buck performed the task at hand as if it were easy.

A better term for Buck was weak, yet he literally flew past of what I could ever expect of him. This also surprised the mares. The fastest of the band was a thoroughbred-looking mule. It flew ahead of the lead mare. All I had to do was ride. The mule turned back southwest and the mares followed after an extremely hard run for at least a half-mile. That's a long distance for a weak horse carrying a man and a saddle at full speed, especially when he was already winded. The miles already behind us had been slow in comparison to that one. Those young mule colts were fast as bullets. They led the mares once they learned which direction to run.

When they turned southwest, I jumped off Buck and loosened the cinch of my saddle. Sweat was pouring from underneath his belly in large streams and forming puddles underneath his heaving belly. There wasn't a dry spot on him. His nostrils were completely opened, revealing the reddened veins and arteries that were to help cool his system as he breathed. Harry was still keeping up with the mares on their northwestern side. He had helped corral them the last time, which were years prior and knew it was imperative to keep up. I couldn't keep up, not without killing my horse. No matter what the loss, Buck would not die of exhaustion at my hands.

The kid yelled occasionally behind the hills to keep me informed. Whether yelling shook the confidence of the pursued horses, I don't know. I can only imagine that it does, for horses are incredibly sensitive as well as intelligent. The mares would either head west or east once they reached Bobby's home corrals, still five miles south and a mile west.

I gave Buck about sixty seconds then jerked the cinch tight and swung on. Buck knew enough to keep up. I was confident that the mares would corral themselves, for they had already tested our speed and durability.

The sleek mule colts, leggy with small bellies in the sparse grazing, actually looked like racers if one ignored their long heads and ears. They could run like antelope, but they were scared and hugged the mares' sides as much as possible. What they wouldn't do was to give in to hysteria in the event heated races were still ahead. If one of the mares got too hot while running hard, she would panic and not turn back, even if one waved slickers in front of her face. Horses will get hysterical. I didn't expect this from the mule colts.

Once the mares had run a few miles, I was confident that they would corral themselves, especially after they've done it before. I also expected that they would slow down after running a few miles. They didn't. Harry knew they wouldn't, which was why I heard him yelling far ahead. They were going to beat us there about a half-mile, which was a bad sign.

Those five miles of hard running over the rough country took its toll on the fat appaloosa. Harry would be there to head them if they ran west of the corrals, if the fat horse was up to the task. He also had a mountain to help turn them back. I wasn't too worried.

The mares weren't about to be stopped at the corrals without a race, hence the word "Spoiled" for the mares did came into play once I arrived.

We were keeping sight of the mares' dust. I actually had to hold Buck back. A cowboy is a cowboy, and a cow horse is no different. Stubbornness always finds its way to enter situations going bad. Most people credit cowboys with something called proud. That's baloney. Without stubbornness, a cowboy or a cow horse wouldn't accomplish half of what they do. I was a Customs inspector and could care less if I ever saw another cattle ranch in my lifetime. I owed the cowboy tradition absolutely zero, especially after the gunsel cowboys today wear their hats while dancing. I am a great admirer of cowboy quality and tradition, but I wasn't about to kill that little buckskin whose proud heart outweighed his brains.

The mares raced the appaloosa west of the corrals and turned back at the mountain. I was hoping Harry would keep his distance, but the rougher country pushed him closer to the mares. He told me later that he had to really push his horse to head them, and without the mountain, he doubted if his horse could've managed.

The mares turned back east and held up at the corral gates without entering. They gave themselves a rest until I arrived. I was hoping that I could give Buck a rest before we actually began penning the horses. Heaven knows that the fat appaloosa needed a rest. He could've trotted over that six-mile run and still be winded.

I made myself as light as possible over Buck's shoulders during these miles and still felt the little horse's heart giving its very best. The mares were still waiting. I pulled up a quarter-mile on a small hill and spotted Harry. He was about a quarter-mile west and that far from the corrals and had already swung off and had his cinch loosened. Everything seemed in order. The mares couldn't go further south, for the corrals were on the border fence. They had already tried racing west. Their only chance was east, my side. I wanted to give my horse a little blowing time, also, but that wasn't going to happen. The mares suspected that I was too slow to head them, since they had to wait, and decided to give my horse the second test.

No problem. We were a little east of them, anyhow. I was surprised that the appaloosa was still on his feet. Personally, I'm never for pushing a horse or an airplane to the outer edge of its envelope. Harry was out of the race, anyhow. He wouldn't be able to back me up if the mares decided to turn back north behind me as I raced the leaders eastbound against the border fence.

When the mares broke east at their very best speed, even to this day, I still didn't believe that Buck was up to the task of turning them. They had a smooth, border fence road on which to run. We had deep and wide washes, cactus and boulders. What was certain, he would give it his best and then some. As the race began, I saw Harry out of the corner of my eye. He was swinging aboard to back us up. He had to try, even though the appaloosa would've fallen within 100 yards.

The mares began to stretch out on the smooth road on the international fence to give them an advantage. Buck still had the rocky arroyos and cholla cacti to face. Since the faster mules colts took the lead and with the mares literally leveling out, I knew that this was going to be worst race yet. Buck sensed this, also. When the first mare broke east of the corral instead of entering it, he was already at full speed over the rough ground. I never asked a thing of him. It was obvious to me that all I had to do was stay aboard.

The up and down country seemed to smooth out as we virtually flew over the shallow washes and slammed into the taller hills. A slower ride would've been rougher. Again, Buck had opened up with all he had. He knew the mares would give this last escape attempt their best shot. Suddenly, I could care less if the mares ever got corralled or not. The rancher was broke and ruined financially, anyway. The money they brought at a sale wouldn't be all that much.

I also knew that this particular run was the last these horses were ever going to have. They were the last horses to ever roam free on the Organ Pipe National Monument after some fifty or sixty years, long before the pioneer Gray and FDR, in their limited and sorry vision, made this magnificent wilderness a national monument.

I leaned forward and spoke encouraging words into Buck's ears, which were laid back against his neck. The wind blew tears of anguish from my eyes. He was jumping arroyos that I didn't think possible and reaching the tops of the next rocky hill with a speed and strength that I never knew existed in such a skinny little horse.

Some of the hills were taller and his front feet would strike the surface some two or three feet below the top at full speed. This is what a remarkable rock horse is all about. His knees didn't buckle, but somehow, divinely, or far beyond my comprehension, the front legs lifted him over the top without slowing us down. It was the most heart wrenching ride of my life!

The mares weren't turning and were abreast of us after a quarter-mile. The young mules were running like thoroughbreds on a track. They knew what the mares wanted them to do. They lengthened their lead on the mares. The lead mare, no doubt the matriarch, stretched herself out to her limit, also. The mule colts were all stretched out, running their absolute best. Buck saw them and didn't give up. He remained stretched out across the rough terrain. I couldn't believe it. No horse of that small size could carry my 170 pounds and my heavy saddle that fast and that far over that rough ground! It was the most remarkable and unbelievable ride of my life. I have been in many races on several cattle ranches prior to college and a federal career.

I didn't then, and I would never ask or urge any horse to do what that little buckskin was doing. One doesn't have to nudge a horse of that caliber to do his job, and I was feeling guilty for simply being aboard him at the time. This time my encouraging words were different:

"You don't have to do this, Buck! Just give it your best shot. No more. They can trap these damned mares if they get away!"

Slowly we passed the mares, which I thought would turn north behind me with Harry too far behind to back me up, but they didn't. Then the faster mule colts couldn't stand the lead without the mares. We weren't too far from Lukeville when they turned back, slightly less than a mile run, before Buck killed himself. The mares found the proper gate to the corrals a back west without trying us again.

The mares corralled themselves. Spoiled or not, they had actually played the game fairly, their last one. The mule colts hit the fence only once before settling down in the dusty middle of the milling mares as we loped to the entrance and closed the gate on the mares for the last time. The horse ranching era on the monument had closed its last page.

I led Buck back toward the corrals with the cinches hanging straight down. Three streams of water poured from his belly like a garden hose was held over his back. The big appaloosa, which did participate in the last run, had even larger streams of water pouring from him. It appeared as someone had turned over a barrel of water underneath him. After we let them blow about a fifteen minutes, I rode Buck slowly the five-plus miles back to the NPS corrals. It was also my last horse race, the best I've ever had the privilege of participating.

Harry refused to move the blowing appaloosa another inch and hobbled him there. He called the port of entry at Lukeville from Bobby Gray's house. Rufus Allen picked him up with the horse trailer where he stood.

What I just described is nothing compared with the old days of rounding up wild mares. The lighter cowboys, usually kids, have ridden circles that would cover as many as ninety miles in a day's time, not at full speed by any means. Their round up would cover hundreds of inner square miles. Their horses were built for it. They were grained with the best feed and conditioned for durability.

Weeks earlier, Buck had swollen knees. Because he was bordering complete starvation, I really didn't expect him to recover. It had been years since he had run. He was small, far too small, for me and my heavy tack to chase loose horses. I was ashamed for having chosen him, but as stated earlier, no other horse in our corrals would've been up to the task.

Buck had my respect long before I gained his--if I ever did. I have ridden far bigger and the most expensive breeds of cow horses by big name ranchers, such as Clarence Scarborough, Jr. His cow horses and race horses have earned him millions. His quarter-horse studs sold for the highest dollars. Hal Bogle, a mule man from the thirties also bred good cow horses, as did Frank Banks, a man named Hancock, Peter McQue, and dozens more like them. None of those horses, in my personal and limited experience, have ever been tested with the intensity for heart and stamina as Buck went through that day.

I've seen many horses fall under their riders that were running too fast for the terrain. I've always managed to keep up, but I would never ask a horse to go beyond what I thought he was capable. If you pay attention to your mount, he will honestly show you what he can and cannot do by his efforts.

Never in the years that I knew him, did Buck ever allow himself to be caught with a bridle as do most gentle horses. Even in the smallest of corrals, Buck insisted on being caught with a rope. He would kick anyone that hemmed him in a corner of a small corral. He demanded that respect as if he might be some old cowboy that had grown too burned out and cranky to properly communicate. One of the cowboys' philosophies, and they have many, is that if you reach your goals without proper respect, you have failed. Buck had that philosophy. He practiced it often. Although he was overqualified, Buck could never be a politician.

If Buck were caught, it was either by a well swung rope or else he came forward to place his head in the loop, which happened about two times in the years Tilton rode him. His mood actually depended upon the length and width of the corral and who was on the other end of the rope. His cow horse heritage controlled his mood swings, and he was never persuaded otherwise.

After he was caught it was bronc time all over again. Sixteen years old or more didn't amount to a bug in a pond to Buck. His game was wild and unbroken. In all his years of being a perfectly gentle horse, he would still lean back on all four feet until his belly almost touched the ground while his antagonist threw the saddle across his back. When real broncs do this, you can expect that they'll spring forward at about thirty mph, taking with them all that's attached, men, ropes, corral fences, sides of barns, anything.

Buck wasn't of that nature. He never sprang forward. One had to understand by his not practicing all these bad actions, an antagonist would appreciate his kindness. Right or wrong, that's the way I respected the old cowboys and cow horses. Humor them or else leave them alone.

The rollers in his nose moved like waves in a pond, snorting ill warnings to any and all people that dared approach him. My oldest little girl rode him in a local parade once. She fed the Customs horses in my care each time I was absent, which were many times over the years. She had never seen a bronc explode from that crouched position as Buck displayed, which is much like the stance a leopard takes before springing for its prey, so Buck's antics never impressed her. I've never seen a leopard spring for its prey, either, but I've read all Wilbur Smith novels.

Even when little Buck was tied to a post or tree and already saddled, the same melodrama had to be performed all over again each and every time he was approached, no matter how many times in a day he was approached, he demanded that you approach him slowly and cautiously. The fury he promised would match a woman's wrath. If he was tied hard and fast and got approached fast, he would leap back against the tie rope and try to break it. I saw him break a large limb from a tree once and drag it a quarter-mile before he was certain that he had taught us a lesson in manners. So approaching Buck entailed the tedious and gut-wrenching phoniness of telling him how bad he was and how scared of him we were. That seemed to appease his tremendous ego.

SCPO Tilton's waxed mustache probably weighed ten pounds. With rocks in his pocket, he would still fall short of 170 pounds, so he was just right for the little horse. Tilton played the game in dead earnest. He missed his calling by not being an actor, although he would laugh during his role at times. He would stop, inch forward, just like Buck was a green bronc, until he touched him, then the game was over. Approach him fast, like I did, he never failed to yank back on that rope with all his might and try to break it, then he would fight and paw and try to break any and everything in sight, including me.

This was quite a show whenever we were camped in the middle of the desert overnight. Buck was always tied to an ironwood or to a rotten branch of a palo verde. Our halters and tie ropes were strong enough to hold Brahma bulls, so he was unable to break them, but he could come close to uprooting the big trees that anchored him often in the desert.

We were camped west of Tule Well in the desert on the Cabeza Prieta Game Refuge, close to the Mexico border. Luis L'amour mistakenly called this windmill Papago Well in one of his books. An excellent writer was Mr. L'amour. However, keeping geography within correct proportion was never a necessary forte in fiction. In other words, he was wrong. Papago Well was thirty miles to the east of us. The only fence within fifty miles of us in any direction was the border. We had ridden west in the open desert at a slow pace for three days. An east-west freeway was about forty miles north of us.

We camped on a bare space of hard pan on the famous Devil's Highway, *El Camino del Diablo,* used by prison wagons between Tucson and Yuma during the nineteenth century. It paralleled the Mexico border, also. We anchored our horses each night to nearby trees with our strong lead ropes, and never camped where one rocky grave or more wasn't nearby. The graves had to be shallow with rocks piled on top of the bodies. Few to none were marked. Johnny pulled a water tank behind his truck that kept our horses watered. Alfalfa and oats were also plentiful in the bed of his truck. When the horses stood tied overnight in the desert, they did it knee deep in alfalfa and with plenty of oats and water.

We had made camp in mid-afternoon that day and made our horses comfortable before we drank, ate, and snoozed for a couple hours. At sundown we watered them again, and again at sunup. They never knew a big thirst on those long trips. We rode them with bridles over their nylon halters. The nylon lead rope was tied to the saddle strings under the horn. No one dared tie one of those seized horses with mere bridle reins in the open areas. Their natural instinct was to escape like any other convict. Bridle reins were kite strings to those seized horses.

Buck would be hard to catch out there in the wilderness. Everyone knew that. Tilton often refused to use normal branches to anchor Buck. He used the entire tree trunk. So after watering them at sundown, Tilton bedded Buck down amid plenty of oats and alfalfa, well under a huge limb of a palo verde. That limb was twice the size of my thigh, even though the palo verde's wood breaks almost as easy as balsa. That limb would require two horses like the little buckskin to break. Anything smaller would've been a match stick.

What Tilton had failed to do that one time was to attach the big nylon rope to Buck's halter. He did an excellent job of tying the rope around the huge limb but not to the halter. As long he stood by the horse's head, it was fine. That was the time, the only time he forgot to fasten the lead rope!

An act that stupid might never happen again inside another 500 years or so, then it has to be performed by someone within the federal services more akin to the U. S. Border Patrol. However, like Tilton, Buck thought that he was attached to the rope.

We ate supper, told jokes and war stories around the fire, and listened to some ignorant-beyond-belief, liberal talk show host on the good-time radio from the Oakland Bay area. We laughed until we became bored with him, then laughed at the irony of even listening to myriads of maniacal ravings. At bedtime I placed my cot about fifty yards away from the fire, out of hearing range of Weldon and Tilton, who both snored in decibels at the thunderstorm level.

At first light it was time to feed and water the horses, then have breakfast.

"Bring a rope!" Tilton suddenly yelled when it was time to water his horse.

I did. The loop was ready but I wasn't about to get close enough in open country to a horse like Buck to toss it. Tilton was frozen solid. His hand was out and he was wooing Buck with the same old sickening "Easy--boy" routine that I've heard hundreds of times. I encouraged him.

Believe it or not, as Tilton approached, Buck stepped back and crouched as if he were about to break the lead rope. The lead rope lay loose on the ground directly in front of his legs. Buck was wild loose. He just didn't realize it. He'd been that way, completely free, all night long!

Tilton played the game by saying, "Easy, boy," twenty or thirty more times. Buck's cup of ego surely overflowed. He crouched back and his nose actually went up as if he were straining against a tie rope! The rollers in his nose were at full throttle and his eyes were showing their whites as his full attention was focused on Tilton. His nose and neck was actually stretching out as he crouched down! That big phony was pretending to be straining against a rope that wasn't even there! He even prepared to set his rear hooves into the dirt as if he were going to uproot a tree or break his tie rope! His nose and neck became one, long line! Incredible--I have never seen anything quite like that! That horse was role playing! His belly was almost touching the ground as if he were testing that tie rope to its maximum strength!

Tilton took his time. I got as close as I dared with my rope, hoping to hoolihand him if he broke into a run, Tilton, not the horse. I wouldn't have stood a chance with that little buckskin at that distance. But I could've roped Tilton and saved him the effort of chasing after the horse on foot.

Lots of horses will stand overnight if they think they're tied. But to stretch back against a rope that wasn't even there? What a phony!

When Tilton touched his shoulder, everyone relaxed. The entire Horse Patrol was out there standing like statues, hardly breathing until the tense moments passed.

After Tilton had secured the lead rope to the halter, Buck was sleeping on his feet again. He reminded me of how he needed the catering to and humoring of a cantankerous, old, spoiled-rotten cow horse! He had made monkeys out of us for years. We supposed it was okay to keep it up.

Chapter 16

The El Salvadorian Disaster

July 4, 1980, a date I shall never forget, nor will the families of victims of the worst and most unnecessary tragedy ever witnessed in the history of southern Arizona's unforgiving desert. They were victims of premeditated murder as well as rape and strong-arm robbery. Such were the motives of Mexico's sourest illegal entrants, the guides or smugglers, sometimes called "Coyotes," that lived in Sonoyta, Sonora, Mexico.

The victims, twenty-two El Salvadorians, consisted of teenagers, older men, and women from thirty to fifty. They were once among the affluent of El Salvador. They lived well in their two-class, socialistic society. Suddenly, as it sometimes happens in socialists countries, they had to flee for their lives. Their government just got ousted and replaced with another revolutionary that wanted everyone dead in the old government. One socialist dictator overthrowing another has been a long time practice in countries south of our own border. Socialist governments have changed little since the Spaniards brought the world's sorriest type of government in the world to North and South America.

These guides or coyotes seldom treated their own countrymen as they treated foreigners. Their foreign clientele would always have money. If they were from anywhere south of Mexico, they would be taken into the interior of the desert, robbed, sometimes beaten, then left behind to die without water. Very few Mexicans will pay a coyote to guide them across the desert. They know how to walk toward a mountain peak and pick out another once that one is passed. They seldom have money for guides or coyotes.

These Salvadorians had money. They were unequipped to walk. The ladies had thin dresses that were expensive and fashionable. Their shoes were light duty sandals, pumps, and light gym shoes. They carried their high heels in their luggage. The men wore their dress pants and shoes with no hats. They had toiletries in their luggage such as shaving soap, lotion, plenty of razors and powder. The women packed perfumes, plenty of underclothes and hose.

All were native of a tropical environment. They had never seen a desert, nor did they have the least idea where a desert might be found. No one advised them in how to prepare for desert travel by foot. Their guides simply planned to rape the women, rob them all, and leave them to perish in the arid wilderness.

Once the Salvadorians learned that they were going to be raped and plundered, they left their money behind after the first night of their attack. They were hardly five miles north of the border fence in a twelve-hour walk! They had no water. Their guides carried their water and food. What they weren't told was that the guides would refuse to share it.

As expected, they became easy picking for the cowardly coyotes. However, the coyotes made fatal errors of their own.

On the previous, night, Thursday, the guides got drunk on part of their advance pay, as it was related to me. The four of them each carried one or two gallons of water. One gallon of water is good for one person to walk one day of daylight, providing they had plenty of rest that night. They entered the United States on Friday morning, July 2, 1980.

Since they didn't walk further than five miles the first day, the Salvadorians didn't begin to die from heat exhaustion until Saturday morning. Many of them died throughout Saturday night. I'm no expert in determining the times of death. I can, however, recognize the cause of death by heat exhaustion under the circumstances. On Sunday morning, some of the dead still had moisture in their bodies, still not bloated and expelling huge amounts of gas. The amount of green flies on the bodies are clues to how much gas is escaping the bodies as they begin to bloat. It's also a clue in how long they have been dead. If I could get within four hours in determining the time of death, I'd feel like an expert, but I cannot.

A young man and woman were lying embraced under thin mesquite limbs as I found them. They appeared peaceful, resting on their sides and facing one another with their arms clinging to one another. I wanted to believe they were asleep. Rigor mortis was strong in their bodies. The flies had found no more than their noses and mouths.

One body bloated in the sun was blackened and swollen to a point where she appeared to weigh in excess of 300 pounds at five-two or thereabouts. She would be the first to die Saturday morning, right before she reached the small grove of short mesquite bushes. She collapsed and died early. The afternoon sun turned her black and slowly began to cook her body. The gas that expelled from her body was strong, but not yet strong enough to attract the buzzards or other carrion eaters.

Three women were found alive in this group. All three were not destined to die of heat exhaustion. All three would have been dead by noon on Sunday, however, from the far more torturous death of dehydration. Two were in their late teens. One proved to be an attractive woman of thirty-two. U. S. Border Patrol airplanes found them and guided us there.

The lady that Tilton and I worked with later told the Border Patrol agents that the lady lying next to her had asked the guide to kill her before he took off with the water. He did. He planned to suffocate her in the sand but there was insufficient sand. He pressed her face down so heavy against the solid earth that he broke her nose while he choked her. This had to be early Saturday night, for she hardly appeared dead to me when we found her on Sunday morning. I shook her ankle time and again to wake her and tell her everything was okay. However, rigor mortis and the green flies collecting at the hem of her skirt told me she had been dead long enough to expel gases.

The guide (coyote) who killed her did not survive. We found him dead two hours earlier that same Sunday morning. He was out of water and had died of heat exhaustion hours earlier.

The coyotes had told the Salvadorians the same story they told all people from the scumbag dictatorships south of Mexico, where many Americans go to spend their vacations. The coyotes told the people to trust them, that the United States police were killers, rapists, and robbers. They claimed the cowardly police never entered the desert except in airplanes. What the Salvadorians heard was believable to them, for they knew brutal police well having grown up among their socialist nation. They had no idea that the United States of America had civilized police forces. They only believed they could find work and homes in the USA if they dodged the police.

The reason they didn't stop and reside in Mexico was similar to why they left El Salvador. It was the same reason Mexico's own people were abandoning it. Socialism. Mexico is different from most socialist countries. It elects its dictators each six years and call them *Presidentes.* In fact, Mexico blatantly calls itself "The United States of Mexico." There are thirty-two states in Mexico--and they are very well *united!* If not, Mexico City would know the reason why in less time than it takes to ask.

"**The** United States Police are dangerous. They are killers. We will lead you across the desert where the police never go. We will guide you and show you the water. We will carry your water and food. You carry your belongings. The police will never find you with us."

The Salvadorians believed them. They paid them in part Thursday night.

The U. S. Border Patrol said there were four coyotes. Actually, I only knew of one, *El Rato.* If there were others, I never saw them. I knew "The Rat" by reputation, who was known to lead foreigners into the desert, yell "Police!" and run back to Mexico with their water. This would be ten or twenty miles deep into the desert after he had collected their money. He was approximately twenty-four years old!

Tilton and I rescued three men one afternoon who had paid The Rat and were left to die in the desert. They said The Rat suddenly yelled for everyone to run for their lives, that the police were coming. Since they were thirsty and tired, they simply sat down to accept their fate with the police. When the police didn't come, one of them walked back to the border and asked Mexico's immigration in Sonoyta, Sonora for help.

The local authorities in Mexico Immigration asked Tilton and me to use our horses to go after the men. We were extremely lucky to find them alive.

At that time, I had a strange thought that I would soon see this "Rat" character dead. I didn't think that I or anyone else would have to kill him. I only believed that I would soon find him dead. Of course, if we had to kill him in self-defense, that would be okay, too.

The El Salvadorian incident made the national evening news everyday for a week. Many articles were written about it. None of which, from any media at any time, depicted anything near the complete truth. I was there and I still don't know all of it. So was the U. S. Border Patrol. What they reported was more true than not, but far from complete and accurate.

The news media were biased against our U.S. laws, much like they are today. They, being the liberal souls they are by nature, found fault with our U.S. Border Patrol and blamed everyone, even U. S. citizens, everyone except those responsible, for the deaths of the El Salvadorians. There was no need to be alarmed at such ignorant talk at the time in 1980. It was how our news media worked, stupid and irresponsible. They call themselves "Progressive," instead of "Backward." Amazing!

I still fail to understand what journalists have against truth in journalism. I cannot understand their editors. I don't understand the biased anchormen on the evening news programs. They report partial truths, half-truths, but seldom report the complete truth. Perhaps it's no longer taught in schools of journalism. Sensationalism sells. This is the only truth that I have learned from them.

One news anchorman reported: "We all must share at least a little blame for that disaster."

Whaat? Let's give this a second thought. Just how dumb does that man think we are? He failed to tell us how we are to blame, just that we were supposed to feel guilt for the many deaths of innocent people from a socialist government? We were to take his word on that? Such a journalist must have possessed a deep gift of astute thinking that's out of his listeners' and readers' reach. I submit that this reporter is incapable of always being fair and truthful in his reporting. The name Dan Rather comes to mind as the rocket scientist who stated that ludicrous suggestion. I only saw CBS cameras at the scene. Whoever it was, I submit that this man could not think deep enough to penetrate his own shadow.

My endeavor in this chapter will present more of the truth of the incident and provide a basis for the disaster. If anyone is at fault here, other than the dictatorships of El Salvador and Mexico, the guides or coyotes, and the El Salvadorians, themselves, then I have no idea who it might be. If Dan Rather wishes to share the blame in this, he's free to knock himself out.

Had the El Salvadorians told the U. S. Border Patrol agents the truth on Saturday, July 3, perhaps more than three people could have been saved the next day. That meant the B. P. would have had to go in after them on Saturday night, and they might or might not have been successful in finding them. Two good trackers in the U.S. Border Patrol worked out of the local station in Why, Arizona. I think they would have been successful. I doubt if I could have saved them Saturday night. The B.P. had already worked their shift earlier that day. They would not have minded the inconvenience but they called us instead. They told us no more than what they had been told. "Women and kids were dying in the desert." Then they went home and went to bed.

That's all the information I gathered. We might have back tracked those apprehended on Saturday afternoon, but the agents were not sure, themselves, in what direction to look. For the Salvadorians they captured were delirious and not willing to tell them necessary information. These El Salvadorians can share in the blame with the air head that suggested all U. S. citizens must feel guilt.

Perhaps the Salvadorians' judgment was obscured by the Mexico guide that murdered their people. I only know that I was there from early Sunday morning to late Sunday afternoon, and I'm not accepting an ounce of blame for their tragedy.

Until that Fourth of July weekend in 1980, I never really believed that even the smallest percentage of people that entered the U. S. surreptitiously would choose to perish when safety was within an easy grasp. Thirteen of twenty-six people perished hardly three miles from the highway! Four of the twenty-six, according to the U. S. Border Patrol agents in the area, were smugglers of people. This would leave twenty-two innocent people to perish. I know that one of those four alleged smugglers perished during the same night as his innocent victims, *El Rato,* The Rat. Varying reports from the B.P. pointed to several smugglers.

I heard that thirteen survived and thirteen innocent perished. I believe that number is correct. It depended upon who was talking and whether or not the agent knew what he was talking about. If the number is true, then the four coyotes perished. No one knows except a very few of the U.S. Border Patrol, and they may not be sure. Too many B. P. officers told too many stories to the news media to be accurate.

I know for a fact that the El Salvadorians did not enter the United States where the U. S. Border Patrol told the news reporters. I know where they entered because Johnny and I later back tracked them from where they perished. After the manner in which the B. P. from Gila Bend, Why, and Tucson conducted themselves that Sunday, I had enough of them portraying themselves heroes.

There were many beautiful women in that party of 22 El Salvadorians. The entire group were educated and accustomed to a high standard of living, who, overnight, found themselves enemies of their own government. They fled for their lives northward with a few clothes and what money they had in their homes. That's where the tragedy began. *El Salvador!* Not here! I don't know if our State Department sent money to both governments in El Salvador or not. Perhaps Dan Rather can explain why our State Department asks our Congress to appropriate our tax money for socialist governments. That is called stealing from the poor to give to the evil, for no one but the leaders of socialist governments receive this money. Not a penny feeds a hungry mouth!

As mentioned earlier, under a hot sun in low humidity, a gallon of water will keep a single person healthy and strong through twelve hours of daylight if energy is conserved with a lot of time in the shade. Under the hot sun, healthy and conditioned men with hangovers will die fast without water to guzzle consistently. The U. S. Customs Patrol received the information from the U. S. Border Patrol about 9:00 PM, Saturday, July 3, 1980: "Fourteen women and children may be trapped in the desert!" They had no idea how many were in the desert. No children were ever found or missed. I found no tracks of children leaving the area where the victims were found.

The B.P. had arrested survivors earlier in the day at approximately 6:00 PM. They told us exactly where they arrested the people on

Highway 85 between Lukeville and Why, Arizona. They didn't tell us how many and I never asked. All the survivors were delirious from thirst. Some had drunk shaving lotion and urine. One older man in the group had died with the innocents before help arrived on a Saturday afternoon by the U. S. B. P.

I looked at the ground at 10:00 PM that night where they were arrested and found no westbound tracks. Tracks are numerous on both sides of the highway that are made daily by illegal immigrants. I called Tilton by radio and told him that the ground was too rocky and too many extra tracks for me to successfully find their trail at night. If any of the B. P. agents thought they could have, then they would have already done it hours before I arrived there.

The one woman that saved them had apparently waited too long in notifying the authorities to save two of the young men. This was possibly due to the smugglers having threatened her and her party with death if she told anyone. This is rumor that salvages some hint of practicality of the entire situation.

This lady might've saved more, but in my opinion, by the time she opened up to the B.P. that found her, the remainder of those that perished was already dead or dying. If not for her fear, we could have looked earlier!

Actually, a higher than average humidity had accompanied the heat all summer long that summer in 1980. A person could be mummified in a three-day period in the lower humidity, give or take a few hours. When the humidity is high enough to register in the desert, it merely adds discomfort to the high temperatures. The last clouds I recalled in the daylight extended back many months.

Any veteran illegal from Mexico knows better than to tackle the long desert treks during the summer months of peak heat. They used the shorter routes or the highways at night. These veteran illegals are the hardest to apprehend. When they see headlights coming at night, they walk off the road twenty or thirty feet and squat down behind a bush. Cars are rare at night. For all practical purposes, the illegal immigrants have the highway to themselves.

It was late Saturday afternoon of July 3. A scared lady, afoot, an El Salvadorian, weary and grimy from dust and in a dress too nice for everyday wear, entered Joe Flores' Chevron Station at Why, Arizona (pop. 50). She quickly purchased three six packs of cold Coca Cola and left without talking--by foot!

Mrs. Flores, the cashier, suspected the worst and acted promptly. No sooner did the lady began walking in the hot sun back south did Mrs. Flores telephone the U. S. Border Patrol's Office in Why, Arizona.

The USBP agents on duty responded and drove south less than a mile before intercepting the scared woman that was loaded with three six-packs of not-so-cold soda pop. She was saving people's lives who were dying of thirst!

She was extremely frightened, they later explained. She wanted nothing to do with the police and refused to explain the urgency of her situation. The agents instinctively knew that she was much more than a simple illegal entrant for a number of reasons. She was dressed too smart, too scared of the police, wasn't used to walking, and lacked sensible footwear. After an hour or two, near sundown, she began to cry and explained her situation. She claimed that people were dying.

She led them to the group she had left near the highway earlier that afternoon as the sun was setting! This was six miles south of Why. She had walked that far and had used that much valuable time. The cowardly and lying smugglers had performed their scare tactics well.

The B. P. found three, perhaps four, depending upon who was talking, dead in the small party in a brushy area near the highway. A young man had gone berserk after drinking shaving lotion and urine. He died while the others attempted to hold him still. An old man in the group had died peacefully. All of the small group were scared of the police and didn't want to talk. They wished to have no contact B. P., even during the pending death of their comrades they had left behind! With this in mind, I find it difficult to understand how Dan Rather could share the blame in their deaths.

Typically, they all expressed their desire to be in the United States and consistently claimed fear of our police. Their hope, perhaps, was that someday the citizens of the United States would sympathize with them and do away with our dreaded immigration officers. No one, not even a priest, could have convinced them that they could have no better friends in the United States than the U.S. Border Patrol.

Fourteen people, perhaps more, were thought to be somewhere in the wilderness. Some were small children, they claimed. This was not true. I counted nine dead and three alive. All were mature people. No tracks of children had left the scene.

The Border Patrol had notified the superintendent of the Organ Pipe National Monument of the situation at 9:00PM, Saturday. Mr. Wallace, a sensible man with thirty-plus years with the NPS, faced too much with too little information. He called Tilton at home, who called me that Saturday night while I was on patrol in a sedan. He ordered me home in order that I could get ready for an early morning's ride. He said that the "Bee Pee" were still receiving conflicting stories from the survivors, and that the whole thing was one big mess. It would be best if we all organized with a central command at the NPS headquarters. Mr. Wallace, the Superintendent of the Organ Pipe National Monument, was a seasoned leader of rescue operations.

The B. P. cannot be at fault here. They couldn't learn the numbers, directions, or anything. In fact, I actually believed that they had already found the whole bunch. It wasn't likely that the party would've split up. It's extremely unlikely that people would perish in the desert some three miles west of the highway.

I was wrong!

The agreement to meet and organize early the following morning would happen at the Visitor's Center and Administrative offices of the Organ Pipe National Monument. This was five miles north of the Lukeville, Arizona Port of Entry. The mission would fall under the direction of Superintendent Wallace. The Border Patrol Station at Why would be present, along with the U.S. Customs Patrol and the Pima County Sheriff's deputies. The meeting would commence at 0500 hours.

Everyone would be fresh in the morning and with the same amount of information. The U. S. Border Patrol failed to show. The County Sheriff was represented by local deputies who were well trained in search and rescue. The Air Branch of the U. S. Customs Patrol from Tucson was present with a Huey 500 D, a neat helicopter on indefinite loan from the U. S. Army. U. S. Customs have used it successfully on many search and rescue missions.

Several vans from the news media were there. I read the letters on one van from Tucson, an NBC affiliate. One of their female reporters had everything that would turn the world's most beautiful movie star enviously green. I can't remember her name. Only my wife was prettier. All three major networks aired the tragic event nationwide later that day and continued to do so.

I saddled Clyde and leaped aboard the monumental palomino that had performed his usual ritual of twisting, head slinging, and dancing around while being saddled and mounted. I had, apparently, erringly placed a watermelon between my saddle and his back again, so we spun and kicked up a few times until I thoroughly understood that Clyde was in charge and could unload me at his discretion, anytime and at any place. I petted his neck and wooed him with humble words, acknowledging his superiority, intelligence, and good looks with all the humility I could muster. It always worked. That horse, a former drug smuggler, had an ego that would dwarf Bill Clinton's!

Tilton yelled something like I was his son or something and to get the hell back to where he was still saddling up. He said that we had no time to parade in front of a pretty reporter.

Clyde did!

Tilton was always slow in saddling. Our corral was 200 yards from the Visitors' Center and well out of view of the cameras. The reporters didn't see me or Clyde, but they surely heard Tilton yell. No doubt, they also heard Clyde snorting and passing sharp blasts of gas from the other end as he crow-hopped all over the place.

At this time the Huey cranked up and went airborne. I was about to radio them that Tilton still needed another twenty or thirty minutes to saddle up, a task that requires about one minute for normal people. But Tilton swung aboard Buck as the helicopter thundered forward. There was no briefing with him or me that morning. I felt like a blind man on an Easter Egg hunt. The Huey was on the same radio frequency as the hand-held radios carried by Tilton and me. I immediately turned the radio off and stowed it inside my saddle bag. Helicopter pilots have never learned how to stop talking into the microphones attached to their helmets once they're airborne. I had already asked one pilot why this was so.

The pilot explained that it was there (the microphone) and somebody had to use it. He said that it was embarrassing and awkward as hell for anyone else to get their lips close enough to talk into the low gain microphones attached to their helmets while they flew. I never asked again.

Tilton told the pilots that we were headed directly north on the highline road paralleling the north-south Highway 85. The pilot flew in front of us but at a faster pace, much to Clyde's dissatisfaction. He wanted to race the chopper. There was an over cast.

The auctioneer-type pilot had already commenced mouthing several sentences involving about 2,000 words each. Tilton mercifully turned the volume down and saddle-bagged the radio. We were in an easy canter, easy on horses and riders, but still in a ground-covering pace. Darkness turned to a hazy gray in the early dawn. The Ajo Mountains would protect us from the early sun but not for long.

For some reason, taking a chance on losing my hat, I looked straight up while the wind whipped past my face. There was still a solid cloud cover. *Very unusual!* That explained the cool temperature. The cloud cover would prove its significance later.

The pilot, pausing long enough to see if anyone was listening to his modest oration, called us. I advised Tilton to ignore him, so he answered as fast as possible.

"Go ahead!"

Ranger Thompson with the NPS was on board. His voice came over the radio from his individual mike. "We have a dead one directly underneath us on the road."

We mentally marked the spot still a mile or so distant and advised them to continue to the scene near the highway some ten miles further north. We would apprise them later of the scene surrounding the dead one.

I cannot explain why, but the dead man's identity suddenly jumped out at me before I even dismounted. He was face down. I had never seen this man, but I had wanted to meet with him for almost two weeks in the open desert. His seriously dead body was what remained of the notorious *El Rato*. He had no identification, yet I immediately believed who the corpse once had been!

I pulled at his chin to get a view of his face. The tiny mustache was there. The cold body, full or rigor mortis, was somewhere in his early twenties. He had stripped himself down to his shorts as many men do when dying of heat exhuastion. As a layman, I guessed he had died about six hours earlier. A green substance oozed from his right ear. The ear drum had apparently exploded from too many freight trains running in his head. He had died a rather painless death, obviously, except for the bursted ear drum. His empty water bottle was perched high in the limbs of an ironwood tree by Ranger Thompson for our benefit. The man had collapsed about one-quarter mile west of Highway 85! Close but no cigar for The Rat. I felt comforted in that I had seen the Rat dead. From that moment on, I gave it no further thought.

"So how can you be so sure that this is The Rat?" Tilton asked, even though he believed the same thing.

It was simple. Here was a guide, a coyote, who had left his party. Who else but The Rat would do that with the water? The empty water jug and the fact that his body wasn't entirely dehydrated indicated that he had died from heat exhaustion, not enough water to keep his body strong. The fact that he had stripped down indicated that he lacked sufficient oxygen to his brain. He had died after the sun went down. He wasn't sunburned and was lying in the open instead of the shade. His bare feet were not scarred or cut. I figured his clothing was somewhere in the premises but I haven't to this day made an effort to locate them. Even though the body lay innocent, I would've been in favor of burning it in order that it wouldn't foul the buzzards.

We made our report by radio. Ranger Thompson later agreed that the body used to house the spirit of the notorious Rat. He had also taken a brief moment to examine the body or make sure that it was dead. The Border Patrol later concurred that the body once belonged to The Rat. Perhaps some of them had seen him.

I salvaged what I could from the television news at home. I don't know who's to be credited with all the information that Tilton and I learned from the three major networks on this search and rescue mission, the B. P. or the creative thoughts of reporters.

The pilot then radioed us moments later that he would have to fly eighty miles north to Gila Bend, the nearest place to refuel his helicopter. The 120-mile flight from Tucson to Lukeville had drained his fuel supply to the half-way marker. We could count him gone for at least two hours.

I didn't know from where he called at the time but later learned that it was from a clearing northwest of us. They landed at that site about three miles northwest. Ranger Thompson tied abandoned clothes to the top of the tall brush in order that we would find it without having to continue back tracking the smuggler.

From the suspect body of The Rat, we had headed northwest. I noticed only once that the gray dawn was still with us but had forgotten about the cloud cover. A mile later we spotted two single-engine aircraft. They circled over the wide spot of green in a distant draw where Ranger Thompson had flagged it. They didn't see us, for they were still a few miles away. We trotted our horses in their direction through the rough country and galloped over the smoother parts.

What happened next is definitely not written to discredit anyone. They are simple facts:

We watched the airplanes circle. The small patch of green was a mesquite grove situated in a large draw in the desert floor. Articles of clothing also marked the spot in trees. We watched as we rode, still trotting and loping as the terrain dictated.

Strange! Other horses were galloping fast around the green spot! *"What in the hell is going on?"* I thought.

I counted at least four riders riding hell bent, single file, in a circle around that large green grove of mesquite and ironwood. I failed to understand the urgency and the waste of horseflesh.

Tilton reined up. "What the hell's going on?"

I could hear the faint roar of a motorcycle. Sure enough, a small dirt bike would circle the green occasionally leaving a tall rooster tail of dust behind it. We called the pilot of our Huey and learned that the two small planes circling the area belonged to the U. S. Border Patrol, that they had been guided there by the helicopter pilot. The airplanes were circling for our benefit, waiting for us to catch up. They had no control over the hysterical B.P. agents riding in circles beneath them.

The riders circling the green were all B.P. agents. I never knew they had horses. Tilton told me later that they rented some horses from town as soon as they learned that Customs had organized a Horse Patrol that was successful in interdicting smuggled drugs. It was some sight, watching the riders circle the area like Indians circling a wagon train in some movie. The motorcycle, when it moved, kept kicking high rooster tails of dust behind it. They were waiting for us to arrive and decided to pass the time in a less boring way. This is what we surmised later.

We arrived and received no greetings from anyone. The riders continued to circle in a fast gallop. Their horses were wet with sweat and winded. Neat piles of folded clothing was everywhere inside the opening of green. It appeared as if someone had spent the night here. On the ground partially underneath rocks was American money, twenties and many paper bills from El Salvador. Again, Tilton looked at me as if he didn't know what to make of this.

"What the hell's going on here, Homer?"

He knew as much as I, but he never passed the opportunity to be sarcastic, so I quickly dug out my best response. "The riders circling us are Indians disguised as the "Bee Pee." They are harmless, but don't stare at them directly or make any move for your weapon. This irritates them even if they aren't showing aggression."

Tilton and I recognized all of them. He still said, "I think they're bee pee. The one on the motorcycle isn't in uniform, but he's an agent, although I don't recognize his face."

I grew tired of the movie game. I made an assumption. "Someone in trouble has camped here overnight. They obviously moved on with lighter loads. They purposely left their money behind to keep their guides from stealing it. So they left here before daylight. Now, you sarcastic horse's butt, what did I leave out?"

"How long ago?" he demanded.

"I have no idea. The day before yesterday. I don't know! The tracks of the women appear about two hours old. Realistically, a day." Then the motorcycle rider zoomed in beside us, scaring Clyde out of his already partially-abandoned mind. The bike rider was an acquaintance from my college years, Sul Ross State College in Alpine, Texas! I didn't recognize him at the time. He lived in the dorm where I was the assistant manager fourteen years prior.

He didn't greet me, either, figuring I was still the same dorm managing jerk that I was in college, so he said later. I stand guilty back then of insisting that all stereos were off at Ten P.M. I tolerated no girlish shouts in the male dorm, meaning no excessive noise from kids that were too old for high school and still too young to be separated from their mommies. The rules were necessary to preserve my sanity--nothing else. I needed to study to make my grades whether anyone else did or not. The library was far more noisier than my dorm, which just happened to be the quietest on the campus.

"What's the matter with your horse?" These were his first words. "Is he a bit spooky?"

"I can only guess," I said. "What're you guys doing over here? I thought everyone was supposed to meet at the Visitors' Center."

One of the riders came galloping in and pulled his horse's head up like a roper training his horse. His horse was lathered and blowing hard. I knew him and always enjoyed his company. He was a fair man that was always friendly and upbeat. While Clyde was dragging me backward again with the bridle reins, I popped off at him first.

"What were you chasing out there, your horse's tail?"

"What's wrong with your horse?" he asked, ignoring the more important question.

The motorcycle rider answered for me. "He's choosey of the company he keeps!"

He ignored that. "Homer, what kept you guys? You're always late!"

The airplanes were circling overhead. The B.P. horseman reported to them over another frequency, that we late arrivals were Charley (Customs). Obviously, the pilots were tired of waiting on us, too.

"People were here!" I shouted to him above the noise of the motorcycle, whose rider revved its engine as if it were about to die each time I talked.

"Yeah! No joke!" he shouted back.

I threw up my hands in exasperation. "So where did they go? You've been circling the area!"

He and the motorcycle rider both pointed northeast. I nodded up at Tilton and swung aboard Clyde. The proper thing to do was to follow the tracks northeast to where the Border Patrol had already rescued them the past evening. That would confirm my suspicions that the entire group was found the day before. Clyde continued to run and march in place while I squared myself in the saddle. The motorcycle rider had followed me right up to the stirrups. I ignored him, silently sending a mental message to Clyde to go ahead and kick the top part of his head off. I called to the horseman:

"You guys might want to keep on circling here in case they come back!"

Tilton murmured quietly: "Or until your horses turn to butter."

Neither of them responded. They just sat there watching us while Tilton repacked his mouth with chewing tobacco. I can imagine that their horses appreciated the break. We left the opening of the circle of trees on the obvious trail of the immigrants. I would've guessed anywhere from fifteen to fifty people had made the trail at first glance. They were in single file, and the trail was deep in the soft areas. Not surprisingly, the airplanes both shot overhead us in the direction of the trail. The pilots could track a visible trail at full speed. I was glad they were there, especially since our helicopter was gone.

Not too surprisingly, either, the four horsemen and one motorcycle sped passed us on both sides, whipping and spurring, spending every ounce of energy their horses could spare. Clyde temporarily lost his mind again. Little Buck didn't seem to notice. I suggested to Tilton that we maintain a sensible pace, that we were in a terribly big desert. Besides, all of this was the bee pee's hummer. Tilton agreed. However, the Border Patrol was only waiting for us. They had agreed to allow us to help them. That was progress, but then, they needed us and knew it. They would be stealing all the press coverage later, since we weren't allowed to talk with reporters.

A mile later the airplanes began to circle again. So did the B.P.'s horses. This time a Border Patrol pilot came up on our frequency. "We have a live one here, can you guys come up here and help her? Hey--there's two more alive!"

Tilton and I both allowed our horses to set their own speed over that fast mile of easy terrain. Horses love to run and race when they're fresh and free from senseless urging. The pilot guided us to the live one with his left wing pointed in her direction. I'm glad he had our frequency. The ground troops of the bee pee had been circling for quite some time now on their winded horses. They sped in and out of an extremely wide area of dead bodies stretched out everywhere. I thought Clyde would surely lose the remainder of his witless brain. Not so. He remained respectful after his mile run.

Again, what happened in this chapter is the complete truth other than senseless conversation between Tilton and myself. Both of us stopped at the live person. The pilot urged us to go 100 yards east and find two more live bodies. I told the pilot to get a handle on his people and direct them there. We were going to have our hands full.

He came back rather emotional. "Just what the hell do you think I've been doing for the last hour? We need some help out here!"

From his tone, I knew that he had now disregarded both of us as useless help. I looked over my shoulder east and was about to go there when two horses reined in to a sharp halt from a hard run at the area of the live people, their horse's back feet underneath them left a solid ten feet of figure eleven skid marks.

I said over the radio: "Your people have found them!"

There was no answer, indicating that he had already switched off their Charley channel and were back on their frequency. A dead woman lay a few feet away. Another woman, about thirty feet away in the open had been dead more than a day in the sun. She was black and bloated. The stench caused me to hold a handkerchief over my nose and mouth.

The live lady's appearance was a picture that I'll never forget. If you've never experienced a person dying of dehydration, here's the most accurate description that I can recall.

She appeared to be a live mummy! Her brown leathery skin was almost paper thin and stretched tight across her skull. Her eyes were flat and well sunken into deep sockets. Her lips were flat and cracked upward a half-inch or more. She couldn't move any part of her body, except her right wrist. It was pointed up with the elbow on the ground and remained there, too stiff to drop back down.

This meant that her blood was like molasses, too thick to bleed and circulate through the muscles properly. She had raised it at the sound of the airplanes. She could not close her eyelids! There wasn't enough moisture for the lids to slide, but I could see them both twitching in an attempt to move. The eyelids were stuck to the dry surface of her flattened eyeballs.

Then I noticed something else! My shadow was suddenly over her head, protecting her eyes. It was rather sudden. *My shadow?*

Tilton and I both looked up at the same time. We both saw the clouds overhead breaking up. We had ridden there at the exact time the sun was coming out! Her eyes wouldn't have lasted another two minutes in the direct sunlight!

Believe me, I'm purposely writing this in favor of the Almighty, Himself. I saw this with my own eyes! So did Tilton. The sky parted and unleashed a terrible atmosphere of oven-like heat during that very moment! I had thought it was still dawn, but the sun was high above the Ajo Mountains. I glanced at Tilton, who was lost in one of his rare, silent moments. We haven't seen an overcast in months!

I asked: "What do you have to say about that, heathen?"

"I think that we happened to be here at the right place at the right time, and don't call me a heathen, hypocrit!"

"Coincidence?" I asked.

"No." he said in a rare, low voice. "Not a coincidence...I don't know! Let's get some water into this lady!"

Her cardboard thin lips had dried and cracked against her teeth as if she might be a dummy in a Hollywood set of special effects. She couldn't move her mouth. It was locked open. Her dried tongue was about the size of one joint of my little finger, or hers. It was only a small stub inside her mouth. That meant she couldn't swallow. I first poured water over her eyes and quickly into her mouth. She began batting her eyelids. After a few seconds, she uttered a slight hissing noise in her dry vocal cords. I thought she might be telling me to empty that canteen into her stomach. I did, a small trickle at a time, slowly.

I lifted her to a sitting position and continued with trickling the water into her mouth. I didn't want to drown her. Had I stopped to think that if God wanted this person dead, she would've already died! He wouldn't have kept that overcast until we arrived in time to save her eyes. I knew she must've swallowed the water without moving her throat. So we repeated the process several times. In seconds her throat was visibly moving each time she swallowed. I poured more water over her eyes when I noticed she was no longer blinking but staring into space with what seemed to be lifeless eyes. I kept my shadow over her face, hoping she wasn't blind. Perhaps she was dying. I didn't know!

After several moments, her lips began bleeding at the cracks. Her skin was still stretched tightly across her skull.

After several more minutes, perhaps we had between a pint and quart of water down her. It must've been misery for her but I did what I thought best. If she regurgitated, I feared she would drown or choke to death. Her widely cracked lips were streaming blood. During this time she was moving the fingers on her left hand. She could blink her eyes and make human sounds in her throat. The water was reviving her, but I still thought she was dying.

She was about thirty years old, and, in spite of her leathery face dried against her skull and teeth, and the skin flat and cracked across her teeth, she was, indeed, a beautiful woman! The dried scales of skin on her lips made it difficult to determine where her lips actually began above her teeth. If I appear crazy, I offer no apology. I saw her as a pretty woman, what we called shiny in college, foxy, fine, and a "Keeper" if we were on a cattle ranch.

Thirty minutes elapsed. She could whisper a few words, mostly about her having a great thirst. She was cold and while flat on her back, managed to cover her upper trunk with a sweater. I helped her, but she continued to straighten it and rearrange it repeatedly. Her lips continued to bleed, yet they were showing signs of thickening. They would stop bleeding once her blood regained some of its life supporting substances. Her skin was thickening and wasn't quite so stretched over her beautiful face.

An hour passed. I heard a helicopter arriving. A truck had already arrived alongside the Border Patrol east of us, who was working with the two other people alive. I later learned that the truck belonged to the county. It was packed full of local reporters with cameras. In fact, after we spotted the truck, we spotted the camera men spilling out and circling what I presumed to be the two live bodies surrounded by four U. S. Border Patrol agents. Tilton made sure he kept his shadow across her face after I moved and stretched.

I turned again to the lady lying face down nearby. She was within arm's reach. And again, without thinking, I shook her leg in an attempt to wake her. She looked alive. Each time I did that, Tilton would remind me that she was dead.

I had moved her head slightly to where I could see her face when we first arrived. Her broken and twisted nose was full of dried blood in the abraised surface. Flies were on the dried blood and flew in and out of her nose and mouth. They were in and out under her dress. Yet I wanted her to wake up. The escaping gas was undetectable to Tilton and me, but not to the green flies. This woman was not dehydrated. She had died from the murderous hands of a coyote prior to her skin drying out from thickened blood. The guide had choked her to death upon her request, I later learned that from the B.P. agents.

The same BP agent told me later that the woman had been raped several times during the past two days, as were all the women by the four guides. The broken nose was a result of that man's *coup de grace*--at her request.

I was still trickling water down the throat of the young woman when the red and white helicopter arrived from the medical center in Tucson. It landed about thirty yards to the south in level terrain. Its wind and dust gave Clyde and Buck the scare of their lives. Both of them drug Tilton in two different directions by the bridle reins as dust showered us. The lady was still eagerly encouraging me to give her water by nodding her head up and down and making noises while the water continued to trickle down her. The mouth of my canteen was covered with blood. So were my fingers and good canteen that was wrapped with gunny sacks to retain some coolness. She had grabbed the canteen several times. Each time I wrestled it from her. I knew that I was torturing her and received no pleasure from it. I didn't want her dying. Regurgitating water was the fastest way for this weak woman to die.

The medics loaded her light body on a stretcher and asked me to give a hand with the stretcher, which I did. One of them had applied an IV needle into her arm and held the solution high with his other free hand. When we first arrived, I didn't think that she had enough of a vein to accept the needle.

I hadn't walked three paces with the stretcher when a heavy hand roughly shoved me from behind, directly and intentionally, right between my shoulder blades! I lost my balance and tumbled forward. But I didn't go all the way down. I held my end of the stretcher up while I fought for balance. Yet I prepared myself for an attack and quickly turned back. My defense was going to be my best offense ever.

The man hadn't really attacked me. He had simply attempted to shove me out of his way without any warning, from behind. He was a BP agent in full uniform, one of those that filled the reporters full of ill facts about the entire incident without knowing anymore about it than anyone else. I knew him well. He was stationed at Gila Bend. He was still there in 1986 when I moved away. He had been promoted to a supervisor by that time, which made sense under such mentality.

I'm left-handed and was coming up from ground level to send my fist all the way through his chest or face, whichever came first, when I saw and heard something else. I must've been moving slower than I thought. A multi-thousand-dollar camera was recording my actions and, thusly, saving my career and myself big medical costs from being treated for multiple wounds. My upward swing died instantly, and my fist did nothing but recover my hold on the stretcher while the agent stepped back with his mouth opened in surprise. Both of his hands went up palms forward.

His face had drained but recovered quickly. He was smiling from ear to ear by the time the swing stopped.

"How're you doing, Homer? Long time no see!"

I said, "Fine. How're you?" I forcefully removed his hand from the stretcher and continued to carry the woman, and, believe it or not, both of his hands stole an inch behind my hands while he scrambled to keep himself between the camera and me. This was what he wanted, to be in the lens of a camera! This is factual! I've heard about truth being stranger than fiction. This was the first time that I had lived it!

I stepped aside and said, "Man, you aren't going to be discovered by movie producers over this!"

He quickly explained that he had thought that I was tired. He apologized and continued in my place. I later learned that two officers almost got into a fist fight to see which one carried the lady in front of the cameras. But my motive to fight wasn't due to stealing camera time. My getting shoved and turning to swing was never aired to my knowledge. The camera had a "CBS" stamped on it. True to form from the cameras and reporters, it was only part of the story. The cameraman never even bothered to look at me as he passed. I figured he would at least issue a sign of human understanding, but no. He probably thought I wanted to be on television. Then, again, I've heard that camera operators aren't any smarter than some of the reporters.

Two officers fighting just to get in front of a camera? Not hardly! I cannot believe I stuck to that stretcher. I guess that I wanted to deny him of the pleasure. I really had planned to either knock that sucker into the next county or else break my fist trying. I have never struck a man, except with a flashlight once when I was a city policeman. It surprises me that the second man I was going to strike was a grossly overpaid, federal officer with the brains of Jimmy Carter.

During this time Tilton gathered our horses, who didn't run far. I walked among the dead bodies, hoping find a trace of life. A young couple in their early twenties lay closely in peaceful positions facing one another. They had embraced prior to dying. No doubt that they had died in their sleep, whether it was at the same time or not. I want to believe that it was. Both appeared to have died with love in their hearts.

They were in a thin shade of a scraggly mesquite with their heads uphill, situated comfortably. The green flies had found their noses. I made the same feeble and senseless attempts to wake them, also. I even begged them to wake up, that it was all over and that everything was fine. I had already felt for pulses on their cold bodies. Nevertheless, hope or hysteria caused a behavior in me that I never knew existed.

I counted nine dead. Three had survived.

The Border Patrol claimed that the two girls they saved were both in their late teens and had dehydrated. They had poured water down them immediately with no ill side effects, so they stated. Neither of the two had choked or made any signs of nausea, according to the officers. Both were pretty, they said. I never saw the two girls, except on television with those same bee pec agents taking turns to nurse them back to health in their arms while the cameras rolled. I could feel good over finding the three alive.

However, such action from grown men turned my stomach. These were the officers that President Reagan would boldly state later would replace the U. S. Customs Patrol! What a slam against us by the most respected president in history! He was he grossly misinformed over the status of too many bureaucracies and was about to make our two agencies, Border Patrol and Customs, richer by tripling our budgets to fight a drug war that had already been won on the ground by the U. S. Customs Patrol!

I had seen the woman's eyes as she was loaded onto the stretcher and was finally out of our hands. They were no longer flat. Dehydrated people usually die with their eyes stuck open.

It isn't funny but I laughed, anyway, partly to relief and partly from the irony. One of the medics, probably the one who accused me trying to fight for a camera position, spoke Spanish. He reported that the lady pointed to Tilton and me and said: "Please give me water to drink. Those men over there would not give me water to drink. I have much thirst!"

This was after the water solution they gave her thinned her blood and made her fully beautiful again, even with her splits lips. Her tongue had already grown to normal size with far too much movement in regaining the lost hours when she was silent. Her body and limbs were fully restored by the intravenous liquid. The IV worked fast, especially after an hour of trickled water down her throat. If I were wrong in my application, then it was due to my ignorance, nothing else. Tilton agreed with me, only he claimed that he didn't know anything about such matters. Somebody had to pretend to be an expert, which was usually me. I had provided first aid to a hundred or more mule riders at the Grand Canyon over five summers of work as a mule guide, but that aid had been to heat exhaustion, not dehydration.

Hundreds of reporters were at the NPS Visitors' Center. As agreed, Tilton and I reported to the superintendent's office, who had spent most of the past several hours on the telephone. His office was packed with BP agents from Tucson, Gila Bend, and Why, all talking inside the small office at the same time with a reporter attached to each man. Several reporters jumped Tilton and me. At least ten reporters were outside the office and held microphones under the bee pee agents' lips as they talked. Oh--how they talked! I've never been in the company of so many immodest heroes!

Mr. Wallace dropped the telephone and stood up to shake Tilton's hand then mine. He was glad to see us. The reporters read this as us being someone important. He wanted us to relieve him for an hour or so, that he hadn't slept the passed twenty-four hours!

"Nothing doing, you cranky old buzzard!" I said. "You know we can't talk to the press. Get a bee pee to stand in for you. You won't get but about 200 volunteers."

"You gotta be kidding!" he yelled in front of them. "They've been in my office for the past two hours! I didn't invite them in here. They didn't even show up for the meeting!"

Reporters were now tugging at my arm and Tilton's, holding microphones in front of our mouths again. We weren't in uniform. "Who're you? Are you the U. S. Border Patrol in plain clothes?"

They were, indeed, inquiring people. Are you the men who found them?"

"No--no!" a bee pee answered for me. "We found 'em! Ask us anything you like."

Again, the total truth. I heard this statement more than once during the five minutes I was there. Mr. Wallace ignored all others and said, "Homer, did you count the dead out there?"

"I did, sir. I counted nine. There could've been more up the trail toward the highway. I stayed in the vicinity of the one lady that Tilton and I worked with. The bee pee were on the east side and closest to the highway."

"Well--I want to know the exact count!" I suspected that he was now disgusted with me, too.

It was then that a Border Patrol agent quickly jumped up from one of Mr. Wallace's chairs and said, "Ask me. I was there!"

"Okay, son," Mr. Wallace said kindly. "I'm asking you. How many dead were there?"

The agent suddenly caught himself. "I--uh--don't know. I think there were nine, but I'm not sure."

Mr. Wallace grinned and turned back to me. I held my hands up and said, "I'm sorry. I looked but couldn't find anymore than nine dead."

The bee pee agent turned and smiled at me triumphantly. He shouldn't have. Several cameras were buzzing directly at him.

The U. S. Border Patrol had recently lost an officially marked car to thieves in Tucson. The thieves stole it from their lot right under their noses in broad daylight. I know they hadn't leaked that to the press. I asked this man, "Have you recovered your stolen patrol sedan? You know, the one stolen off your lot right under your noses, the one that was well marked with red lights on top of it and full of radios?"

More cameras zoomed in on him.

That felt good. I ducked out and heard the desired effects. Mr. Wallace was slapping his knee with his usual loud laugh, the other was the bee pee agent answering honestly with all the dignity he could muster.

A reporter followed me out and asked my name. I explained that we weren't allowed to talk with the press and gave him the number and name of our Public Affairs Officer in Houston. He would know more than I inside an hour.

My youngest daughter told me that she had seen me on television for an instant later that day, Tilton, also. I had only checked for the progress with two of the survivors, but I do not remember the cameras. I thought she was teasing me.

A day later I saw my skinny image on television in the CBS Evening News broadcast. I had, indeed, turned around and faced the camera!

The news reports stated that two of the four smugglers of the group of twenty-six had died. Two were eventually prosecuted, according to the Border Patrol who fed this information to the news media. Again, I cannot begin to guess where the live coyotes were during the rescue, or if they were of the group the B.P. had arrested the day before. I sincerely doubted they had arrested any of the smugglers.

Several BP agents of the Why Station told the press what they thought had happened. The group had entered near a place called *Quitobaquito* ten miles further west. It was an oasis in the desert with shade trees, a pond, and a spring, the whole works. It's fifteen miles west of the Lukeville Port of Entry. They probably had entered a day or two earlier and had walked some thirty miles, according to the agent who had plenty of words but no facts. The first party of the dead were found some 16 miles northwest of the Lukeville P.O.E. on Highway 85. That was the news media's report to the public. The last part was correct.

On the following Tuesday, Johnny and I rode to the green where we first found the B.P. agents circling it. We found much clothing still neatly folded. It remained there, to my knowledge. Some of the paper money was scattered into the brush by a dust devil. The large coins were still neatly stacked. Most of the money was still under a rock. Investigations can last for months. I wouldn't have touched the money for the Lotto's winning ticket.

We back tracked the large group of illegal immigrants. They did not enter southwest at Quitobaquito. They entered the United States due south of where they perished four to five miles or so later.

Johnny and I found three places where they had stopped. Plenty of imprints on the ground indicated several people had lain down. The group had entered exactly five miles west of the Lukeville Port of Entry. Five miles west of safety! The lady that the Border Patrol aircraft found for Tilton and me was dying only three miles west of Highway 85!

Suddenly, a voice from a draw called to us. Johnny and I stopped. A pot-gutted man stood up and called to us again. He was an illegal immigrant, sipping dirty water from what used to be a plastic milk carton.

He was belching loudly and often, a bad sign. It meant the man had been regurgitating and the acid in his stomach was making a lot of gas from the water. He was already in shock, which explained his big gut. His stomach was flattening amidst all the blood collecting within his trunk's walls. He quickly regurgitated the sips of water and swallowed more. His brown face had paled. Both Johnny and I dismounted and quickly emptied the milk carton of its dirty water down his back. Johnny rinsed it and filled it half-way from both our canteens.

I asked him to sit in the shade and talk to me. He did. He blabbered like a crazy man. Actually, he wouldn't shut up. His brain was lacking oxygen. He explained that his legs had simply stopped functioning, that he wasn't hurt or anything. He kept slapping them as if they had been naughty. *No servicio! No servicio!* (They don't work!)

He repeated it a dozen times or more, burping, regurgitating, and sipping more from his water bottle.

Right or wrong. I took his water bottle and poured part of it behind his head and on his wrists. I splattered his crouch area and feet and let it trickle down his back and under his belt. He thought I was attempting to poke fun at him and did a certain amount of struggling. Johnny giggled at my efforts to cool the man down and to save him from further shock. I forced his head between his knees while he sat.

Moments later, he could walk and talk much better. He slapped his legs several times, as if punishing them again. He said that he would be going now and thanked us for the water.

Instead of allowing him to walk, I helped him to mount Clyde and led him to the nearest road. Johnny called our Houston, Texas Sector with his hand-held radio and asked them to send a ranger to our position. We had another man down that needed a forced rest prior to his illegal trek northward.

Ranger Dexter met us and applied water in the same areas that I already had. This brought more giggles from Johnny. Actually, the ranger was acting indignantly as if we didn't have the sense to pour water over the body's warmer spots. The man was still pale and needed rest. Apparently, the only sense the man could make from any of this was Johnny's giggles. Dexter assured us that he would hold him until the sheriff's deputies arrived. They would take him to a center in Ajo where illegal immigrants could obtain free medical benefits. During this time, they would notify the Border Patrol.

The man continued to explain to Dexter that he was feeling much better and that his legs functioned fine, that he must be going. He slapped his legs and pleaded to me when he saw that Dexter understood even less Spanish than me. I explained that he must go with Ranger Dexter and sleep twenty-four hours. This frightened the man terribly and had to be physically restrained with handcuffs.

Johnny's personal laugh only sounds like a giggle. One has to know him. He's both tough and intelligent. I thought he was going to laugh himself silly as we had to apply the handcuffs. I think the man was interpreting our actions as a planned sexual perversion of some sort, all due to Johnny's silly laugh!

Dexter understood none of this. It's just as well. I still wanted to shoot him for cutting that fence around our water hole. We bid Dexter farewell, that we didn't want to be around when this man told his story to the Spanish speaking deputy later.

Rumor Control had management of the U.S.B.P. stating that they were displeased with the B. P. agents for having talked with the press so much, telling stories and giving personal opinions as to what happened: "It was plain murder." One had said on the evening news. That was true, one of the phrases I remember hearing from my friend on nationwide television. He was also the one who talked to me that morning on horseback, one of the four we saw running their horses in circles. He resigned from the U.S. Border Patrol a few weeks later and returned to his home in western Arizona.

The El Salvadorians were not granted refugee status by the State Department, even though they were escaping political persecution, the exact requirements to grant them political asylum had somehow eluded them. With all the exceptions to Immigration laws, there's a good chance that they're still with us, but Rumor Control claims they were eventually deported.

One of the B.P. agents stationed in Why, a neighbor living within a couple blocks, showed me a letter from a good-hearted soul in Alabama. He learned the agent's name from the television evening news, and wrote him a lengthy letter. His letter was an explanation in how dig a well. He said it would work to depths to twenty feet, which must have seemed halfway to China to anyone in Alabama. He said all one had to do in his neighborhood to dig a water well was to use a pair of post hole diggers. The public water well in Why, Arizona is 1,100 feet deep.

As far as I'm concerned, the Alabaman had written this bit of information to the correct source. I'd further venture to guess that the B.P. agent responded with this: "We don't have to dig wells out here in the desert in Arizona. We get all the water we need from the faucets inside our houses."

Actually, the agent did respond respectfully to the Alabamian explaining that our groundwater in the desert is hundreds of feet down. It's heartwarming to know that people do care, even though they might think that we never had the brains to dig a well and had chosen to die of thirst during the hundred years that this part of Arizona had been settled. So be it. I have lived to witness our nation in a crazier state.

Chapter 17

Chola, A Customs Patrol Horse

This beautiful, blue-roan filly was seized from drug smugglers early one morning by the Indian Customs Patrol Officers on the Tohono O'odum Nation. Three other horses were involved. Each one carried 200 pounds of marijuana. All four were almost too exhausted to move away when they were ambushed by the officers. The two smugglers that led the horses surrendered without incident. This happened nine miles north of the Mexico border in 1976. She was only two years old but large enough to work for the greedy smugglers. The 200 pounds of marijuana she carried cost approximately $20,000.00 in Mexico. They could have afforded her food and rest.

The shabby name tacked on *Chola* was undeserving. *Chola* is a Spanish word for females of ill standing. She died early in 1994 at age twenty still carrying the name. However, when her name was used it was respectful, and no one equated her with the name.

She grew into a pretty mare from her exceptional breeding. Her temperament was ideal. Weldon trained her for every aspect of the patrol. She stood perfectly still with gunfire all around and was gentle enough to drag a wounded man to safety by simply hanging on to a stirrup. She could turn on a dime, as they say in horse circles when discussing the reining or handling of a horse. Weldon's two small children could ride her safely anytime she wasn't used for government work.

Following her official seizure, *Chola* wasn't sold at a Customs public auction with the three others. The chances of her dying from underfeeding and exhaustion ruled out all potential buyers. If she lived, she was a keeper for the U. S. Customs Patrol. Over a period of three years, twenty-two horses were seized from drug smugglers. Tilton kept eight of them to be used by the U. S. Customs Patrol. The others sold for 10 to 20 dollars each to local ranchers, who would sell them to the killers for a huge profit.

Tilton carried her to the National Park Service's corrals located in the brush about five miles north of the Lukeville, Arizona Port of Entry.

The sight of her depressed me. She lay on her stomach with her nose resting on the ground. Next to her nose was a small pan of sweet horse feed. Also, in easy access, was a pan of water. Her eyes were sunken and all the flesh on her skeletal frame was drawn tightly around her backbone, hips, legs and neck. She barely lifted her mouth to draw a sip of water and slid her nose away, letting the few sips of water to drain from her lips.

Tilton's faith in her recovery was remarkable. I wanted her euthanized immediately but kept it to myself. She would be dead, in my opinion, before we could haul her to a veterinarian in Buckeye about 110 miles north.

I told Tilton that. That's why he would attempt to nurse her back to health. He had done exactly the same thing with Buck, Clyde, and Speck after I recommended that he have them put down. However, they were not in such a sorry shape as *Chola*.

Several weeks later, *Chola* was the beautiful young filly she was supposed to be. Her dam and sire had to be top quarter horses. Mexico's horsemen bred many good horses. How she fell into the hands of smugglers, other than being stolen, no one knows. Buck had been stolen off the Indian Reservation and worked as a cow horse for years in Mexico. He was stolen by or sold to smugglers. Clyde was also a well bred horse of show quality, a big palomino much like the many "Triggers" of Roy Rogers. Yet he had spent his career as a cow horse in Mexico before the smugglers captured him and began to work him to death. I asked Tilton to call Weldon in Douglas, Arizona to see if he wanted *Chola*. He said he had already made the call. He had finally done something right.

Weldon was skeptical until he saw her. She became his Customs horse at first sight and remained that way seven years when he left the patrol to join Internal Affairs. She developed a sweet and trusting disposition. She also did her own thinking. She was good for roping and snubbing broncs. She never protested against work. All that knew her loved her.

Unfortunately, at age eight, while residing in Walker's corrals, *Chola* fell in love with a high-priced stallion residing on a neighboring ranch. No one will say how she attracted his attention, but it happened. The two found each other and made a baby.

This was big news to the U. S. Border Patrol in Douglas and Lukeville, Arizona. Ugly rumors arose, something like this is illegal. Now, I just dropped you a hint in how a certain U. S. Attorney in Washington, D. C. learned about a Customs mare getting pregnant near Douglas, Arizona. I think the B. P. suspected Weldon of trying to steal a horse from U. S. Customs. With Weldon's background, I don't think he needed the money. I know for a fact he's anything but a thief, but that's how our sister agency saw us. We were always getting in their way of becoming famous for interdicting smuggled drugs. Anyway, their goals were to move us off the border.

What's the damage of the Customs mare getting pregnant? Zilch. Nevertheless, a typical letter to our District Director and Branch Chief from the U. S. Attorney's Office in D. C. caused U. S. Customs in D.C., Region and District to reach voice octaves above the *Star Spangled Banner.* It eventually filtered down to Weldon, the dirty culprit.

The U.S. Customs attorney's letter was the complaint, since he needed to protect his source, stating that it (having a Customs mare bred) was a clear misapplication of government property--if not abuse, etc., ect. To me, that's typical U. S. Border Patrol lingo. Any U. S. Attorney is a busy person--even in D.C! He hardly had the time to care if a Customs mare got herself pregnant or not. Weldon stated it right a few weeks prior to his promotion into Internal Affairs, "What the hell does he know?"

The Washington attorney never really searched for a prosecutor and would have had to do it, himself. I don't think he wanted Weldon prosecuted, but he had responded to a report of some sort from an anonymous source. A sure bet was that he was ignorant of President Reagan's love for our horse patrol. Our straight and fair U. S. Customs Service Commissioner William Von Robb also loved our horse patrol, yet neither man ever made a public claim to this effect. For that matter, neither one had so much as publicly acknowledged the existence of the U.S. Customs Patrol in its entirety! The patrol was the most successful drug interdicting force in the U. S., but neither of these two great leaders had a need to know it for reasons of lower level bureaucracies.

The press had always gone for the easier stories and praised the works of the U. S. Border Patrol, a popular agency, which held the reputation of being our only defense against the U. S. invasion by illegal immigrants. They were our primary defense against illegal intrusions but this nation's defense was poor at best. Stuffed teddy bears could perform the same job, almost, with the same results, and much cheaper!

Ill information to the press is the exact core of why our "Drug War" exists today. Ill informed journalists with too little time to write their articles correctly have a great need to pry during an interview. In other words, most of the fault of the Drug War today is solely the fault of the U. S. Customs Service's departmental heads immediately after President Reagan took office. These lower department heads wanted to build a federal empire like the U. S. Border Patrol had built.

An officer of the U. S. Border Patrol did, however, continue to dig for details to convince our regional commissioner that Walker was attempting to steal the colt--all on the word and speculative thoughts. The same B.P. agent, later went to the state of Arizona to see if I had registered the colt to myself, Weldon or the U. S. Customs Service. The jealousy of this U.S. Border Patrol agent definitely overtaxed her mental capacities.

Had the majority of the American public known that the U. S. Customs Patrol actually existed, that it was the strongest and most successful drug interdicting force in U.S. history, that the so-called "Drug War" was about to be won in the smuggling facet, history would have been far different today. Taxpayers could have watched our many billions of tax dollars go to some huge private company like GMC instead of the Drug War. The tax dollars wasted for the drug war went to a useless agency of the U. S. Customs after the patrol was eradicated. The U. S. Customs Air Force, itself, gained close to a half billion dollars each year to apprehend little drugs.

I personally think we would have won the smuggling end of the Drug War completely by 1990 on the land, sea and air. In fact, the U. S. Customs Headquarters barely terminated the patrol in time to save the drug smuggling enterprises. I seriously mean that. *Why else would they have done it?*

First, the Customs Patrol was set up as a temporary agency. It was to relieve the higher waged special agents from working in the field. One must understand that the special agents positions are all white collar work. They do not work in the field. Considering the millions they collected each year from fraud in shiploads of items imported into the United States, they were underpaid.

This is the difference between "Field" work and "Office" work. The patrol officers are workers in the field and are, therefore, paid a lesser salary.

With this in mind, the special agents of U. S. Customs created the Customs Patrol to perform their field work. Never in their lifetime did they believe that common field workers would be so successful! The special agents stood idly for a decade and watched their creation steal the publicity from them due to the highest seizure of drugs entering the U. S. in history. However, the Customs Patrol, the leaders in the huge stats of smuggled drugs, in land, air and sea, was never mentioned to the public. The U. S. Customs Service, the entire enterprise, received the credit, and this was modest due to Customs never having the need to impress Congress for a higher budget.

Their million-dollar fraud cases made the back pages while the Horse Patrol and cases of marijuana seized from smugglers stole the Customs magazine's headlines.

To worsen matters, during the ten years that the patrol stole the in-house headlines from them, the few individual creators of the Customs Patrol had been promoted to Headquarters in D.C. They had created the agency and they could terminate it. And terminate it, they did!

However, jealousy wasn't the prime motive. *Empire Building* is responsible for the termination of the Customs Patrol, including the successful Horse Patrol. With Empire Building in one's agency, greed and power accompanies it. Since the taxpayers foot the bill, they can sit at the top of the empire and enjoy their domain. It is very prestigious to head a huge, federal empire.

Since 1971, or there about, U. S. Customs agents enviously watched the U. S. Border Patrol of the Justice Department scream to the news media for more money and more manpower. They have done this for years! The Border Patrol heads claimed they couldn't control the immigration problem without money and manpower. Money was never a problem for Congress. *It grows on trees!*

For thirty-five years to date, the Border Patrol heads claimed that their unsuccessful attempts to stop the flow of illegal immigrants was due to a lack of money and manpower. Yet, they received more money and more manpower each year, what they wanted. The U. S. Border Patrol grew into a large empire. The influx of illegal immigrants also grew to gigantic proportions at the same time! They were apprehending repeaters and counting them as individual entries.

From 1971 to 2005 the U. S. Border Patrol grew from 1,800 agents to 9,000 as my memory depicts. It's still growing. The immigration problem, meanwhile, tripled and quadrupled! More money and more manpower meant absolutely zilch in controlling the flow of illegal immigrants from Mexico and China. Congress has always known this as well as each president knew this during each of their terms. So long as they have a scapegoat to blame the influx of the illegal immigrants, the Border Patrol, they are in the clear. Yet the new media, ever so politically correct, could never blame the poor souls who actually did work hard to stop the flow of the illegal immigrants. The B.P. arrested them at the border and deported across the border almost within the same hour, only to arrest the same ones later. I personally apprehended the same man three times in the same 8-hour shift! Many of us did. He was deported across the fence in order that he could enter the United States illegally again. Each one of those three apprehensions counted as three to add to the apprehension statistics of the U. S. Border Patrol. It was turned over to Congress. The higher the number the more impressed Congress became. This is how the U. S. Border Patrol was successful in the *Empire Building* process.

U. S. Customs heads wanted a piece of this pie and President Reagan was their man to provide it, as would any other man recently elected President of the United States.

The termination of the Customs Patrol simply meant making all 800 officers special agents. With the promotion came raises. With their newly acquired budget from a new administration, they hired many more special agents off the street. The small number of special agents grew from approximately 1,100 in 1982 to 4,000 a few short years later. The influx of smuggled drugs, however, is still with us!

Cheap politics, from my viewpoint, not all in Congress, has changed the attitude of this nation. Our politicians are unmercifully controlled by the news media, which causes this country to face further extinction on an hour to hour basis.

I wish to be clear with this: We in the Customs Patrol have never been outnumbered by smugglers--not even in ten to one odds against us! We have never screamed for more money and more manpower until 1981! Our leadership did this for us. We never wanted it, except we wanted decent vehicles to drive. I wanted more horses.

Chola had saved U. S. taxpayers an immeasurable amount of money during her years in the horse patrol, at least half-way into the six-figure bracket, or millions in comparison with the drugs seized by the 4-million dollar airplanes that are expensive to fly and interdicts little to zero drugs after the horse patrol was terminated. Her work wasn't measured in dollars until she was removed from our force, after we abandoned the land patrols and joined the Customs forces already in the air.

The smugglers had fed *Chola* too little and worked her unmercifully. The youngest of a working horse's age is two years. Her ruthless owner had already doomed her to deadly exhaustion and malnutrition within a few torturous days!

Weeks or months after meeting *Chola* the first time, and while working the day shift at the Lukeville, Arizona port of entry, I stumbled into *Chola's* former owner--I think!

Mere suspicion for such a crime against *Chola* and the other seized horses warranted a broken nose. Heavier suspicion warranted death by a two by four. We have no such laws for Mexico's smugglers. They're only tried for smuggling, not for being the horse-torturing scum that ranked almost as low as pedophiles. With no punishment for their crimes against decency, it serves to endorse the natural animosity between horse lovers and horse abusers. In other words, people like myself took horse abuse by the smugglers personally.

The suspect smuggler was a citizen of Mexico and possessed one of our Immigration Service's famous Border Crossing Cards. He was a "laugh-it-up" comic about fifty. His Spanish was good, and he appeared to be a big buddy-on-the-spot with one of our two Immigration inspectors at the small port of entry in Lukeville, Arizona. That morning I heard this inspector laughing it up in the other room, as did most everyone within a fifty-yard range. He called me to join them.

Behind the hysterical mirth was the Mexico citizen showing the Immigration inspector a couple rolls of recently developed snapshots from a good camera. A crowd of three or four curious locals had already gathered round, laughing heartily. I elbowed my way into a good position only to be let down. The pictures were nothing but a stallion servicing mares. This was humor? The inspector thought I was losing my perspective by not reeling into leg-slapping glee, so I grinned a little for the sake of politeness.

I suppose such acts aren't private when a stallion does it for money. The pictures depicted three different, well-bred mares being serviced. The lighting was different in a few pictures, as were the horses that stood in the background, proving that all three weren't serviced the same day. The pictures, of course, were to convince the owner of the mares that the proper stallion had performed the service in the proper time sequences. Horses aren't exactly rabbits in the propagation area and one breeding every other day is plenty to keep the stallion's breeding benefits strong. Stallions will breed until they're exhausted everyday if they had their way. The pictures were for legitimate business purposes. At that particular time, however, the pictures were used as pure pornography!

By observing the strange man from Mexico, I could imagine that he'd turn a rock into a sex object if he could realize a profit. Amid his laughter, he appeared to have an air about him that I detested. I read him as a low principled jerk with a filthy personality. He wore clean clothes, was smooth-shaven, and had a new hat, which was of poor quality from the Mexico side. To me, this man could've been someone without a conscious or soul, a complete psycho. His pale green eyes were icy cold, an unusual Mexican to be sure! His swarthy complexion was made darker by our desert sun. He was over confident and appeared to be a braggart.

I imagined all this by one simple observance. He wouldn't meet my eyes, yet he wasn't the type to be easily humiliated. He certainly was no introvert. Once you've seen a two-legged coyote, you've seen 'em all, as they say in the west Texas cotton fields.

I asked the six-foot-three and 220-pound Immigration inspector that claimed Boston as his hometown if I could see the pictures again. He was hysterically thumbing through the stack of neat photos for the third time.

He passed the stack to me. "Yeh--I thought you might like 'em! Does something for you! Huh--huh? Yeah?"

Sure enough, standing in the background among other horses was the blue roan filly in two pictures! She was far too poor there, also. This told me the pictures of the stud servicing the mare were many weeks old. It was time, possibly, for the owner of the stud to prove what stallion bred the mares.

"Who's the owner of these horses?" I asked, trying not to raise suspicion. Anyone working around good horses is always proud to reveal the owner's name. Such men deserve recognition, which is righteously an international concept.

The man shrugged. "I don't know." He was too fast and had already read me. On the other hand, perhaps he thought it was none of my business, for he knew that many of his horses had already been seized recently by Customs Patrol officers. I didn't push it. Some people lie in order to save embarrassment, others lie to save an arrest. He gathered his pictures and left in a less gleeful mood.

I asked the inspector how long he had known this funny man from Mexico.

"Years and years--yeh--yeh--yeh! Dirty--dirty, that man--oh yeah! He doesn't smuggle through the port but I wouldn't trust 'im. No--no! Know what I mean? Gotta watch 'im! Yeh--yeh."

"Yeh--yeh." I replied unintentionally. The man was as contagious as the flu. Know what I mean?

I said, "The blue roan filly that the Indians seized a few months ago are in one of those pictures."

"Aww--come on--come on! All hosses look alike! You can't tell me that you saw a strange hoss one time and recognized it later in a picture! Jeez! No one can do that. No--no--neeuuu! Ain't possible! No--no--no!"

The man was limited for sure. "I just did it," I replied half convincingly, not wanting to argue with a tree stump, especially an Irish one. "If he owned that filly, I can seize that picture and take him into custody before he walks back into Mexico."

"And who in the courts would believe it was the same hoss? All he has to do is say that the hoss was stolen. Know what I mean? Huh--huh? Yeah?"

"You got a point. At least we know who the smuggler with horses is."

I confronted the horse owner alone days or weeks later while working the evening shift as an inspector. I didn't see him come through the port of entry, yet he was leaving on foot by the gate, meaning he had merely walked around the port. He was walking back to Mexico from the store across the street with a sack under his arm. It was 11:00 PM. I caught up with him a few feet short of the border. Several Mexico Customs inspectors were standing curiously nearby. They knew him, apparently, to be a smuggler. We were nose to nose.

He felt it before I said it. He was no horseman, simply someone who dealt with them. But he knew that I had recognized the blue filly that had just been taken from his pack of smugglers. Guilt sounded from him as if he shouldered a "Ghetto-buster." I could do nothing but I wanted to do something. I called him a goat. Then:

"We still have four of your horses." I stated in my best Spanish. The big inspector had told me that he spoke no English, but I had an idea that his English was better than my Spanish. "They are very poor."

The man only returned my cold stare.

"You have no tongue? You have no jokes? Your smuggling with horses is finished on this side of the border. Do you understand me?"

He said something, most of which I couldn't understand. He had attempted to walk around me while delivering his response. I think it was about me coming to Mexico, or not going to Mexico for some reason or other.

He was wearing a blue denim jacket. His boots were the best Mexico had for sale.

He walked briskly by the curious inspectors on the other side of the wide cattle guard in the border fence, who looked questionably at him, then at me. "No more than a goat, him!" I explained and left.

The big inspector reminded me of Victor McLaughlin, the great actor, the only man alive who came close to whipping John Wayne, one on one, in a movie. *The Quiet Man* is a true classic. This inspector was nearing retirement age. He spoke to me about my lack of professionalism, which had only succeeded in making me feel worse. It wasn't smart to tell the smuggler what I had told him. It certainly wasn't among any of the things within my job description. I had really wanted to goad him into attacking me. What astonished me is that I didn't think that I had talked within the inspector's earshot.

I immediately set the inspector at ease. "Are you going to miss him and his dirty pictures or what?"

He laughed but not at my stab at humor. "No--no--no! I'm just trying to tell you that you can't say that to just any...body. Know what I mean? Just a word of caution. Right? Yeh--yeh. This place may be remote, but we work under the same set of rules as everyone else. Know what I mean? Yeh? Yeh?"

"No." I said and walked passed him to tend my own affairs. If I ever caught the smuggler away from witnesses, north or south of the border, I'd whip him with whatever was handy until he was in no better shape than the blue filly, a point where his survival was questionable. That was a fact and that's all there was to it. If that hair-lipped the Irish-blooded inspector, well, as they say in west Texas, "Life isn't just one big keg of cold beer."

Deep down, I wanted to kill or beat no one senseless, regardless of their capital crimes. Perhaps this is why I told the smuggler in advance, which was dumb at best.

He laughed louder. "Miguel has friends!" he said to my back. "He'd kill you for fifty cents! Yeh--yeh! You--me, his mother! Know what I mean? He's no good! Nooo. Know what I mean? Yeah?"

The other Immigration inspector later asked me what was going on between me and the funny man, Miguel. I explained the whole episode to him. He said if I had any physical proof of my suspicions, other than dubiously recognizing a horse in a picture that I had only seen once, he would gladly lift this man's border crossing privileges.

I placed my nose within inches of his. "Just what in the hell does a man like Miguel have use for a Border Crossing Card? He comes and goes as he pleases between ports of entries."

The inspector turned away and dismissed me as a lost cause. I had never doubted that he would lift Miguel's card. Apparently, entering the country illegally under the fence some 100 yards west of the P.O.E. to smuggle drugs wasn't sufficient for him to lift a card. The law clearly states that if an Immigration inspector merely wants to lift a Border Crossing Card, he can. No reason is necessary. Border Crossing Cards are, after all, a courtesy granted our border neighbors.

That was the last time any of us ever saw Miguel, the man with jokes and pictures of horses breeding. The local, infamous horseman had mistakenly surmised that we officers north of the border had all our acts together. He did move on and smuggle in another location; namely, the Sasabe, Arizona area. The Customs Patrol Officers on the then *Papago* Nation would soon seize more of his horses.

The horses used to carry the drugs were ill bred and cold blooded, ideal to sell at Customs auctions, hardly worth the 10 bucks they brought. The Indian officers told me that the horses belonged to Miguel. There was no doubt in their voices.

The afternoon that Weldon unloaded *Chola* into my corrals, many years later, was a mixed blessing. He had hauled her half-way across the state that day from Douglas to Why, Arizona where I lived. Her belly was quite large with her colt.

The day also marked the torturous closing of our blessed horse patrol days. I had one other officer remaining, Johnny. After he transferred to another station as a special agent, I would be the sole horse patrol officer. Tilton and Garcia bailed out when the first breath of foul air reached us. From that point, I could only work day patrols. However, we still had three years remaining before I'd have to leave my horses and transfer to a cushy job. Weldon was wisely getting out while a good job in Customs was available.

The baby arrived about two weeks later. He fell under the expert care of my fourteen year old daughter and *Chola*. The taxpayers would have to feed the baby two years before it could be used in the patrol. I trained the colt for free. I did it on my days off and on

Customs time. It would cost Customs about 200 dollars to feed him in his first two years. I used him on daily patrols during his training period. The backpackers, what few there were, smuggled in other areas.

My daughter named him "Duncan" from Shakespeare's "King Duncan." He inherited *Chola's* personality, and, in spite of his being spoiled rotten by *Chola* and my family, he was the easiest colt I have ever trained.

Chola was the finest horse to ever reside in my corral. Buck and my personal horse were no slouches, either. Duncan made an excellent saddle horse with many gaits that all came naturally. He had a fast running walk and a fox trot that felt more like pacing. I never knew which of the gaits he practiced due to my lack of experience with gaited horses, and bending over to watch his legs move was out of the question. That colt could and would dodge like a cutting horse. I often led *Chola* just to get her out of the corral and break up her boredom. I loved *Chola* as if she were a friend. She walked or trotted freely beside us as if she were led. I was also fond of Duncan, her spoiled brat colt. He was full of personality.

Buck, the oldest Customs horse remaining after Speck and Clyde had to be put down, stood idly in my corral. He knew his time was coming. He had resided with me almost two years with his head hung over the south gate, longing for Mexico, hating my guts, along with any other man that had ever walked toward him with a rope. Buck had three other horses for company, yet his depression worsened. And, like many older men, he often had to be filled with mineral oil to pass undigested food. *Chola* and her colt did nothing for him, either. That was understandable. The colt, while small, had bugged him constantly by nipping at his long eyelashes or roughly pulling his tail like a puppy playing tug of war.

Buck was getting old and wanted to die where they had worked and almost starved him to death. His accumulated fat without much work all those years with Customs was the type of prosperity he never fully appreciated. He had, of course, undergone surgery early in life and had no use for the opposite sex other than what's found in a platonic relationship. He was a cowboy's horse. He didn't like horses or men, not even the little colt that bugged him constantly. He was the toughest little horse I have ever ridden. He came to us with an attitude and never grew out of it. Yet I loved him equally with Chola, my horse, and Duncan.

Sadly, after President Reagan was sworn into office, the remaining Customs Patrol Officers were suddenly placed under the command of the Office of Enforcement, the special agents of U. S. Customs. The Customs office in Tucson openly detested the Horse Patrol. This was for no other reason than the horse patrol was successful. The commissioner of Customs, William Von Robb, was too high on the totem pole to help me fight the approaching battles with jealous agents that outnumbered me fifty to one. Like our esteemed President Reagan, he trusted his subordinates to do their job in the most expeditious manner. That was a tremendous mistake, and it would cost the taxpayers billions during the approaching years. Blanket promotions for hundreds of Custom Patrol Officers into special agents had already been effected.

In spite of the fact that the horse patrol in the desert was the most practical and cost effective tool in federal law enforcement, horses were not "Chic" by current standards. Horses outgrew their usefulness to U. S. Customs during the 1940's, long after the heydays of bootleggers entering the United States from Mexico. It mattered little that dangerous drugs replaced smuggled liquor in the same remote areas. Horses were obsolete. They didn't measure up with the progressive standards of the 1980's.

That's my best and most honest explanation for eliminating horses from U.S. Customs.

Six months after I was transferred to the Albuquerque, New Mexico Air Branch in 1986, the smuggled drugs returned to the Lukeville area in force. I do not believe that it was due to my absence. I think the smugglers finally realized that the U. S. Border Patrol posed no threat to their lucrative business on the border's desert area. The Horse Patrol had been an active threat against their business. Tilton and Franklin were brought back to Lukeville as special agents. What they did was continue to patrol to seize the drugs while writing something else down on their paperwork, such as "We caught this load due to investigations."

What coincidentally transpired was that the drug smugglers were getting hit too often on the east coast by the Coast Guard, who eventually gained Customs authority to seize property and make arrests. The smugglers did return to find the border in the Lukeville area as wide open as it ever was. More Border Patrol agents were hired, and, they, too, had more search and seizure authority. Nevertheless, the drugs kept coming.

Perhaps we should have suggested that Congress build a 700-mile fence on the border to keep the smuggled drugs out of the country.

The Border Patrol grew larger and began to put smuggled drugs on their top priority, even if it meant odd hours and getting out of the vehicles. Their drug stats, however, remained at the same low level as it always has.

They had a reason for their failure to stop the smuggled drugs. It was made public: "We need more money and more manpower if we're going to do U. S. Customs work!" .

The U. S. Customs Office of Enforcement placed special agents back in the Lukeville area to assist Tilton and Johnny. They were granted absolutely no patrol authority. They may as well have worked out of Bowling Green, Kentucky. The cost of the Drug War began its long, successful ascent in what used to be our area for the Horse Patrol. Tilton failed to slow the drug smuggling. It remained strong. With horses, he could and would have shut it down completely as he once did. As they say at the west Texas crap tables: "Win some, lose some."

However, the same U.S. Customs Officials that terminated their successful Customs Patrol took up the U. S. Border Patrol's astonishing cry: "We need more money and more manpower!" It worked. Highly paid Customs agents number into the thousands, yet drug smuggling is still lucrative to the cartels. The end is not in sight.

Once, during his training, Duncan ducked his head and decided to toss me from my cushioned saddle. I yelled the word "NO!" He stopped immediately and backed his ears in protest. He tried it again later. The same thing happened. He had learned the word well, as all my colts learn long before they're trained to carry people. Had he actually gotten into bucking that day, I think he would have stuck my head in the dirt.

Months before my being transferred to Albuquerque, Duncan was coming age three. All the Customs Patrol Officers had left Lukeville in order to pursue their careers with modern technology in law enforcement. I was growing older and nearing retirement. Going to an academy to learn special agent skills sounded too much like a culture shock. I was left alone to run the station with one secretary, who had kept the station in good running order during its heydays of narcotics seizures. She was transferred into the Inspectors Division without my approval.

Prior to transferring, I rode Duncan and my personal horse almost every day, extending my job as long as possible. I searched diligently for signs of smuggling. The Indian officers, who also worked for me, had my attention as the station's head was to make schedules and sign annual leave. They did well without my supervision. They found little evidence of smuggling in their area.

My work days grew to twelve hours. I loved my family but the Office of Enforcement had my home number, so I stayed away as much as possible. I carried a hand held radio in my saddle bags. Fortunately, the radios were limited to small distances in the remote desert. If a Customs aircraft flew into my area, and it happened often, I would talk with it. Management often sent me messages via Customs aircraft pilots from Tucson. If the messages were too demanding, I could no longer read them. Then I was called into Tucson for personal meetings, which amounted to a waste of time and fuel costs. They simply wanted to control me, nothing more. I kept insisting that they were in complete control of my entire existence. They refused to believe that. I spent far too much time looking for signs of smuggling—my job! My job was obsolete, along with my status as an officer.

My horse patrol completely disappeared from under me by July, 1986. The harassment from our Tucson office became brutal and unnecessary. It was the same at the Indian's station at Sells, Arizona. The Indian officers had worked hard and loyal for years. They deserved none of it. They feared for their jobs because they could not be transferred off the reservation.

My special agent bosses stopped one form of harassment after I warned them, and they would take up another from a different angle. They simply wanted to push the last Horse Patrol officer, a social embarrassment, out of the service. Its passed seizures meant nothing. Drugs smuggled into the United States meant nothing to them in the "Big Picture." I could only figure, personally, that the hierarchy in Washington, D.C. welcomed the drugs returning to the Mexico border. They had learned well that the U. S. Border Patrol could yell for more money and more manpower each year. The immigration problem continued to triple and quadruple. The same should work for drug smuggling.

The one and only solution to our immigration problem was to exterminate the socialist government of Mexico and turn it into a capitalist society. We could then allow competition reign in their industries with living wages for a work force.

Today, the U. S. Customs Service's empire is enormous. At one time in the late 1980's, an assistant commissioner in D. C. was bragging that he would have a Customs office in every city in the United States, which included Bowling Green, Kentucky. He accomplished this feat. His empire is still far reaching.

When Commission Von Robb learned that I had dumped the horses to another federal agency, he didn't like it. Too bad. He saw to it that the Indians would have horses to ride in the Horse Patrol so long as they existed. Rented horses came to the Sells, Arizona Station after my transfer to Albuquerque. I really don't know if they have ever seriously patrolled on the horses since I left them in 1986. National news has aired them occasionally, but I sincerely believe they did nothing but photo ops with the horses.

Chola and her three-year old son, Duncan, along with four horses from the Sells, Arizona Station, were transferred into the U. S. Fish and Wildlife Service. This service had recently purchased a ranch near Sasabe, Arizona to save a species of quail. This service hired a working cowboy. I provided him the horses.

The cowboy and I stayed in contact until I retired in 1992. *Chola* died suddenly and unexpectedly. The four horses from the Sells, Arizona Station were never ridden. The cowboy rode Duncan year after year on that ranch, who is twenty-three years of age at the time of this writing.

In Albuquerque where I was transferred to be out of Tucson's hair, I rode in the back seat of a large jet. I ran the radar and FLIR. After a couple of years, I was responsible for detecting one load of smuggled drugs with the FLIR and radar.

I worked it another four years and caught zilch. The other fourteen officers working the radar interdicted nothing during this time. It cost approximately 1,200 dollars to get the big jet off the ground. I don't know the cost of fuel, but it was high. But stats weren't as important as the prestige of modern technology with extremely high costs. Why?

I can surmise that drying up one's well would put one out of a job, as the saying goes. If the Border Patrol were successful in stopping the illegal flow immigrants, where would thousands of jobs go? If the Drug War was won, what would thousands of special agents do?

Chapter 18

The Red Lantern

No one in my office has ever spotted a UFO in our desert region of the United States. I still don't believe they exist. I cannot believe any vehicle from another planet has ever visited our planet. I will admit, however, that we have an abundance of strange phenomena in our own planet that has never been explained. I can prove my reports in this chapter, not just by witnesses, which are abundant, but by your own observance if you wish to see it. There is nothing added. It all happened as depicted.

In the late seventies and early eighties, I worked in pairs with horse patrol officers in vehicles as well as horses. I trusted them for their intelligence, honesty, and for their integrity. If I found them equally willing to work with me, I took it as a compliment. I chose my partners carefully for safety's sake; otherwise, I worked alone.

We never talked about extraterrestrial craft, UFO's, Bigfoot, or ghosts. We were already buried in the confusion of our own world.

Tilton and I both received calls from district about vehicles spotted at night on the border in a remote area on the western side of the reservation. The exact location is three miles west of Papago Farms. This is about 30 miles inside the southwest corner of the reservation. It was a hot smuggling area, so we planted a sensor there that would transmit vibrations to our monitor in Why, Arizona, about 40 miles distant. The immigrant smugglers had even made a gate in the fence years prior to our arrival. We wired it back. They cut our wires.

We often responded to the sensor planted there at 11:00 PM. We waited where the desert road intersected with the north-south highway. This desert road is about twelve miles long. It's a rough road and we had plenty of time to drive there from Why, Arizona to apprehend the load of illegal immigrants.

The vehicle lights in question were spotted twelve miles from our position on the highway on night by a special agent from Tucson, who decided to watch the border for his own information, and to record our responses. I'm sure the Tucson office was also curious. We backed our patrol vehicle under a palo verde tree and waited for the vehicles to travel the twelve miles west to our intersection. We had plenty of time, for the road they had to use was too rough for anything but slow traveling.

We worked this sensor often and we apprehended many smuggled loads of illegal immigrants, but only one load of smuggled drugs. I was not on duty during this seizure. This road was the only way out of that remote corner.

A north-south highway reaches almost to the border from the state highway between Why and Tucson. No one stepped even close to that hot area without ringing monitoring bells in our homes and our office.

A printout also gave us the exact time and how many hits. It wasn't difficult to determine the hits and time in relation to a vehicle being driven through the fence. The process of crossing the fence required about ten to fifteen minutes, for they always rewired the fence. Vehicles crossed there often in the mid-seventies. After Tilton and his crew seized a few loads of narcotics from that gate, they practically stopped. Nevertheless, a load of illegal immigrants would occasionally pass through there. We always caught the illegal immigrants and notified the Border Patrol so they could deport them by turning them around and allowing them to re-enter Mexico in order that they catch the again for more stats.

We actually received no sensor hit on this particular night. What brought us there were the reports of car lights in that location. Some special agent had driven to the abandoned buildings of Papago Farms and spotted numerous vehicle lights moving about in that one are. He called Tilton by telephone, as did our district office. We usually drove all the way to the corner to check our sensor. But since there were vehicle lights already on the area, we simply waited at the intersection of where the desert road reached our point on the highway.

Johnny was an expert with the sensors. He worked with the same ones in Viet Nam. In fact, they belonged to the U. S. Army. The sensors were a valuable tool against smuggling of any type through the border fence.

The lack of sensor hits where the cars were accumulated at the crossing raised questions. My explanation for this was that the battery was either dead or else the sensor's radio had stopped transmitting. Actually, no battery went dead when Johnny maintained the sensors. They never failed. When I was with him one time, he had to point to the antenna among the tall grass stems before I could find it. They appeared one and the same. The wires, of course, were cleverly under dirt in the grass that Franklin carefully poured over them.

Each time a report of car lights reached us from that area, we always drove there the next day or as soon as possible. Not once did we ever find evidence of vehicles in that area. Yet there were reports of cars with bright headlights in that very area! Our own officers had seen them from the eastern position at Papago Farms. The problem was there was no longer a good road from Mexico to the crossing. Even getting there from Papago Farms on our side, the sand was too loose and deep with too many mesquite bushes. Instead of driving the three miles to the crossing, one had to drive twenty miles back north, fifteen west, and twenty more to our location.

Nevertheless, we always hauled our horses to the location in the daytime and thoroughly searched the border fence. Not once did we find evidence of vehicles anywhere. Thus, special agents from Tucson, at the request of Internal Affairs, checked on those lights and made sure that we answered the reports. We didn't require I.A. or special agents to check our work, but when they did, they found us capable and thorough, whether it was reported that way or not, we never learned.

We always looked for tracks of vehicles, horses, and foot traffic. Nothing! Yet the reports of car lights there were precise by people who knew the country! They always saw these cars on this portion of the border anywhere from 10:00 PM to Midnight. All of them were always on our side of the border.

We consistently treated the reports with respect. At least someone out there was on our side and wanted the drug smuggling to stop. Besides, Tilton wanted to get out of the office and ride his horse.

When we looked at the area the following morning horseback, it was the same story. No tracks of a single vehicle passed in that area.

Since our office reported no sign of automobile traffic in the area, an agent would keep driving in secret to the reservation to check our honesty the second and third times, plus others we probably didn't know about.

While checking on us, however, the agent stood the chance of getting run over by drug smugglers. They were cautioned about that. So the agent would find a high spot and hide his vehicle so he could watch the hot spots on the border with binoculars, always at night.

IT was on this night at approximately ten-thirty, we received a telephone call from two Indian Customs Patrol officers. Johnny and I were called to ambush the smugglers. By the time we arrived, they would be upon us in less than thirty minutes. We were always hidden long before any vehicle would have had time to drive to the intersection over that rough road and get northbound on the highway.

Upon arriving and hiding our vehicle, we saw the headlights about one-half mile distant coming our way. I turned to Johnny. "We didn't get here any too soon!"

Johnny was not only scientifically and high tech minded, he was good natured and easy company. He not only refused to argue or complain, he could discuss some subjects with firm authority. I learned a lot from him. We had about a minute before that car would be arriving.

The headlights were not much closer after a moment, however. I would be calling Tilton by radio later to report that our "device" wasn't working. This meant that Johnny had allowed the batteries to go down. This was okay because Tilton already knew that Johnny was as dependable as a Timex watch. I knew it as well. Harassing Johnny to his face always made him grin.

We had a car approaching and it wasn't blacked out! *Strange!* We had caught several vehicles coming off that road. All of them were blacked out.

Johnny knew that the sensor was working fine. The car was spotted at the crossing point and had come our way, yet it had not set off the sensor! Regardless of the possibility of this happening, we were witnessing exactly that! We waited with apprehension. Apparently, there was a new crossing place on the border fence. I thought of that. Johnny doubted it. I did, too. The country was too rough for vehicles in other places.

After sufficient time elapsed, Tilton, who was already awake and notified of the spotting, called and asked out status. I didn't like using the radio at this time. The car just stopped on the road in front of us with its headlights on and seemed to linger there in hopes of pulling us out of our hiding place. Its headlights would retreat back to what I thought was a half-mile and come forward to about a quarter-mile from us before it stopped. I was ready to crank up and go after it on the dirt road. If we were being baited, then I was all for chasing it. Of course, better judgment depicted differently.

"The car's headlights were backing off and then getting closer." This is how I reported it by radio. This went on for a half-hour. The vehicle was not smuggling men or drugs. It wasn't even getting close to the highway!

Tilton wasn't buying that. He asked, "Do you think that you need to go after it on the road or what?"

"To tell the truth, yes." I told him so, then the headlights grew larger. The car was coming out! I told him this within a few seconds.

A moment later, with the headlights appearing to be floating in place, I called Tilton and said that it was no car at all." Then he was definitely curious.

I said it as it happened. "What we are seeing isn't anything that I have witnessed before. They appear to be headlights but they are about ten feet in the air, not on the ground. I'll keep you informed."

The headlights caused no shadow of Johnny standing in front of our sedan.

I radioed Tilton a few moments later. "We're going in to investigate. I don't know what we are seeing, but I can tell you now that no one has seen a vehicle out here in this entire area!"

I said this because the watchdog special agent was listening. His report would be contrary, but he had his chance to drive over by highway. It would require the better part of an hour. We would wait. As it was, we heard nothing from him.

We drove in after the headlights in earnest. The headlights backed away and disappeared in the heavy brush close to a dry lake bed a mile in front of us but still facing us. I was driving a sedan but could still manage at least three miles before the road grew too rough. We drove to where the headlights had lingered on the road. There were no tracks!

We drove another half-mile, well out of sight of our ambush site. Still, the headlights came back on and came within a half-mile of us from our position on the road. The lights were on the road. We waited. It kept its distance. I chanced driving on the sandy road another half mile to search for vehicle tracks. There were none! The headlights were equally as close at they were while we waited at the highway. We drove further. Still no tracks! Johnny and I stepped out with our flashlights to search the ground away from the road in the event it was merely paralleling the road. Still no tracks! The headlights were leaving no tire marks underneath them.

We had driven into the desert at least three miles and finally reached the trees. The headlights disappeared in the mesquite bushes and trees as we watched them. It wasn't a matter of anyone killing the lights. They had faded into the trees leaving no tire marks!

We drove back to the highway. I called Tilton and reported no tracks of a vehicle, that we were possibly looking at a mirage or a reflection, but from what vehicle lights? He said we would check the area for tracks tomorrow. I was overwhelmed or completely confused. Johnny, during this time, said nothing except to say that he saw no tracks.

Back at the intersection of the road and the highway, the headlights were back on us again! We stepped out and waited. They weren't bright enough to blind us. They were soft and didn't jiggle on the ground as if they were traveling on a dirt road. They seemed to float. Johnny said nothing. I was ready to go in after them again.

They grew larger, then disappeared for a moment. They came back no closer than they were prior to growing larger. They were exactly over the dirt road! I finally asked Johnny what he thought was happening. He refused to comment on what he didn't know and stated it that way. Then they grew larger again. I ran back to our vehicle and made sure the engine started. Johnny stood in front of the hood. He remained silent and still. I chewed him out good. He had better get in or I'd leave him. He didn't budge.

Then the headlights disappeared again. They came back on further away. I got the sedan ready again for the chase. Johnny still wouldn't budge. They disappeared again. The second time I was getting suspicious about something. I stood on top of the hood near the windshield in my stocking feet and could see the headlights in the distance. There were many headlights in the area of the sensor. The watchdog special agent checking on us was correct. The headlights were there without a doubt. They were twelve miles distant in the desert.

I discussed this with Johnny, or made a feeble attempt. I did the talking.

He said absolutely nothing. He agreed with me but had little to add. He was well read and had already learned to use a computer before the rest of us had ever seen one.

I also had to admit something else. No one could actually see the headlights on the border if they were on the ground. From our position, we were on the opposite side of a long rise in the road. That was a fact. I saw what I thought were vehicles gathered at the crossing twelve miles away, but with the rise between us, they lights had to be twenty feet in the air. I would have had to stand on a twenty foot tower to see the headlights where our sensor was located twelve miles away. Yet I had seen them. This could only mean that the lights were a mirage in the air about twenty feet off the ground. There were mesquite and ironwood trees taller than I while standing on the hood. Johnny agreed.

"Ghost lights," I suggested.

Johnny chuckled and went dead pan on me again. It was quiet out there, an ideal time for panic and to make wild guesses, not a time for serious thought. Johnny could be trying at times. I felt a great urge to panic and start running in circles.

The headlights returned to the same distance again and again. They would disappear for a time then reappear. The vehicle lights were still at the sensor location after fifteen minutes. Johnny stood on the hood and saw them. But he also knew that neither of us could see the border from where we were. These lights were definitely in the air some twenty or thirty feet. Ground fog could supply the base for the reflection from lights that had to be at least twenty miles distant in Mexico or fifty miles away in Sells, Arizona.

Tilton came back on the radio asked what was happening. I told him that we had headlights coming but they haven't arrived yet. This, of course, made no sense to Tilton. He said he would wait for an explanation.

I would guess another hour elapsed from the time we were there to the time that all the lights disappeared for good.

I called Tilton back and reported that the lights were all a mirage, and I am quite correct. Johnny finally agreed. The headlights were from a highway approximately twenty miles into Mexico and reflected to the stratus clouds above us to the stratus clouds on the ground that night. I saw no clouds in the sky. I am unable to explain why the mirage lights were exactly above the road all the time with all those square miles of desert to play about. It had to be mere coincidence. We drove home.

All this time, the watchdog from Tucson wisely had nothing to say. I saw the lights exactly where he thought he saw them. He was about fifteen miles east of the lights that were thought to be at the sensor, almost thirty miles from where we sat. Had he commented, he would have had to report it. What he was seeing was also above the ground about twenty feet.

The watchdog probably thought that Johnny and I were dirty and had allowed a load to go through. His other choice was that what he saw was a mirage on the ground. There were no sources for the lights to be there. Apparently, he had bought my explanation, for we faced no questions later.

Why did I call it a mirage? A college professor at the Sul Ross State College where I attended, a "Dr. John," as he liked to be addressed, had his Ph.D. in physics, his Masters in physical geology, and was one of the smartest men I have met. He explained the famous Marfa Lights to our class one morning. He said an invisible ground fog is responsible, which is nothing but a stratus cloud resting a couple feet off the ground for a mile or so. It was scattered too thin to be visible, yet there is sufficient moisture in the air to reflect headlights. The balls of light traveling the length of the old runway near Marfa are those of reflected headlights from the highway a mile to the north. No brush or trees to break up the light. Each headlight on a traveling car a mile away mirrored its reflection much the same way a fish sees out of the pond and past its banks to approaching ground dwellers.

I asked Johnny if he knew the explanation of the Marfa Lights. He didn't, but then, he hasn't seen them, either. He simply said that he didn't believe they existed. No point in attempting to inform Johnny of anything he didn't understand. If the Marfa Lights were in the legend on a map, he would know them well.

Nevertheless, I attempted to explain that the headlights we saw were from vehicles on a highway. I might as well have been talking with the man on the moon.

He said, "What highway? The nearest one was twenty miles to the southwest of our position. He would know. He studies maps in his spare time. The next day we tested the sensor. It was working fine. There were no vehicle tracks.

Johnny didn't buy into Dr. John's theory of reflected lights. I did. It is the only possible solution for the Marfa Lights.

However, only a few years ago, I heard that the lights were seen long before vehicles were invented. Strange, I had never heard that before Dr. John's theory became popular. To this late information, I say, "Phooey!"

Still, I had to know at least a part of Johnny's sound mind. "So what do you think we saw?"

He thought for awhile before answering, long after I had given up on him answering at all. He finally said, "I don't know."

TWO miles south of our position is a village on the *Tohono O'odum* Reservation, formerly called *Papago.* Another mile south of the village, the land, which appeared flat, is actually a long slope uphill, which makes the border out of sight. One had to be almost at the border fence before it can be spotted. Part of this is due to the tall brush, saguaros, mesquite, palo verdes, and ironwood, not to mention the underbrush.

So Mexico's surface was invisible to us, except for a short distance. The land, which appears flat, simply goes uphill for awhile then downhill. People or vehicles cannot be spotted until they are in range of level sight, which isn't far.

From our position where we were parked, the foothills of the mountain range southwest of us in Mexico were not so rough that a highway could not be constructed through them until our tax dollars made it possible. A highway is there. It leads to Santa Anna, Sonora. Behind us on the highway, from one of the higher hills, which was a mile north of us, only a small portion of Mexico could be seen. I tested this with binoculars in the daytime and at night after Johnny's and my encounter with the headlights that did not exist. For at night, I have seen many pairs of headlights approaching the border from Mexico where it isn't possible to see them. None of the headlights ever reached the border fence. I have lost much time waiting for them. So has Johnny and other CPO's. There is no road, but the country can be traversed with a vehicle. Paths and wagon trails had grown numerous south of there over the decades. A gate is in the border fence to allow the Indians to pass to and fro.

I would guess that the headlights we saw, or thought we saw, approaching from the south would have to be thirty or forty feet in the air before they could be spotted, even from the high point on the hill from the highway.

The Indian officers have seen these lights for years. Other CPO's, prior to Johnny and me, have seen them. No one wished to express his opinion, and treated them as if they didn't exist, allowing someone else to bring it up. This is what I do best, bring things up. Sometimes people will talk. Johnny, I think, wasn't sure if he had seen anything of this world or not. He was a man of logic and practicality. If it wasn't explainable, then it didn't exist. The headlights, in his mind, were gradually ceasing to exist.

Tilton did buy into Dr. John's theory of the Marfa Lights after I explained it to him in my limited ability. He called the Indian CPO's. One of them talked to him.

"We often wondered how long it was going to take you guys to discover those lights. One officer drove in from the east at Papago Farms to locate them. He said about five cars were milling about for about an hour before they disappeared. The next day he drove there and found no tracks. He thought it was funny. He called them "Ghost lights," and after that, we don't pay them any mind."

Much later, I attempted to explain to the Indian officers how the vehicles from about thirty to fifty miles away managed to reflect their lights to the low spot where the ground fog settled near the sensor.

Whether they bought into Dr. John's theory or not, they didn't say. But I was told a dozen ghost tales by them.

First, I was asked if Johnny and I saw any shadows from the headlights. The answer was no. That was proof to them that they were ghost lights. While Johnny stood between me and the headlights, I thought they were close enough to cast Johnny's shadow on my windshield. There was no shadow, even though the headlights appeared rather bright.

The officers laughed. They claimed that reflected light cast shadows. They thought they had me.

I'm not sure that reflected light over such a distance can cast light sufficiently to make a shadow.

One of them told me a story. The same two of them witnessed what one was telling me. They found tail lights in front of them that were northbound on a dirt road. They attempted to catch the tail lights and chased them about four miles over the road before they just disappeared right in front of their eyes. This country was dusty. They left a wake of dust behind them that would require about twenty minutes before it dissipated in the stillness. The car in front of them made no dust. They had me again. The reflected lights remained above the road as it twisted to and fro across country!

I explained that they were driving in a ground fog too scattered to be dense enough to see and that they were chasing their own tail lights. I could not comment on why there was no light in front of the tail lights, except this: "At best, I don't know."

"Okay," one of them said. "How would you explain the 'Irrigator?'" The irrigator often walks the dike of an old pond that was supposed to irrigate a small patch of land on the nation. He always carries a lantern with a red light. It moves to and fro on the dike. What's the source of his red lantern?"

I asked, "Did you see a shadow of a man that would be lit from the red lantern?"

"No. But what difference does it make?"

"Refracted light," I explained. "It cast no light."

"Maybe you ought to know something, Homer. The irrigator was there in the 1950's. He always carried a lantern with a red glass around the flame. He's been dead almost twenty years! The bugs and flies don't come to a red light or anything colored. That's why he carried the red lantern when he was alive. He walked the dike with the red lantern just like we see from time to time on some nights."

"Well," I said, still unconvinced of the supernatural, "That's coincidental."

"Well." he said. "It's something, all right."

I didn't tell them anymore of my personal theories. I believe that all of us see what we want to see at times and we all believe what we want to believe. This is what Johnny was dealing with during the hour we watched the approaching headlights. He had to be sure that it wasn't him. The two of us could not have been experiencing the same hysteria over such a long period of time. Over a period of years of seeing the same thing, I don't think it was anything close to hysteria. I think we saw reflected lights from the headlights of automobiles, wherever they might be.

One night on routine patrol,Johnny and I were southbound on the same highway on the reservation. We caught up to the U. S. Border Patrol, who was also patrolling. I turned our red lights on and pulled them over. If they were going to be present, I didn't want us conflicting with each other. During our conversation, I learned that they had permission to be on the reservation, which I doubted. I think they were calling the Tribal Council's bluff and were poaching for drug smugglers, a practice in which they have often done in the past. Customs had permission to be on the reservation, not the U. S. Border Patrol. The Indians were not invited into the Border Patrol like they were into the Customs Patrol, so they weren't allowed on the reservation.

I told them that we were going to sit on the border and that they were welcome to join us, if not, don't try to assist us in a chase unless we ask. They were not pleased, and I had to agree to their same rule. Since most of our stops were illegal immigrants, that was no problem.

I followed them south on the road until we reached the hill where the headlights in Mexico could be seen. I saw the headlights, too. They looked real. I stopped beside them.

I said, "What you're seeing there, partner, is a mirage. There's no car there. We're going on to the border in the event there is a real car coming from Mexico."

This was a new guy. He wasn't about to be taken in by me. He said, "We'll just wait here for the car to pass us. Then, he's ours."

I said, "You can have this car. But when we fall in behind a car that comes from Mexico, don't help unless we ask for it." I drove on.

Those guys never practiced tact. I saw no reason to waste it on them. Johnny and I parked on the border. There were no cars south of us.

An hour or so later, here came the Border Patrol. "What happened to our car?"

He had thought that we had turned it around.

"You didn't see it?" I said, not liking his tone. "It came right passed us about an hour ago."

"No it didn't! What happened to it?"

Johnny enjoyed this. "I'm telling you, man. It came right passed us. It might have stopped in the village. It was yours, so we didn't bother it any."

"No it didn't! We were watching."

I had enough of this. His tone rankled me. So I stepped out and tried one more time just to make it legal, then I was going to punch his lights out. "Look, if you can tell that it didn't stop in the village and it didn't pass you, then you might want to listen to me this time, because there has been no car passing through here. One hasn't even approached."

I'm glad that he accepted that. I explained the mirage to him, that it originated from the Santa Anna Highway. He nodded, and they both left us. He was probably telling his partner how lucky I was that he didn't punch my lights out for smart-mouthing him. The man appeared as intelligent as a French tourist lost in a curio shop at the Grand Canyon. Who could possibly think we would turn a car around in Mexico just because it was the Border Patrol's call?

In the first place, it would be our call, not theirs. It was theirs if the vehicle contained illegal immigrants, which the B. P. had the least interest. They wanted to appear worthwhile and seize a load of smuggled drugs. Johnny and I weren't there to appease their ego. Later that night, while parked in the area where Johnny and I first spotted the ghost lights, here came the Border Patrol again. It was the same officer, only this time he wasn't so mad.

"What's up? You guys have something hot or are you just here killing time?"

I said, "We're still waiting on that car you saw a few hours ago. It should be here anytime now."

He laughed. "I think that was a mirage."

Johnny chuckled and said, "You never can tell."

My wife and I stepped out of our car after arriving home in Lukeville one night. It was a rare night, there were scattered clouds overhead. I just happened to look up and spotted a tiny light in the sky traveling at a tremendous speed. It moved to the side inside a tenth of a second a few times and almost made a ninety degree turn before it disappeared. I called my wife's attention to it.

She looked up and said, "Uh-hmm."

"Yeah!" I was excited. That was a car light's reflection in the stratus clouds we can't see."

"Uh-hmm."

My wife was a sharp lady. Her interest in strange phenomena went no further than merely chuckling at a headline on a sensational tabloid in a grocery store. She had to take care of all my academic problems in math and English, and all of our children's as well. My job was to handle all the difficult stuff like what channel to watch on TV. I had just seen what many other people have seen and called it a UFO. Their explanation was that no craft of ours can make those types of maneuvers at such a high speed. So they had spotted a UFO! What they didn't figure is this: No craft, UFO or not, can maneuver in our atmosphere at such a high speed, not if it's a solid. It would burn up in our atmosphere. When a reflected light moves in the moist areas of air, which isn't consistent, it will show up from where the air is the most moist. As for the speed, if the cloud is 2,000 feet above our surface, then a car's headlight would be about ten times faster above us than it would be on the ground. If one can hold a long fishing pole in hand, then whip it to and fro, the end of the pole is much faster than it is at the wrist. The same principle applies to a reflected light from the ground. The Marfa lights move at the same speed the car travels, for it is almost within reach at our level on the ground.

I have experienced no ghost stories. From the time I've spent outside at night and in the daytime, if a UFO was in my area, I would have seen it. I think. Johnny misses nothing. He most certainly would have seen one. We have both witnessed meteors dissipating in our area and have seen the melted debris falling from its wake. Little streams of smoke or steam follow the bits of debris down to the ground. This is quite common in southern New Mexico and Arizona.

I flew in small aircraft and in our radar-equipped jet about four times per week several years prior to retiring. Most of this was at night. I have seen lights that I thought were in the air far away, but they were not. They were reflections immediately outside on the cabin's Plexiglas. If one stares at them or fixes on them, they can appear miles away. They can be red or green or a combination. There might even be several of them, some of them will be blurred. Some commercial airline pilots report them as mysterious aircraft. The large majority of them do not. The lights will move exactly at the same speed as the aircraft moves. It will last several minutes. The compressed air passing over the canopy has to be dense enough in moisture to pick up the right or left's wing lights, sometimes both. The reflections are about one-eighth of an inch, or less, off the Plexiglas. If you place your finger on the inside wall of the Plexiglas, one can see the width of the Plexiglas, and there will be the light a fraction of an inch away. Remove your finger, and the lights can appear several miles distant and pass through what seems distant clouds. Most pilots explain these lights the same way I wrote them.

All of the lights of UFO's can be explained in this manner, whether they're immediately overhead or not. However, people believe what they choose to believe. I choose to believe Dr. John's theory. He made a lot of sense.